ESCAPING THE SELF

ALSO BY ROY F. BAUMEISTER

Identity: Cultural Change and the Struggle for Self (1986)

Public Self and Private Self (ed., 1986)

Masochism and the Self (1989)

Meanings of Life (1991)

ESCAPING THE SELF

Alcoholism, Spirituality,
Masochism, and Other Flights
from the Burden of Selfhood

ROY F. BAUMEISTER, PH.D.

BasicBooks
A Division of HarperCollinsPublishers

Library of Congress Cataloging-in-Publication Data
Baumeister, Roy F.
    Escaping the self: alcoholism, spirituality, masochism,
and other flights from the burden of selfhood/Roy F. Baumeister.
        p.   cm.
    Includes bibliographical references and index.
    ISBN 0-465-02053-4
    1. Escape (Psychology)   2. Self.   3. Self-destructive be-
havior.   I. Title.
BF575.E83B38 1991
155.2—dc20   91-70063
                                                        CIP-

Contents

v
271798

Preface

For several years I have sought to understand our modern culture's overriding fascination with selfhood and identity. This fascination has permeated the society, and academic research has been touched, too. Indeed, starting in the late 1970s, self and identity formed one of the most popular topics of study in the social sciences, as well as exerting strong influence on the humanities. My own interest in the self and identity began as part of that movement.

But if I have ridden the self bandwagon, I have done so with some skepticism. There is something not entirely healthy about our culture's fascination with selfhood, something vaguely indecent, problematic, perhaps even dangerous. However beneficial overall, most major social developments exact costs as well. Usually the problems become apparent only gradually and long after the benefits have been embraced.

So it is, I think, with selfhood and identity. Our culture has moved selfhood to center stage and has developed an extensive vocabulary of self to inform a prolonged, admiring discourse on the subtleties and possibilities of selfhood. Meanwhile, the costs of this fascination attract less attention.

These costs, dangers, and problems constitute one of the most interesting and important areas for scholars to investigate today.

By now, nearly everyone has agreed on the importance of self-esteem. Hundreds of studies, dozens of therapies, and even an official commission of California notables have explored the benefits of positive self-esteem. It is clear that low self-esteem is unpleasant to experience and is linked to a variety of pathologies. But high self-esteem is probably not an unmixed blessing, and an undiscriminating effort to raise everyone's self-esteem may not be the best thing for society. After all, arrogance and conceit are manifestations of high self-esteem, as is the overconfidence that results in errors of judgment with potentially catastrophic consequences. Weren't self-importance and overconfidence two of the factors that embroiled the United States in Vietnam? This tidal wave of interest in self and the incipient backwash of its negative aspects forms the context of this book. In a previous book (*Identity: Cultural Change and the Struggle for Self*), I undertook to explore how the modern form of selfhood became so problematic, and in another (*Meanings of Life*), I examined how modern society has begun to use selfhood in a new way to help make individual lives meaningful and fulfilling. In this work, I have sought to explain some of the dangers and problems that arise from the modern heavy emphasis on self, and then to show how these dangers and problems lead people to seek ways of escaping from self.

Escape is an understandable response to an overemphasis on the self or to problems of the self. Escape is neither inherently bad nor good, although value judgments can be made about particular forms of escape. It is hard to see suicide or alcohol abuse in a very positive light, but the enhancement of individual consciousness through religious or spiritual exercises—which also require escape from the self—may be one of the supreme goods on earth.

I have always tried to let the data lead me wherever they indicate, rather than holding fast to a particular viewpoint or hypothesis, and as a result, I often end up far from where I started. This book in particular evolved out of a series of projects that I began with very different goals. For years, I have been laboring to pull together insights the social sciences can offer about how people find meaning in life, and I have researched a wide range of topics for relevant data. At one point, several years ago, I hoped that my theories about meaningfulness in life might shed some light on the opaque mystery of sexual masochism. I planned to spend a few hours in the library to learn what was known about masochism. It soon became apparent that masochism bore little relation to the search for meaning in life, but it posed such a striking contradiction to psychology's principles and generalizations about the self that I felt challenged to try to understand masochism on its own terms. And so, laying aside my project on life's meaning, I read more deeply the literature on masochism, collected data, and slowly began to make sense of this great puzzle. The contradiction between psychology's theories about the self and the phenomenon of masochism is no accident or illusion—it is the very essence of masochism: masochistic practices are designed to thwart, unmake, and obliterate the self, at least temporarily. I came to see the core of masochism as a way of escaping from one's knowledge of oneself.

My research on suicide led me along a similar path. As with masochism, I began with the hope that suicide would shed light on the meanings of life. But as I read the voluminous literature on suicide, it soon became apparent that most suicides are not responses to an entire life but rather narrow reactions to current or very recent problems. Moreover, suicide seems to center on a certain type of problem—problems connected with the self. The urge to lose self-awareness emerged as a central feature of the presuicidal mental process.

For me personally, masochism had been a frustrating topic to study because so little research has been published. There were many questions or hypotheses that I simply could not find answers for, because it is so difficult to collect data on masochists. In contrast, researchers have been collecting and publishing data on suicide for over a century, and there is no paucity of information. If anything, the scholar interested in suicide encounters the opposite problem—there is so much information that it is difficult to master. But this problem is offset by the intellectual opportunity that the abundance of the suicide literature affords: the odds are that something can be found to address almost any broad question one might pose. The excitement and stimulation of working with such a rich, varied, and huge mass of information was one of the high points of my career in psychology. I know that for many people the concept of suicide evokes deeply personal and usually traumatic memories, but for me it is associated with the happy recollection of an extraordinary intellectual adventure.

Through the topic of suicide, I was able to develop my understanding of the process of escape in much greater detail than had been possible with masochism. Once I finished with suicide, the core of the theory of escaping from the self was nearly complete. A crucial further development came with the recognition of the differences between masochism and suicide. I realized that the initial motivation to escape oneself could take several forms. This became particularly obvious when I looked into the writings about religious and spiritual experiences—for these, too, talk about getting rid of the self. It would be foolish to argue that the aspiring Zen master, the sexual masochist, and the suicidal sufferer are driven by identical motives and mental states, despite their common effort to escape the self. This book contains my first exposition of the multiplicity of motives that direct people to seek escape.

For the reader with professional interests, the scholarly basis of this work has been laid in a series of journal articles. My work on masochism was published in 1988 in the *Journal of Sex Research* and in book form the following year. The year 1988 also saw the publication in the *Psychological Bulletin* of my review article on self-defeating behavior. As reported in that work, my coauthor Steve Scher and I found that normal people do indeed show patterns of self-destructive behavior that existing theories fail to explain. We concluded that the desire to escape from aversive views of the self was one theme common to many self-destructive patterns.

The *Psychological Review* published my work on suicide in 1990, and an early overview of my general theory about escaping the self appeared in the published proceedings of the Ontario Symposium. At the symposium on which the later volume was based, Todd Heatherton approached me with the comment that the research literature on binge eating contained some relevant studies. He and I collaborated on a review of that literature, which will be published in 1991 in the *Psychological Bulletin*. A laboratory study by myself and Tom Dixon, dealing with escaping the self, will also be published in 1991.

I owe personal and intellectual debts to several people who helped me assemble this work. Todd Heatherton, now a professor at Harvard, made the greatest contribution, and he deserves most of the credit for my understanding of binge eating. Jay Hull (of Dartmouth), Claude Steele (of the University of Michigan), and Bob Josephs (of the University of Texas) generously shared their work and thoughts on alcohol. Tom Dixon, now a psychotherapist in Chicago, collaborated with me on collecting data.

I am very grateful to Dianne Tice, my colleague at Case Western Reserve University and now my beloved spouse, for her insightful critiques and suggestions on all phases of this work. I thank Bill Swann and Dan Gilbert for hosting my sabbatical at the University of Texas, where I was able to develop the initial ideas and write most of my book on masochism. I am also grateful to the many people who have provided constructive feedback over the years, including Swann and Gilbert, Janet Polivy, Peter Herman, Roxie Silver, Dan Wegner, and Jamie Pennebaker.

Lastly, I am indebted to Jo Ann Miller and the staff at Basic Books for their guidance, help, and encouragement. For me, writing a book always contains some aspect of leaping into the unknown, but they improved the odds of a safe landing.

ONE

Identity: Paradise or Prison?

Long ago [the human being] formed an ideal conception of omnipotence and omniscience which he embodied in his gods. To-day he has ... almost become a god himself.... But ... present-day man does not feel happy in his godlike character. —Sigmund Freud, *Civilization and Its Discontents*

Throughout history, people have longed for an ideal society. They have often held a vision of the promised land: of living at peace, without starvation or disease or poverty; of having plenty of good food to eat, and being able to marry the person one chooses.

It would seem that modern, middle-class life in the United States embodies these dreams. Not only do we have superb food and shelter (much better than the crowned heads of Europe enjoyed throughout the era of royalty), but we also enjoy peace and safety, excellent medical care, social stability, and personal freedom. Technology has given us capabilities that surpass the magical powers of ancient fairy tales—to fly, to communicate with people across great distances, to view images of strange lands, to cure injuries and sicknesses that once would have been fatal.

Despite these advances, there are surprising trends. Suicide rates are high and rising, especially among young people who seemingly have a lifetime of unprecedented opportunity ahead of them. Sexual masochism is on the increase, especially among wealthy and powerful individuals who seemingly could enjoy any pleasures they want. Drug and alcohol use are increasing throughout the population. Unusual foreign religious cults are flourishing and attracting large numbers of young people.

Some suggest escapism underlies these trends, but that seems an inadequate explanation. Why would people so blessed want escape? One could understand the need in societies that suffer war, famine, poverty, or other hardships. But whence comes this need in modern middle-class lives that seem full of comfort, pleasure, and security? U.S. history has been characterized by a steady *in*-migration. People escape from other places and come here. Why would *we* want to escape? Nor is it the miserable, deprived, and oppressed among us who are inclined to escape: Suicide flourishes in the middle class, masochists are drawn from the well-to-do, and alcohol use pervades the population from top to bottom.

Amid these self-destructive behaviors, we seem fascinated with ourselves—witness the popularity of books on "the identity society" or "the culture of narcissism." This fascination may hold the key to the paradox of self-annihilation and self-aggrandizement. Modern society has made much of the self—perhaps too much. The demands of creating and sustaining a modern identity are becoming increasingly burdensome, and as people's lives center even more on maintaining a certain image of self, the desire to escape from this burden grows ever greater.

WHAT IS THE SELF?

We all use the term *self* several times every day, especially if compound words like "himself" and "herself" are counted. This frequent usage doesn't mean that everyone could furnish a clear and precise definition of the term—indeed, its very familiarity may make it especially hard to define. The problem is compounded by specialized usages like those introduced by the psychoanalysts Carl Jung and Heinz Kohut. In this book, I will start with self as a grammatical reflex, a point to which things refer. When saying or thinking "I" or "me" or "my," the self is what we invoke. Those terms, and the forms of action implied by their usage, refer precisely to the self. People say, I am an American, a teacher, a swimmer, a stamp collector, a man or a woman, a future executive, a parent, a tenant, an honest person, a good friend, a Hoosier, a Christian, a liberal. These predicates define the self. Each of us is a composite of such definitions.

One could say the self consists of a physical body and a set of definitions. There is little question that the self begins with the body. Philosophical analyses of self and identity nearly always assume the physical self and primarily consider whether the body is sufficient to define identity.[1] As young children begin to learn who they are and form their concept of self, the body plays a central role; only later do they add such refinements as values, personality traits, and privileged access to inner experience.[2] The history of the concept of self in Western culture began by equating self with physical being and only gradually were nonphysical notions added. Indeed, recent history has seen an escalation and expansion of inner, nonphysical attributes to the self.[3] We have come to regard the inner self as vast, stable, unique, important, and difficult to know; and we presume that it contains thoughts, feelings, intentions, personality traits, latent talents and capabilities, the wellsprings of creativity, the key ingredients of personal fulfillment, and the solutions to many of life's problems. Indeed, the very notion that you can look inside yourself to find the solution to a dilemma would be regarded as absurd in cultures that don't share our overriding faith in the inner self.

Certainly, the self does seem to consist of more than body. People identify themselves with far more than physical attributes. They have social roles, memberships in family and other groups, reputations, career histories, bank accounts, plans and goals, personal values, commitments, obligations, relationships. Identity is linked with rights, privileges, duties, options, goals; with past and future possibilities. These are not properties of the body like hair color or weight. Identity is made of meaning, not of atoms and molecules.

Self can be understood as a physical entity overlaid with meaning. It is a biological organism as well as a socially defined being. A human being is an animal that moves and sees and craves and feels, but a human being is also a symbolically defined member of a community—the beast with the credit card and social security number. That the self is a construct (meaning superimposed on a physical, animal being) is vitally important for understanding how people can escape the self, as we will see in this book.

Because the self begins with an animal being, it is endowed with needs and wants, just like the vast majority of nature's organisms. The self has to deal with the natural appetites for food, sleep, warmth, comfort, and sex. There is good reason to believe that the human being comes endowed with a *need to belong*, that is, a need to be a member of social groups and to form interpersonal relationships or bonds.[4] The need for esteem may well derive (at least in part) from this need for social belongingness. Unless others regard us favorably, we may end up alone. Somebody has to like us or find us attractive, desirable, or useful. People internalize this need, and so they feel a strong need for self-esteem. Hundreds of experimental studies have confirmed that people are strongly motivated to maintain favorable concepts of themselves,[5] both in their own minds and in the minds of others.

Another major part of the self is a quest for *control*. The self wants to believe itself to be in control of its environment, of its relationships with others, and of itself. When real control fails, people develop illusions of control.[6] The origin of the desire for control is not clear. Some theorists believe it innate and point to the way many species explore their environments, practice and rehearse mechanisms of control, and show pleasure in mastery. When deprived of control, they exhibit irritation, resentment, pathological resignation and helplessness, even illness and death. Other theorists point to nurture instead of nature, and therefore stress the socialization of the need to take charge and show initiative. Either way, there is no question but that the selves of people today are oriented toward control. The self is an agent that acts on the world.

The self is closely linked to one's emotional repertoire. Pride, shame, guilt, anger, sadness, and many other emotions refer to whether the self is doing well or doing badly, and to how other people regard the self. Failure may arouse either no emotion or intense emotion, depending on whether the self is implicated, and depending particularly on whether other people see the outcome as reflecting on one's self. After losing a contest, for example, people may feel upset and humiliated if they think an audience sees them as incompetent pretenders; proud if seen as doing better than could be expected in the face of overwhelming odds; or little more than minor frustration if seen as victims of bad luck.[7]

The self is linked to many standards. These include norms, values, expectations, and goals. People have idealized concepts of how they would like to be[8] and evaluate their activities by discrepancies between what they are and what they would like to be. They also feel obligations and responsibilities, and if their actions violate these, they feel distress.[9]

THE OVERGROWN, OVEREMPHASIZED SELF

The theme of self dominates recent trends in our culture. In the 1940s, Erik Erikson coined the term *identity crisis*, and it became a catchword during the placid 1950s when various groups, such as women and minorities, did indeed begin to question anew what their true nature was and what their proper place in society should be. In the 1960s, the quest for self took people in many different directions, including an expansion of humanistic psychology movements aimed at exploring the human potential, the use of "consciousness-expanding" drugs that were purported to reveal important insights from deep inside the self, and the increasing interest in Eastern religions and mysticism that used age-old techniques to unlock spiritual treasures buried in the mind.

In the 1970s, spiritual discovery and psychological cultivation of the self gave way to more mundane forms of self-development, such as assertiveness training, and the self-absorption captured in the phrase "the Me Decade" or "the Me Generation." At least in stereotype, interest in the self degenerated in the 1980s into mere selfishness, although the interest in discovering and cultivating the self continued.

This increasing emphasis on self can be seen in the relation of self to other basic values. Several important studies have concluded, for example, that people have recently come to place a higher emphasis on self than on marriage and family, in sharp and direct contrast to previous generations. One important scholarly work contrasted the treatment of dilemmas in women's magazines across several decades and showed an increasing emphasis on self.[10] In the 1940s, marriage was the basic value criterion used for evaluating the individual. To be a good person, you had to be able to sustain a good marriage. In the 1960s and 1970s, marriage came to be evaluated on the basis of its contribution to individual satisfaction. If the marriage was constraining, it was the person's right and even duty to get out of it. Once upon a time, the self was the servant of the marriage, but today people feel that marriage should serve the self.[11]

Ideas of the self vary across time and place. The way people think of themselves is heavily dependent on their culture. For example, in Asian societies people tend to see themselves as deeply woven into their families and other groups,[12] and the concept of self is accordingly based more heavily on being part of the group than on being unique, autonomous, and independent. In our society, in contrast, people emphasize what is unique or special about themselves.

This emphasis on the individual self is unusual in the history of the world, although these days it is spreading from its base in Europe and North America to other lands. Even in Western history it only goes back a few centuries. Before the Renaissance, people placed much less emphasis on unique qualities, talents, and potentialities; instead, people tried to conform to standard models, and what mattered about a person was how well he or she fit the ideal rather than in what ways he or she was different. The Middle Ages produced few autobiographies, because there was little value seen in the special, particular details of one person's life or personality. Biographies presented their subjects as fitting the ideal models, and were—to our view—shockingly indifferent to factual accuracy.[13] Miracle stories were freely borrowed, for example, so that the same miracles showed up in the biographies of many different saints. The point, however, is not that the biographers were poor scholars, plagiarists, or imbeciles, but rather that factual accuracy did not matter, because individuality was a trivial concern. The goal of writing a biography was to inspire and edify, so that readers would come away from the book with a better understanding of the ideal Christian life and a greater desire to make their own lives conform to that model.

Only after the Renaissance did Europe develop a fascination with how each person was different, special, and unique. Gradually this interest developed into a cultural demand that a person ought to strive to be unique. By 1800, it had become an article of faith that each person had unique personal qualities and a special destiny that he (to a lesser extent, she) could either fulfill or fail to fulfill. The culture inculcated the idea that each person had a great potential.[14] This new belief was heavily intertwined with the new movements for individual freedom. Countries that were made or remade during this period, such as the United States and France, relied heavily on principles of individualism and the rhetoric of individual freedom and opportunity.

These centuries that saw the growth of individualism also saw the growth of a new escapism. Elsewhere, I have traced the remarkable parallels between the rise of individuality and the rise of sexual masochism,[15] a parallel that suggests the need to escape from oneself grew in concert with the increasing construction of that self. As the culture began to expect each person to be autonomous, special, unique, and to cultivate inner potential in order to achieve his or her specially assigned destiny, the burden of maintaining the self grew— and the desire to escape from this burden. I am convinced that many of the paradoxical behavior trends that we see today, such as the rise in suicide rates among people who seemingly ought to be enjoying a comfortable, secure life, result from our culture having taught each of us to construct an *overgrown* self. There are several important reasons that our culture has done this, and the positive benefits of this obsessive concern with self should not be denied. Self has become vital to our concepts of human fulfillment, freedom, autonomy, adjustment, happiness, love, and creativity. But there are costs.

THE BURDEN OF THE SELF

A useful illustration can be found in the aristocrats of past centuries. They formed a small part of society, but they (especially the males) were encouraged to cultivate a great egotism, in the name of pride. The need to defend their pride produced a wide variety of constraints on their behavior: In some periods, any slight insult was regarded as thoroughly intolerable, to the point that the man had to fight a duel to expunge it.[16] Many people apparently willingly suffered injury and death over seemingly trivial insults.

A hypothetical analogy to something other than the self may be helpful. Suppose society gave each person an enormously large, beautiful, and expensive house, and suppose that maintaining it was assigned to be one of the most important purposes of the person's life. Suppose, too, that there were no such thing as home insurance, so that if something happened to your house, you would have to deal with the loss and problem on your own.

At first, each person would be delighted to have such a wonderful possession and would experience great joy and satisfaction. But then it would also make great demands on the individual's time and energy. Considerable upkeep is required for a house, and the larger and more elaborate the house is, the more upkeep is involved. Moreover, because everyone would be equally concerned with owning a marvelous house, comparisons would start to focus on small details and imperfections. This would lead to a general obsession with minutiae and anticipating all the things that could go wrong. Meanwhile, one would tend to forget that this excessive concern was preventing one from traveling and perhaps enjoying other pleasures or opportunities that one might have had if one did not have this house.

Before long, people would find themselves tied down by their houses, perhaps feeling like servants rather than owners. This is not to downplay the continuing positive aspects of owning a fine house, for there would continue to be moments of pleasure and enjoyment. But there would also be many times of worry, concern, and even feelings of being trapped and obligated. People might begin to wish for vacations, for the chance to be free for at least a brief time. And if something bad happened to the house that could not be easily fixed, people would have to live in distress, knowing that everyone who passed by would see their disgrace.

So it is with the modern self. Each person in our society has received the burdensome gift of the overgrown self. We enjoy the positive, attractive features of this self-orientation, but we may fail to appreciate how much it costs us as well. The upkeep on the modern self is greater than we tend to realize, as is the scope of lost opportunity and the investment of time and energy.

People find themselves repeating, if on a small scale, the fate of Donald Trump, who became a symbol for the American scene at the end of the 1980s. Trump, a very aggressive and wealthy businessman with a consuming egotism, craved wealth and power and publicity, and so he made highly visible deals and renamed everything he could—airlines, hotels—after himself. He wrote a book about what a great businessman he was and even marketed a board game named for himself. Ultimately he succeeded in producing one of the most overgrown selves in the history of the world and appeared to have attracted all the attention he craved.

Then his wife caught him with his mistress and that, along

with various other complaints, led her to file for divorce. His businesses faltered at an unfortunate time, and he found himself facing bankruptcy. He was ordered to sell off some of his businesses and personal toys and to rein in his flamboyant lifestyle. Meanwhile, the media gloated over his humiliation. Both his marital and financial embarrassments made headlines, and he was rumored to be suicidal. There are many lessons to learn from the Trump saga, but one of them is certainly the stress and risk involved in sustaining an overgrown ego. Having worked so hard to impose his personal egotism on the national attention, Trump had to suffer through having the nation laugh at him when he got egg on his face. Millions of people suffer money troubles and marital problems every year, without being made a laughingstock in the national press. But once he had compelled the big national eye to see him at his best, Trump couldn't avoid its cruel gaze when he was at his worst. And so this overgrown image of self that he had cultivated so carefully changed from a source of satisfaction and fulfillment to a tragic, painful burden.

Consider the range of things we all do in order to maintain a proper image of self for ourselves and for the external world. We struggle to gain prestigious credentials. We read books and take courses on how to make a good impression. We discard clothes that are not worn out and buy new, more fashionable ones. We work hard to devise self-serving explanations for failures or mishaps and fight to make others take the blame. We go hungry to make ourselves fashionably thin. We rehearse conversations or presentations in advance and ruminate about them afterwards to try to imagine what went wrong. We undergo cosmetic surgery. We endlessly seek information about other people so we can have a basis for comparing ourselves. We engage in fistfights with people who impugn our respectability or superiority. We grope desperately for rationalizations. We blush and brood when something makes us look foolish. We buy endless magazines advising us how to look better, make love better, succeed at work or play or dieting, and say clever things. Maintaining self-esteem can start to seem like a full-time job!

The modern age is so in love with self that it has built it up all out of proportion, oblivious to the costs and faults in such a preoccupation. Like someone in love or someone addicted, there is an obsession with the self. Drug addicts may only dimly sense how much time, effort, and money are being poured into supporting their habit. The self habit is like that. We know that it brings us pleasure and that it structures our lives. We don't fully see what it costs us.

Escape from the self is a direct outgrowth of the emphasis on the self. To be sure, all cultures have had some notions of selfhood, and at times the need to escape has arisen for individuals in all cultures. But it is especially powerful and prevalent in cultures like ours that place such a premium on the individual self.

≈≈≈

ESCAPE: GOOD, BAD, OR INDIFFERENT?

To escape from the self is to free oneself of the struggle to maintain a certain image. It means to give up on the motivations that are a driving force behind so much of human behavior, namely the quests for esteem and control. It means to dodge the pressures, demands, obligations, responsibilities, and other factors that plague the modern self and make life stressful. It means stopping the emotional roller coaster that one rides with one's concept of self. It means to forget all the grand, complex, abstract, wide-ranging definitions of self and become just a body again. This may be an attempt to get rid of unhappy feelings, or it may be a rest break from the daily struggle, or it may be a first step toward creating an entirely new self. But it requires manipulating one's mind in particular ways so as to remove one's awareness of the full extent of one's identity. To escape from the self means to forget who you are—at least for a while.

This book is concerned with what people do in order to get away from themselves. As we shall see, a large variety of actions fit into this category, and they have often been misunderstood—as individual, isolated patterns; as limited responses to specific events; or even as part of some broad pattern of self-destructiveness. To understand the behaviors properly, we must appreciate how they are related to the self and how they allow us to escape from our awareness of who we are.

One frequent explanation of drug abuse, suicide, and similar behaviors is low self-esteem. Raising self-esteem is sometimes touted as a panacea. The talk-show host Oprah Winfrey recently devoted a television special to self-esteem, as if to explore what its great powers would be. The state of California established a commission to determine how best to promote individual self-esteem among its residents. A seemingly endless stream of pop psychology books, cassette tapes, and self-help programs promise to raise our self-esteem and, as a consequence, bring wealth and happiness.

The point seems to be that if we could all somehow feel better about ourselves, our problems would vanish. Ironically self-esteem seems to depend heavily on feeling superior to other people.[17] Most evaluations depend on comparisons with other people—IQ scores, for example, are meaningful only in comparison with the scores of others. There are obvious practical limits to *everyone* feeling superior to everyone else. Nor is high self-esteem necessarily good. Consider the example of people who feel dejected about their inability to understand complex money matters. Suppose we simply raise their self-esteem and convince them they are financial geniuses. Is this going to be in their best interests in the long run? After they have invested the family money and lost it, the value of self-esteem alone may appear doubtful.

This is not a contrived exercise. The late 1980s witnessed a variety of investment patterns by wealthy, influential men who allowed their egos to guide their actions. We have already mentioned Donald Trump. Another was Robert Campeau, the Canadian investor who bought Bloomingdale's and other U.S. stores with a view to building a retail empire. His vision of himself included grandiose schemes of wealth, power, and influence, and he allowed these optimistic, self-flattering illusions to cloud his business judgment. As a result, a slight downturn in the economy was a disaster for him: heavily in debt, he found himself unable to make his payments, and his optimistic forecasts of great financial success failed to pan out. He returned to obscurity, chastened, impoverished, and humiliated.

The notion of escape has been touched on in various contexts, such as the recent debates about drug use, but it has been widely misunderstood. Two misunderstandings are particularly problematic. The first simply groups all forms of escape together. In this view, people have escapist impulses simply because of stressful concerns in life. But the need to escape from oneself is *not* the same as the need to escape from problems, oppressive conditions, or life stress in general. Escaping the self is a response to problems associated with how people feel about themselves.

A dull or empty life may lead someone to seek escape into heroin abuse, the sexual thrill of casual promiscuity, or extensive television watching. Such responses do not necessarily involve the self. The person may be content with who he or she is, and feel no need to forget the self. After all, consider the high rates of heroin use, sexual activity, and television watching among the underprivileged classes in the United States today. Studies show that these groups do not lack self-esteem—if anything, they enjoy higher self-esteem than is found among the more privileged groups.[18] But simple escapism is rampant. Activities that emphasize escape from the self in particular, such as sexual masochism and binge eating, tend not to be found among disadvantaged groups. These disadvantaged individuals are apparently escaping from oppressive conditions and an unattractive environment or from the demanding stresses of difficult lives and uncertain jobs. They do not seem to feel the need to forget who they are. Rising suicide rates among young black males do not necessarily contradict my argument: The demands on them to sustain favorable reputations contribute to a very stressful form of egotism that can well account for their growing need to escape the self.

A second misunderstanding about escapism is that it is inherently bad. When society senses escape, it is quick to condemn. Partly this may be seen in the attitudes toward heroin, LSD, and other mind-altering drugs. Escapism has been associated with them, and so the desire to escape becomes tarnished with their unsavory aura. U.S. society has a long tradition of being practical and realistic, and anything that takes a person away from reality tends to attract disapproval. The recurrent debate about watching television often focuses on its unrealistic depictions and its capacity to promote escape from reality.

But the need to escape from self is not necessarily bad. A more evenhanded understanding of this need and its manifestations is long overdue. True, people can become involved in dangerous and harmful activities in the pursuit of escape from themselves. But escape can also be harmless—even beneficial. In chapter 9, I will argue that escaping the self is necessary to fulfill some of the highest ideals known to humanity, as embodied in religion and spirituality.

Perhaps more to the point, the fact that people do so many things to escape suggests how important their need is. If our society were to close all those avenues, the result might be extremely harmful. People clearly *want* to escape, and they may also *need* periodic escape. To prevent escape might well be to increase stress, with a resulting rise in suffering and pathology.

I am not advocating that society indiscriminately promote escape. But if we understand more about what is involved, we might learn to live with ourselves more harmoniously. And we might learn to serve our underlying needs in ways that could reduce the unpredictable and potentially harmful effects of escapes.

Suicide and spiritual fulfillment are extremes, but consider the more intermediate forms of escape: alcohol use and sexual masochism. Sexual masochism, despite its somewhat unsavory reputation and deliberate bizarreness, appears to be neither helpful nor harmful. Most people who engage in it don't end up injured or sick. Nor does it make them better people. It simply provides an effective escape that is treasured by a certain minority. It is an unusual form of sexual play, and that is all.

Alcohol, however, produces a range of effects, both harmful and beneficial. Some people become addicted, with ultimately devastating effects on their physical health, family relationships, and careers. Others find pleasure and relaxation in the moderate use of alcohol. There is some evidence that moderate use of alcohol is linked to favorable effects on health. So is alcohol use good or bad? The answer is as mixed as the modern self.

THE PARADOX OF ESCAPE

A difficulty with escaping from the self is that it is a paradoxical task: The self must itself decide and carry out the process of removing itself. Moreover, in what sense can a person be rid of self? One can't get rid of one's body and still live, although one can perhaps forget about it for a while. One could conceivably have one's attention focused on something so that one forgets one's physical being. But most escapes from the self seem to focus attention intensely on the body. Drinking alcohol or binge eating direct attention to physical sensations: The person becomes absorbed in physical feelings. Likewise, sexual masochism emphasizes bodily awareness—the absorbing mixture of pain and sexual pleasure will call attention *to* one's physical being, not away from it.

The answer to this paradox is that often escape from self directs attention to the body precisely as a means of taking attention away from other, more meaningful aspects of the self. As we saw, the self is composed of both a physical body and an accumulation of meanings. Escape from oneself is directed at getting rid of those meanings—that is, of shutting them out of one's mind. Sometimes it is necessary to emphasize the bodily self as a way of escaping from the meaningful self.

Escaping the self is thus not a matter of removing the self entirely, but rather of shrinking it down to its bare minimum. In particular, one gets rid of many of the definitions of self that are causing trouble. The minimum self that a person can have is the body. There is no way to avoid having a body. But if one's self is reduced to only being a body, that is quite a feat, and many sources of distress, worry, concern, and threat are removed. Escaping from the self is, more precisely, an escape from identity into body.

For example, let us suppose that you are an adult man, of medium height and weight, an engineer, a college graduate, a Republican, an environmentalist, a husband and father, a former high school honor student, a Methodist, an employee of Able Industries, a distant cousin of a movie star, a homeowner, and (you hope) a future vice president of your corporation. These definitions connect you to the distant past and future, as well as to places and events and people far distant from you now. Thus, meaning links your physical self with many other people, places, times, and events. To escape from yourself is to lose awareness of all those connections. During escape, your awareness of yourself shrinks to the immediate present. You become only a warm body, probably sitting in a chair right now and holding a book, feeling certain sensations from your immediate environment. Your awareness of self shrinks to the immediate time and place (the room you are in, here and now) and to the short-term movements and sensations of your body.

Escape from the self is escape from the *meaningful* aspects of the self. As I have written elsewhere, sexual masochism affords escape from identity by emphasizing body.[19] That is, the sexual masochist forgets the symbolic identity consisting of professional roles, ambitions, obligations, reputation, all with a certain past and future. Instead, the masochist is aware of self only as a body, in the immediate present, feeling pain and pleasure. All the meanings of self are forgotten.

Meaning plays an important role in escape from self. If a person can stop engaging in meaningful thought, the self will almost automatically be stripped down to the bare, physical minimum. Normally, people are constantly thinking in meaningful terms. We analyze, elaborate, remember things, have associations, draw inferences and conclusions, tell stories. Everything that happens to us is saturated with meaning—it is interpreted, compared with past similar events, evaluated against standards or ideals, put into context, rationalized, described, questioned. Much of this thinking involves the self. You analyze the events you experience in terms of what they mean for your goals, reputation, opportunities, vulnerabilities, obligations. We don't simply ask, what does this mean, but rather what does this mean for *me*? As long as we analyze experience in this way, the self is heavily involved in a meaningful fashion.

To escape from the self requires finding a way to stop the mind from its habit of meaningful thought. The mind must be directed to stop at the level of sensations and impressions, or just to observe events without exploring all the implications for the self. Of course, sometimes that is precisely what drives the need to escape. When your lover leaves you, it is distressing to dwell on what that means for you and about you. Now you will be lonely. Now you will have to explain to others. Maybe you are unlovable, undesirable, unattractive (in fact, didn't your ex-lover say something to that effect before slamming the door!). You will need to find a new partner and build a new relationship, but if you are indeed so unsuitable as a partner you may have to change. So what are your main faults, and which of them can you remedy? To dwell on all these faults at one time, while still feeling full of sadness and hurt, can be extremely unpleasant, and perhaps not particularly productive. Getting the mind to cease its meaningful thought will be a great help. A strong dose of alcohol may be just what a person wants in order to blot out those thoughts pertaining to the self.

Escaping the self involves the mind and the body in a strenuous and sometimes dangerous effort, all in order to enable us to forget who we are. Let us now examine what sorts of events bring people to the point of wanting to undertake this difficult and paradoxical task.

TWO

―――――――――

Why Escape?—
The Burden of Self

*But as I looked in the mirror, I screamed, and my heart shuddered: for I
saw not myself but the mocking, leering face of a devil.*
—Friedrich Nietzsche, *Thus Spake Zarathustra*

P eople seek to escape from the self for three main reasons: to avoid thinking bad thoughts about oneself,
usually in the wake of some calamity; to find temporary
relief from the stressful burden of maintaining an inflated
image of self; or to seek transcendence in the very act of
shedding the self. These escapes appeal to different types of
people in different circumstances. We will find many shared
features among them, but the different bases of the escapes
also produce differences in the patterns of escape that
people actually use.

―――――――――

CALAMITY:
FORGETTING THE UNACCEPTABLE SELF

For most people, self-awareness is highly evaluative. It is difficult to be neutral when thinking about ourselves. Instead,

21

we constantly measure ourselves against standards.[1] Am I smart enough to handle this task? Is my body slim and sufficiently well proportioned to attract members of the opposite sex? If I wear this outfit, will people laugh at my poor taste in clothes? Am I performing as well as I should, or well enough to succeed at this job? Did I do the right thing? Dwelling on negative answers to such questions generates a variety of unhappy emotional states. People may become angry, depressed, or anxious.[2] There is some evidence that unpleasant emotions tend to cluster. In any case, it is clear that people typically want to stop feeling these emotions as soon as possible.

The first, and most obvious, reason for escaping from self-awareness is because such awareness is acutely unpleasant. Normally this occurs when events cast the self in a strongly negative light, making the self look incompetent, unattractive, immoral. When you feel stupid, clumsy, inadequate, unlovable, you want to stop thinking about yourself. There is considerable evidence that people prefer to view themselves and wish others to view them favorably. People strive to maintain existing concepts of self or to enhance them with new positive features.[3] They resist taking on negative views of self. To hear that you are not as beautiful as you thought, or not as talented, or not as capable, is painful. A loss of esteem is aversive for nearly everyone.

One might ask about people with low self-esteem. Don't they want to confirm that they are worthless, incompetent, unattractive? In fact, people with low self-esteem do not see themselves in a wholly bad light. "Low" self-esteem is only relatively low (typically it is medium).[4] People with low self-esteem want to view themselves favorably; they want to succeed, to be accepted and admired, just like everyone else.[5] Even persons who are targets of discrimination and prejudice and negative labeling from the society at large hold relatively favorable views of themselves. Indeed, they seem to score slightly higher on self-esteem than persons of privileged classes![6]

Alas, events do not always cooperate with our preferred views. We fail, fall short of expectations, are rejected, or behave in ways we may (if only later) regard as wrong or unacceptable. And certainly we act in ways that make others view us critically, even if we are able to rationalize our behavior in our own eyes. Despite our desire to avoid loss of esteem, events can seem to conspire to threaten us. Events have this power to make self-awareness unpleasant because the self is generally considered to consist of stable properties. Each event thus seems to reveal something about the *permanent* features of the self. Failing a test doesn't simply mean that you had a bad day; it implies that you are stupid or ignorant. People may manage to avoid these implications, pointing, for example, to other tests on which they have done well. But the fact that they have to deal with the implications at all is revealing. The event, the failure, suggests that you are stupid, and for at least a moment, it is up to you to convince yourself—and others—to the contrary. The same holds for moral traits. One lie makes you a liar, and it is not easy to reestablish yourself as an honest person, even if you have told the truth on many occasions in the past. Indeed, moral traits may be especially intractable in this regard.

Sometimes people can dismiss an isolated failure without losing much self-esteem, but other times this is not so easy. When I was in college, a fellow student rebelled against a course he disliked during his senior year. He stopped attending class or doing any work and skipped the final exam. As a result, he failed the course. But his self-esteem was not affected. He was a senior and had achieved top grades all through college; indeed, he graduated with honors and prizes despite that F. And of course, the failure was largely due to his decision not to bother trying to do well on the course.

But imagine another student failing the same course—a

first-semester freshman, someone wondering if he or she really is smart enough to succeed at a prestigious university, someone who was trying to do well in the course, someone who hadn't already accumulated a record of A's to prove academic competence. That same F grade would be much more upsetting to that student than to my friend: That grade would suggest failure and incompetence. Under such circumstances, it can become very painful to think about oneself. To look in the mirror is to see a failure, a loser.

Experiments with mirrors and cameras—which have become standard tools for researchers trying to make people self-conscious—confirm this effect. When events cast the self in an unpleasant light, people avoid anything that makes them think about themselves, such as a mirror. For example, after receiving a bad evaluation, people were quicker to leave a room in which they faced a large mirror than after receiving a good evaluation. Other people receiving the same bad evaluation, but in a room without a mirror, did not show the same hurry to leave—it was the combination of the mirror and the bad evaluation that people wanted to escape.[7]

In another study, male subjects met an attractive woman and received a "first impression" rating from her.[8] Unknown to them, she was helping to conduct the experiment and gave half the men, chosen at random, an uncomplimentary rating: She described these men as boring jerks she had no interest in meeting again. These men showed a desire to avoid cues that reminded them of themselves. Self-awareness appeared to be acutely unpleasant for them, in contrast to the men who received an approving response from the woman. A similar effect was found in another experiment where people were induced to act in ways contrary to their beliefs— reading aloud statements that contradicted their own personal attitudes.[9] The feeling that they had betrayed their personal convictions made self-awareness painful for them.

The importance of permanence was suggested in yet another study.[10] Here, everyone received a bad evaluation. Some people were led to believe that they might improve on their weaknesses, while others were led to believe that their weaknesses would be permanent. The latter were more inclined to escape from self-awareness (again, this meant leaving a room lined with mirrors). While it is unpleasant to think we have faults, it is especially unpleasant to think that we have lasting faults.

People vary in susceptibility to feeling bad about themselves. Some people are better at keeping the multiple aspects of self separate, so that a failure and bad feelings in one realm don't carry over into others. For example, if someone regards herself as an executive, a mother, a good athlete, and a wife, and all of these identities are unconnected, this person may find an athletic failure easier to bear because she can comfort herself with success in other realms. It is when all parts of the self are linked together that failure makes a person most eager to escape from thinking about himself or herself.[11]

This last finding points the way to understanding how personality factors (such as the complexity of the self) may play a role in escapism. As long as the focus is on escaping the self, traits of the self may prove decisive. A concept of self that has many different, loosely related parts is relatively resistant to threats. It can be compared to a mansion with many rooms and wings. If there is a calamity in one wing of the mansion, residents can retire to another wing and remain comfortable there. In contrast, if the concept of self is like one large room, even a very nice room, there is nowhere to go to escape from a calamity. When a calamity occurs, it is necessary to leave the house altogether.

Another factor is self-esteem. Of course, a single calamity can occur to anyone, regardless of the level of self-esteem, and laboratory studies have failed to find any consistent relationship between self-esteem and the need to escape the self following a personal failure. But self-esteem may be linked to the perceived frequency of embarrassing, humiliating, and degrading experiences. People with low self-esteem feel that they fail often; people with high self-esteem think that they generally succeed and are good at most things. In one experiment to investigate how people respond to failure, the participants performed a task and were tricked into thinking that they had failed.[12] People with low self-esteem took the failure to heart and set about trying to improve their abilities so as not to fail again. People with high self-esteem, however, were unwilling to tolerate failure, and they generally preferred not to spend any more time on the task. One of them, when told that he seemed to have low ability at this task, replied, "Yes, this must be one of the few things I'm not good at." (The interviewer had to struggle to keep herself from laughing aloud!) For him, clearly, failure was an unaccustomed experience, and he wanted to be sure that we knew this.

The lower the self-esteem, the more common the need to forget the self: Addiction researchers have concluded that many different forms of addiction share a common feature in appealing mainly to people with low self-esteem.[13] Addiction is, of course, only one end—a very troublesome one—of the spectrum of escapes. But it does indicate that constant feelings of low self-esteem may be linked to frequent desires to forget the self.

Clearly, there are many things that can cast the self in a bad light. Failure at a task or test is only one type of threatening event. Finding out that your spouse or lover is romantically involved with someone else is often a major threat to self-esteem, because it implies that you aren't desirable enough to keep your partner's interest.[14] Becoming the victim of a crime is often lowering to one's self-esteem, because it undermines one's view of oneself as the sort of person who deserves to have good things happen.[15] Even contracting a serious disease like cancer can pose a threat to one's self-esteem.[16] At a more everyday level, self-esteem can be damaged by any sort of failure or bad evaluation, whether from authority figures, friends, lovers, or even strangers.

In short, events that carry threatening implications about the self make people want to escape. They want to forget about their identities if worries are associated with them. This motivation for forgetting the self tends to occur as a crisis. A particular event, a calamity, creates an acutely painful or unacceptable implication about the self. Often it is unexpected. (To have expected it, the person's view of himself or herself would have had to allow for the likelihood of the unhappy event, and so the event would come as less of a shock to self-esteem.)

The typical sequence of events includes a discrepancy between what you expected or wanted and what actually occurred. This is blamed on the self, with the result that the self is linked to some undesirable traits. The self-blame is significant: It is not just that things go badly, but that they reflect badly on you. The result is an unpleasant awareness of self as falling short of its own standards and expectations—a highly undesirable emotional state you wish to end or escape. This scenario seems to produce a sudden and intense desire to do something to obliterate awareness of self. The method of escape may be chosen haphazardly, based on whatever is immediately available and powerful enough to have the effect. A person may fail to take adequate precautions or consider long-range effects, and this type of motive to escape can produce dangerous consequences.

In essence, in a crisis that provokes escapist motivations, reality falls short of what one wanted or expected. Such a disappointment may arise either because one's standards and expectations were too high, or because events were especially bad. For example, a study of suicidal women showed that most of them were seriously disappointed and frustrated by the level of intimacy and closeness in their marriage or romantic relationship.[17] The gap between expectation and reality was huge—regardless of which might be out of line. For some of these women, the disappointment was attributable to male partners who were aloof and withdrawn, and so the woman's quite normal and reasonable expectations were not being met. Susan, for example, seemed to have a fairly standard idea about how spouses should interact, but her husband, Donald, seldom initiated conversations with her, answered her only in monosyllables, rarely had sex with her or showed affection, and seemed to have no interest in being with her or hearing about her feelings. Feeling isolated and lonely despite being married, she was driven to attempt suicide.

In other cases, the male partners seemed to be willing to be close and intimate to a normal degree, but the women held unrealistic expectations for intense intimacy. Ellen was typical of this group. Her husband, Bill, was much more willing to spend time with her than Donald was with Susan, but nothing Bill did was enough. Ellen thought Bill should anticipate all her needs, empathize with all her feelings, and share all his feelings with her; that he should phone her often during the day, tell her each night everything he had done, and hear about every little thing she had done. To him, she seemed unable to tolerate being alone for even a minute, and he soon came to find her demands for intimacy were intrusive and excessive. Ellen too attempted suicide. Bill and Donald were miles apart in their capacity for intimacy, but both their wives ended up feeling left out. The disappointment was the same, but in Susan's case it was due to external factors, while in Ellen's case it was due to excessively high expectations.

When misfortunes or setbacks occur, people can either blame external factors and exonerate themselves, or take responsibility and blame themselves. Escapist motivations arise mainly among people who follow the latter path. If you can blame your troubles on other people, on the government, on nature, on divine will, on an enemy, you don't end up feeling so bad about yourself that you have the urge to escape. In contrast, self-blame transfers the onus of misfortune onto the self. It compounds your suffering by suggesting that you will receive more misfortune in the future. If you decide that your lover left you because she or he was neurotic, unstable, and incapable of true intimacy, you simply need to pull yourself together and find someone else. But if your lover left you because you are unattractive and unlovable, then you probably should expect others to treat you the same way in the future. That's the sort of conclusion that makes people want to forget themselves.

SELF AS STRESSOR: THE BURDEN OF EXPECTATIONS

It seems obvious that people want to forget about themselves when something makes them look and feel bad, but the self can be a source of constant stress even without a major failure or setback—indeed, this may be the more common experience.

Research on stress has produced a number of surprising findings, including the fact that a person can be under tremendous stress *even if nothing bad ever happens*, as was shown by the classic "executive monkey" experiments performed by behavioral biologist Joseph Brady and his research group in the 1950s.[18] The executive monkey worked six-hour shifts pressing a button to avoid electric shocks. Typically, these monkeys performed very effectively and received only a few shocks. Yet after about three weeks, the monkeys died. Ulcers were found to be the cause. As was demonstrated repeatedly, the shocks themselves were not responsible for the ulcers, for other monkeys who received the same number of shocks showed no ulcers or, indeed, any harmful effects at all. The stress became fatal without requiring anything bad to happen: the relentless demand for constant vigilance and effort to ward off the threat of harm killed the monkeys.

Subsequent researchers refined and elaborated Brady's work, only confirming the key point: You can be under a great deal of stress without ever experiencing any harmful events. Failures, rejections, disappointments, and other calamities can indeed produce stress, but stress can occur without any of them.[19] Stress is typically a matter of the *anticipation* of something bad happening. You can get an ulcer just from worrying about how your kids will turn out or whether you'll be fired. The stress occurs even if your kids turn out fine, and you keep your job until retirement age. Some people go through life full of misery, struggle, and worry despite the fact that, viewed from outside, their lives seem to be charmed with constant success and good fortune. I have a good friend who's done precisely that for fifteen years. Each time something good happens, he feels good for a short period of time, but then reverts to worrying about the next disaster. As far as I can tell, none of these disasters has ever materialized, and indeed life has treated him remarkably well. But he has been almost continuously miserable. Instead of enjoying his successes, he is always worried about some future failure.

In short, it is the *threat* of something bad, not the actual occurrence, that creates stress. This principle is very important for understanding the need to escape the self. Certainly, some calamities make people want to forget themselves, but we all must live with the *vulnerability* to calamitous experiences even if the feared disasters never come to pass. The more elaborate the self, the more it is at risk of constantly falling short of standards and expectations. Each performance, each evaluation carries the risk of falling short—and hence the risk of unpleasant emotional states. People don't want to feel bad, yet the higher the expectations that surround their definitions of themselves, the greater the risk of feeling bad.

This constant vulnerability is especially stressful for certain groups. Professional athletes, for example, are constantly required to perform their jobs before large audiences, maintaining a heavy burden of appearing competent and effective under difficult circumstances. Likewise, politicians have to sustain a larger-than-life image of integrity, compassion, and competence, despite constant scrutiny by the news media looking for faults and frequent challenges by opposition candidates who do their best to make the politician look inept, indifferent, or immoral.

The more we invest in the self, the more we have to lose. The need to escape the self can therefore occur without any negative feelings about the self. Indeed, the most successful and outwardly perfect self may produce the greatest inclination to escape, because the higher standards create the greater vulnerability and hence the greater stress.

It is easy to predict that crises and calamities will foster a need to escape, but if stress arises from constant threat and vulnerability, when exactly will escape be sought? Stress research suggests a simple answer to this question: It doesn't matter. The conclusion from many studies is that it is very helpful to have some time off, but one can schedule this time off at any point. Vacations and work stress make a good analogy: It doesn't matter much *when* you take your vacation, but it is important that you take it sooner or later.

This principle has been demonstrated under the rubric of the "safety signal" hypothesis. The studies show that it is highly stressful to be continually exposed to threat. Even if the danger remains, if there are periods when you can be sure that it's safe to relax, stress is greatly reduced.[20] Just having a sense that you *can* escape the danger is comforting.

In one classic study, people were exposed to unpredictable noises. Most of them were able to cope, but at a cost: afterward their frustration tolerance was reduced and their ability to perform effectively was temporarily diminished, both symptoms of stress. Only one group of subjects showed no negative effects of stress. These people had been told that if necessary, they could press a button that would turn off the noise. They were asked not to press the button if they could help it, and in fact *none of them ever tried to turn off the stressful noise*, but they thought the escape was available in case they needed it. That belief alone reduced the harmful effects of the stress.[21] These results can be applied to the problem of escaping the self: An occasional period in which one is relieved of the burden of selfhood can make a large difference.

The notion that the self is stressful furnishes several predictions about patterns of escape. Calamities can trigger an urgent need to escape, such that people will look for any quick and powerful technique without necessarily considering long-term consequences, while the stress of self suggests a regular, confirming need for brief episodes of escape, which can be foreseen and planned. A person can fit regular escapist patterns into his or her life, almost like a hobby. Of course, the person may not think of the activity as offering escape from the self but simply find it enjoyable to develop a hobby or pastime that clears the mind of the concerns, worries, problems, preoccupations, and other matters that attend the ordinary identity.

The use of regular, predictable patterns of activity to relieve stress has implications for how people will escape. People who want to find some respite from self on a regular basis will probably use much safer and more manageable means than people who find themselves in an unexpected crisis and desperately look for something quick and powerful. Alcohol, for example, can be used either as an emergency response to a crisis, or on a regular basis to provide a temporary relief from stress. When a major personal setback occurs, such as a demotion at work or being jilted by one's beloved, people may go out and get drunk—paying little attention to issues like safety (that is, making sure there is someone else to drive home), health care (considering the harmful effects of severe drunkenness), or how one will be able to perform tomorrow morning in the midst of a major hangover.

Other people may use alcohol on a regular basis to deal with such stresses of self as maintaining the right image at work. These persons may come home from work and immediately drink a martini or two, which they find relaxes them and lets them enjoy their family life without constantly worrying about their career. This use of alcohol may become a regular part of the person's life-style, but it is likely to be kept within limits. If the person has something important to do the next morning he or she may refrain from drinking, or at least may stop at one drink. The person may take fewer risks and chances with health or injury. And if there is a need to stay completely sober one evening or one weekend, it is no problem to skip the alcohol. The person needs the escape to occur periodically, but it doesn't have to be on any particular occasion.

Similar conclusions emerge from comparing two other escapes that will be covered in later chapters, masochism and suicide. Sexual masochists use their activities to remove their ordinary identity, but they appear to organize these activities into their lives in a safe and planned fashion. They don't seek out unusual sexual experiences in response to a particular calamity, but rather find a regular basis for playing these games (as they refer to them). They are extremely careful about physical safety. In contrast, suicide is typically a response to an immediate calamity. Often the person has not really made a considered decision to die, but feels so bad that he or she seeks oblivion through drug overdose, or takes great physical risks that focus the mind on the immediate present. Unlike the masochists, who usually experience no harmful effects of their escape, suicide attempters frequently end up dead or seriously injured.

The notion of stress of self also permits one to predict which types of people will be most prone to engage in various escapes. Politicians and professional performers have already been mentioned, but any group of people whose selves are linked to high standards or expectations, or who are constantly threatened with loss of face, will tend to be exposed to greater ego stress and will therefore have a greater need of periodic escapes.

Assuming that historically recent demands on selfhood increased the stressfulness of the self, one may predict that this cultural change would produce an increased need for escaping from the self. Thus, the early modern period should show an increase in various forms of escapist activities, especially the ones that involve regular, stress-reducing patterns. There is no reason, of course, to assume that this cultural change would also increase the frequency of calamity-driven escapes, although some overlap is plausible.

ECSTASY:
DISCARDING AN IMPEDIMENT

A third motive to escape the self involves the positive attractions and benefits of being rid of the self, getting away not *from* but *to* something. This distinction parallels "freedom from" and "freedom to" in Erich Fromm's classic work, *Escape from Freedom*, although his analysis portrayed escape as essentially a regressive rejection of individual freedom rather than a response to the difficulties of selfhood—or, here, a state enjoyable in its own right and conferring benefits and advantages to the individual, such as increased opportunity for creative work or spiritual advancement.

There is a long history of recognizing that loss of self entails bliss. The very word *ecstasy* derives from Greek roots meaning roughly "to stand outside oneself." Religious experience is perhaps the most obvious form of this escape from the self. As chapter 9 will show, high levels of spiritual attainment require dissolving the ego, feeling oneself merge with God or with the totality of being, and overcoming what spiritual sophisticates refer to as the illusion of separate, individual selves. Self is regarded as a substantial hindrance to spiritual advancement by religions all over the world. Even Christianity, whose mystical tradition has generally been of secondary importance, has always condemned the self and treated self-ish behaviors as sinful. According to Christianity, salvation requires overcoming self-orientation, and this is all the more true in religions that emphasize meditative or other practices designed to achieve salvation before death.

Western society has never emphasized spiritual mysticism or meditation, but people have long sought ultimate experiences through love. Love, too, requires breaking down the walls of individual selfhood. In Christian doctrine, the supreme experience of God's love involves merging with God and losing oneself in divine bliss.[22] More secular lovers think of love as merging with another human being.[23] Our culture is fascinated by the way in which two people become one when they fall in love. Love is probably the most popular secular ecstasy in our society, and it is commonly experienced as the overcoming of individual selfhood through merger with one's beloved. Losing oneself in union with another human being is a form of escape from self, and a highly fulfilling one.

Other losses of self also yield benefits. It appears that the highly satisfying experiences of immersion in stimulating, creative work involves a loss of normal self-awareness. This experience has been termed "flow," and it involves a sense in which the individual merges with the task.[24] Some authors have even proposed that one learn to overcome self-awareness in order to perform optimally at certain sports, such as archery or tennis.[25] Laboratory research has also shown that people perform best on a range of skill tasks when they manage to escape from self-awareness. In contrast, preoccupation with self tends to produce nervousness, anxiety, and choking under pressure.[26]

In fact, the longstanding and widespread problem of test anxiety seems to have concern with self at its core. "Test anxiety" refers to the pattern of unpleasant feelings that ends in a student's being unable to perform up to his or her capability during a test: The person knew the material when studying the night before, but when sitting in the exam room faced with the blank sheet of paper, is unable to summon up the knowledge that is needed. This problem appears to result from focusing attention on the self. When people who usually suffer from test anxiety are distracted from themselves, their performance improves significantly. Indeed, they end up doing as well as anyone else.[27]

Creative performance may also suffer from self. Anyone who has been asked challenging questions in public knows how surprisingly hard it is to think creatively while a group of people are staring at you. The struggle to create has often led people to experiment with mind-altering substances that they hope will take them out of themselves and thus enable them to produce their best creative work; examples range from poets like Samuel Taylor Coleridge or writers like Aldous Huxley, who sought to use exotic drugs to help them create great works of literature, to many modern writers, such as those in the recent "Lost Generation," whose alcohol abuse turned out to be counterproductive. Musicians have undoubtedly been the most assiduous devotees of drugs and alcohol in the search for creative stimulation. The short history of rock music is full of triumphs and tragedies linked to the use and abuse of these self-negating substances.

The self is also a barrier to sexual fulfillment. When Masters and Johnson revolutionized the field of sex therapy, one of their key discoveries was that self-awareness is a powerful detriment to sexual performance and satisfaction.[28] Sexually dysfunctional men and women often appear to be watching themselves closely during sex, and they evaluate their own performance by measuring it against standards and expectations. This "internal spectator," as Masters and Johnson labeled it, is often excessively critical and interferes with response and pleasure. For example, a man may worry whether his erection is hard enough, and so during sexual play he pays close attention to how hard his penis gets. If it seems at all limp, even for a moment, he may react with panic, which usually contributes to further loss of erection. Thus, a cycle is set up, involving self-awareness, anxiety, and lack of erection, each contributing to the next.

Likewise, a nonorgasmic woman may watch herself during sex with an attitude of skepticism about whether she will be able to have an orgasm. As intercourse continues and she does not have an orgasm, the internal spectator keeps her painfully aware of how much time has elapsed. She starts to feel that now it is time for her orgasm, and now it is overdue. She thinks her partner must be getting impatient, and she wonders what he privately thinks about a woman who can't seem to enjoy sex. She wonders if he will reject her if she doesn't reach orgasm quickly. The increasing urgency of the demand for orgasm is counterproductive, and again, the cycle leads to frustration and prevents satisfaction. Another aspect of self-awareness that is often detrimental to sexual satisfaction involves egotistical approaches to sex. For some people, sex may be a performance or a conquest, a way to show off their excellent technique or their ability to charm many partners. In these cases, too, sexual pleasure is impaired.

The techniques of sex therapy developed by Masters and Johnson were aimed partly at getting rid of the internal spectator. Overcoming self-awareness is an important factor in restoring people to normal sexual responses and enabling them to find pleasure and satisfaction in sex. Of course, this technique is not limited to sex therapists. Many people use simple techniques for reducing self-awareness to increase their sexual pleasure. Some people drink wine or other alcohol before sex. A hot bath, a back rub or massage can focus attention on the body and away from the symbolic identity. Just the act of removing one's clothes can help strip away symbolic identity and work roles, allowing one to become merely a body, which is the prerequisite for sexual pleasure.

The individual self holds center stage in modern Western culture, and that is not about to change. There are strongly positive aspects of selfhood and identity seeking that are very important to people, especially in our modern culture. The self is a major source of ideals and values, and it holds the promise of such forms of fulfillment as fame and reputation. People want to find, know, express, and cultivate their inner selves, and presumably they receive important satisfactions from these activities. But even if the self is not burdensome or stressful in any way, people seem to experience a wide range of benefits from temporarily escaping themselves.

THREE

The Self Against Itself

It is not love we should have painted as blind, but self-love.
—Voltaire, *Correspondance, à M. Damilaville*, 11 May 1764

Psychologists have long been fascinated with the human penchant for self-destructiveness. From procrastination to suicide, people seem to do things that will bring them distress and loss. How can rational beings behave so irrationally? What could be more basic than self-preservation? Yet people often behave in ways incompatible with self-preservation: harming themselves, compromising their values and goals, or defeating their projects and ambitions. Indeed, after observing human behavior for decades, Freud was moved to conclude that people possess an innate, instinctual mechanism that drives them toward destruction, harm, and death.

Much of this book is devoted to patterns of behavior that have self-destructive aspects and that have long been interpreted by psychologists as self-defeating, such as masochism, suicide, and alcohol abuse. But in fact we can find no basis for concluding that people are driven by self-destructive motives (apart, that is, from people who are mentally ill). Escape, not defeat, is the key to understanding what people want when they end up hurting themselves. Even suicide, which seems the quintessential form of self-destruction, is apparently motivated more by the desire to escape than by a genuine desire for harm: Unsuccessful suicide attempts are extremely common—and may be quite successful escapes.

In this chapter, we will take a fresh look at this and other self-destructive tendencies. How normal are they? What are the causes? Researchers have a lengthy catalog of self-defeating or self-destructive ways, but the reasons and causes behind these behaviors have not turned out to substantiate popular theories. For one thing, the role of guilt has never been confirmed. Guilt makes people feel bad, and it makes them want to stop feeling guilty, and it even makes them want to do something positive to offset what they did that made them feel guilty. But no one has been able to show that guilt makes people want to suffer, or that we harm ourselves or seek punishment as a way of handling guilt.

Perhaps this should not be surprising. When people break the law, for example, they rarely seem to want to be punished. If accused, they usually hire a lawyer and do whatever they can to escape punishment. The key to understanding self-destructive behavior, at least among people who are not mentally ill, seems neither guilt, nor self-hatred, nor a death instinct—but rather a desire to escape and forget the self and its problems. The person wants immediate relief and will accept risks and costs to get it.

DELIBERATE SELF-HARM

The first question to ask is whether people are ever primarily guided by a desire to harm themselves or defeat their projects. What circumstances produce such tendencies?

Trying to Fail

Despite considerable research into the question of whether people deliberately try to fail or to do badly at some task, few cases have been substantiated, and even these are not unequivocal. One early theory was that people who expect to fail will try to fail, because they want to confirm their expectancies. This idea is related to the familiar notion of a self-fulfilling prophecy, that is, that what people expect tends to come true *because* they expect it. In the case of self-defeating behavior, we would have to believe that people want their beliefs to be confirmed more than they want to succeed with their projects. The studies cited to confirm this view are questionable, and careful follow-ups have been unable to repeat the findings.[1]

Another idea was that people with low self-esteem will try to defeat themselves to confirm their low opinions of themselves. In particular, these people might "reject success," that is, respond in a negative way to success: If they regard themselves as worthless or incompetent, they might feel uncomfortable doing well and therefore sabotage something that seems to be going well. This idea has received little support, though people with very low self-esteem don't react to success the same way others do.[2] Most people respond to an initial success by investing themselves more heavily in that same sphere: If you win an important tennis match, you will tend to devote yourself more to tennis. People who hold confirmed low opinions of themselves don't seem to make such changes in response to success.[3] Or they even withdraw, unwilling to risk a subsequent failure that might discredit the success or preferring to work on their shortcomings rather than on things they are adequate at.[4] Still, this is not the same as rejecting success. People with low self-esteem desire and enjoy success as much as anyone else.[5] They might tend to believe criticism more than praise or find failure more plausible than success, but emotionally they prefer positive feedback.[6]

A related notion is the idea that women in particular have a "fear of success." This idea surfaced about two decades ago, in connection with evidence that some women imagined aversive consequences connected with success.[7] In a study conducted by Matina Horner at Harvard, people were asked to make up a story about an imaginary person who received top grades in medical school. If the subject of the story was identified as female, women tended to complete the story with unpleasant events—for example, the brilliant student was rejected by her friends and ended up unhappy and lonely. The evidence for this fear of success has never amounted to much, and now may be time to pronounce that theory dead once and for all. One researcher recently examined the data and found no conclusive evidence to support the belief that women (or men) fear success.[8] Women may not try their hardest when working with a man who holds traditional views of male superiority,[9] at least if the man is attractive in other respects, but this is hardly a case of trying to fail. Such a woman is primarily working on a different task: making an impression on the man.

People do try to fail—if failure can make them look good in some other way.[10] Highly anxious people withhold effort if succeeding would set them under a burden of expectations for continued success.[11] Others may let the boss win a racquetball game to avoid making a powerful enemy. They may let a child defeat them at some contest, in order that other adults will regard them as mature and supportive, or to encourage the child. All of these patterns involve trade-offs whereby the person gets something positive by failing. Based on our current knowledge, we cannot say that people desire failure or self-harm under any circumstances.

Choosing to Suffer

A second type of behavior that could indicate deliberate self-harm involves choosing to suffer. If people follow a certain course of action in order to experience pain or loss, we could assert that they have self-destructive motives. The question, then, is whether normal people ever choose suffering when they could escape or avoid it.

There are very few situations where psychologists have found anything resembling deliberate choice of suffering.[12] These choices occur only under fairly limited conditions of moderate unpleasantness, like receiving a few electric shocks or eating a caterpillar: If the person is first made to expect the unpleasant task, but later given a choice, the person may indeed choose the unpleasant task over the neutral one. These people seem to choose unpleasantness as a consequence of expecting it. Their psychological processes are based on the belief that there is no alternative, and momentum from these processes leads to the choice to suffer. This is not the same as having a deliberate desire for harm. Instead, the people face up to the necessity of suffering, resign themselves to it, and deal with it in their own minds. Only after these steps have been completed will a person actually choose to suffer.

There is evidence that some people entertain the superstitious belief that by suffering now they can be better off later. These people seem to think that they are destined to get a fixed quantity of suffering in life, so the choice is between suffering now and suffering later.[13] This idea has strong resonances in religious doctrines that God will comfort the afflicted, or that the next life will compensate people for what they have endured or suffered in this life. Under the harsh conditions of life in the Middle Ages, roving sects of flagellants marched from town to town, stripped naked to the waist, lashing themselves or their neighbors with small whips. They hoped that the spectacle of their suffering would convince God to ease up on the many afflictions He had visited on them.[14]

Even these cases, however, don't really qualify as deliberate self-harm. None of these people desired harm for its own sake or as an end in itself. Rather, they genuinely expected benefits to follow from current suffering. In fact, the goal is *escape* rather than harm to self: By choosing to suffer now, the person hopes to avoid further, future, or greater suffering. As in the cases of trying to fail, the person chooses to suffer as a means toward achieving some attractive, desirable goal. There may be occasional or isolated cases in which people wish for suffering and failure, idiosyncratic responses that elude laboratory studies, no matter how carefully designed. Researchers have been unable to set up a situation in which people in general will want to fail or suffer. No situation or experience researchers could devise has been able to generate self-defeating intentions.

TRADE-OFFS

Pure self-destructiveness may be something of a myth, but it is clear that people do exhibit a variety of patterns of self-defeating behavior. They sabotage their own performances, endanger their health and well-being, undermine their material goals, and even condemn themselves to emotionally painful circumstances. There is no evidence that people *desire* these unpleasant outcomes, but they do choose them when the alternative is an acutely painful awareness of self. When a person's image of self is at stake, many other concerns become secondary. Harm to self is accepted as a cost of avoiding unwelcome thoughts of the self as incompetent, unworthy, unlovable, unattractive, or otherwise deficient. Let us take a look at some instances.

Self-handicapping

Self-handicapping is an excellent example of a self-defeating trade-off, creating obstacles to one's own success that can furnish an excuse for potential failure.[15] Self-handicapping is a strategy that prevents one from getting valid feedback. The student who fails to get enough sleep the night before a major exam can blame a low grade on the lack of sleep and avoid being labeled as stupid. The alcoholic whose life is in a shambles can blame his or her problems on the bottle rather than personal inadequacy. The under-achiever can attribute a lackluster record to not trying hard, which is better than lacking talent.

Such patterns can start early in life, especially if parents encourage it. Jane, my neighbor, once told me about her son's schoolwork. "He gets C's because he won't apply himself. He could easily get A's and B's if he worked harder, but you know how boys are." She said this with an indulgent smile. We all recognize this sentimental tolerance for the smart young boy who can't be bothered with the busywork school-teachers assign when the outdoors beckons. As long as her son didn't put forth maximum effort, Jane could sustain her belief in his great potential. But what if he tried his best and still got C's? It is hard to imagine her smiling so indulgently while saying, "My Johnny works as hard as he can but only gets C's . . . I guess he's just kind of dumb." Under such circum-stances, it becomes risky for Johnny to work hard at his schoolwork, for if he still got a C it would puncture this bub-ble. Once he learns that he must never take a chance on doing his best and failing, a career of underachievement is born.

The other side of the self-handicapping coin is that if a

person does succeed, he or she gets extra credit for overcoming the handicap. Success always looks good, but it looks doubly good if you haven't practiced or studied much. Every so often Johnny would come home with an A, which would confirm Jane's belief in his great potential—especially because she knew he'd gotten that A without even trying. Indeed, some people try to have it both ways by practicing or studying secretly.[16] That way, they get the benefit of being prepared, but they can pretend they haven't prepared much, so they reap the extra credit of appearing to succeed despite a handicap!

Thus, self-handicapping is a strategy that makes you look better regardless of whether you succeed or fail. The conclusions people make about you based on your performance are improved—they attribute failure to the handicap, not to you, and they attribute extra ability to you if you do succeed. The catch is that, objectively, it makes you more likely to fail. Not trying, not practicing, not sleeping, being drunk—all these do in fact impair performance. Self-handicapping is thus a trade-off that sacrifices actual performance quality for the sake of attributional benefits. The self-handicapper is protected from the implications of failure, at the cost of increased likelihood of failure. Reality is sacrificed for illusion, and it is often a bad bargain.

The harmful effects of this self-defeating trade-off may show up only gradually, over a long period of time, whereas the benefits may be more immediately apparent. Self-handicapping typically sacrifices only a certain *probability* of success, receiving in exchange fairly *certain* attributional benefits. A person worried about an upcoming performance might feel it is better to fail with an excuse than without an excuse, and so the person may self-handicap. The possibility of failure was real, so on a short-term basis the person may feel that he or she has lost nothing while gaining valuable protection against a humiliating outcome. Over the long run, however, self-handicapping will cause some failures that could otherwise have been successes, as the laws of probability do their work. Self-handicapping is stacking the deck against yourself, and you can't beat the odds forever.

Consider the athlete who arrives in training camp with a heavy burden of expectations, thanks to being chosen high in the draft or having been sought after by many teams. Suppose this person copes with the pressure of expectations by not exerting himself to the maximum during practice and suspending training each time a minor injury occurs. His supposed great potential is never disproven, and he can retain the respect of the others without having to perform at a stellar level. In the long run, however, the lack of stellar performance may prevent his career from reaching its potential. He may then develop a drug or alcohol problem and put his career on hold. It seems terribly self-destructive, and it is. But he has achieved one crucial goal, which is to preserve the image that his talent and potential were sensational. If he had gone out and tried his best, he might still have failed to perform at a stellar level, and then everyone would have known him to be mediocre.

Self-handicapping is typically caused by some insecurity about one's ability to succeed. A particularly important type of scenario is one in which you somehow accumulate a record of success, but don't privately feel that you really did it— or that you can do it again. Secretly, you may think you were just lucky, or that things worked out better than you deserved, but other people see your success and conclude that you are brilliant. And they expect you to keep up this high quality of work. This combination of high external expectations plus inner lack of confidence—pressure plus insecurity—is very oppressive and stressful, and studies show that it does in fact make it very difficult for people to perform as well as they should.[17] Perhaps it shouldn't surprise us that people facing such a tough situation are especially prone to resort to self-handicapping.[18] After all, if failure seems very likely, taking on an additional handicap doesn't matter much, and protection from the implications of failure becomes increasingly important.

Self-handicapping, then, is a trade-off that sacrifices some of your chances for success in exchange for bolstering your *appearance* of competence. This is not exactly the same as processes of escaping the self, but there is an important conceptual link: What looks like self-destructive behavior—not trying hard, not preparing for a presentation, not getting enough sleep before an exam—is motivated by the desire to save oneself from looking bad. Escape, not harm, is the goal.

Substance Abuse: Getting Drunk or Drugged

A second self-destructive trade-off involves substance abuse. Alcohol, tobacco, and many other drugs have been shown to have harmful effects on personal health, as most users know well. Yet people continue to use these substances, often to excess. (Since every package of cigarettes contains an explicit warning about its dangers, it would be hard indeed to avoid realizing that smoking is harmful!)

Alcohol use is sometimes motivated by self-handicapping,[19] as discussed in the last section, but there are also other reasons for drinking and taking drugs. One obvious reason is that these substances cause pleasant sensations.[20] They make you feel good. They also help you stop feeling bad, especially by helping you to escape from yourself. Alcohol reduces one's awareness of self,[21] and smoking may do the same.[22] Less is known about illegal drugs (the illegality makes it much harder for scientists to conduct research with them), but it seems likely they have similar effects. We'll return to alcohol in chapter 7 to examine its power for producing escapes. For the present, our concern is how alcohol and other substance abuse constitutes self-defeating behavior by offering some benefits, but with the potential over the long run of producing extremely damaging results to health, finances, relationships, work, and other important aspects of life.

Substance abuse resembles self-handicapping in two further respects. First, its benefits are immediate, whereas its costs only become apparent later. Having a few drinks makes you feel good right away, but the hangover doesn't come until morning, and the liver damage or the disruption of career and marriage doesn't become apparent for years. Second, the benefits of substance abuse are fairly certain, while the costs are often a matter of probabilities. Smoking doesn't *guarantee* that you'll get cancer or emphysema—it just increases the odds.

Most important, the role of escaping from self is central. People use alcohol to lose self-awareness, not to destroy their livers. Smoking may have similar effects; for example, nervous people find that smoking gives them something to do with their hands, and the preoccupation with smoking activities can help take the mind off one's worries about looking bad or feeling stupid. Thus, like self-handicapping, substance abuse is a form of self-destructive behavior that is motivated by a desire to avoid thinking badly of yourself.

Health Care: Disobeying the Doctor's Orders

The medical establishment has long suspected that people fail to take all their medicine as prescribed, to get the full recommended rest, and to follow the rest of the advice of their physicians. Recent evidence confirms a startling disregard for professional care and advice. In different studies, compliance rates with doctors' orders have ranged from a high of 82 percent (still only four out of five patients) to a low of 20 percent.[23] People only keep about 75 percent of the medical appointments they make, and when someone else (such as a spouse or parent) makes the appointment the no-show rate rises to 50 percent. Likewise, compliance with long-term treatment programs is only around 50 percent.[24]

The self-destructiveness of disobeying doctors' orders seems obvious. Physicians prescribe medicines and other forms of therapy in order to maximize the patient's chances of surviving and recovering. To disregard this expert advice is to take often serious risks of slower recovery, recurrence of problems, more severe or frequent illnesses, and even death. Yet, as we have seen, noncompliance rates run from 20 percent to 50 percent, and occasionally even higher.

People don't like to think of themselves as sick, and complying with a health care regimen may constitute an unpleasant reminder of illness. For example, when a disease has aversive and obvious symptoms, people comply and take their medicine, but when the effects of the disease are not obvious, people are less likely to comply. A particularly dangerous pattern arises with treatments that make the symptoms go away before the patient is fully cured. In such cases, people are notoriously prone to stop taking the medicine once the symptoms clear up. Once they are able to forget that they have a problem (with the symptoms gone nothing reminds them), they discontinue treatment. This leaves them vulnerable to relapses and other complications. Sometimes people have symptoms that are wholly unrelated to their disease, yet they discontinue treatment if the symptoms disappear—a very dangerous pattern in dealing with a serious disease.[25] Patients who regard their symptoms as intolerable will seek treatment and generally follow it. When symptoms are not so bothersome, however, people comply much less, regardless of the severity of the disease.[26]

The common thread seems to be that people want to escape from *awareness of the self as ill*. While there are other reasons for not following the doctor's orders—people don't like treatments that are painful, expensive, or inconvenient —the need to escape from one's sick self is an important one.

Revenge and Embarrassment

In 1668, the Duke of Buckingham, a leading figure in the British government, was having an affair with the wife of the Earl of Shrewsbury. They were not especially discreet about it, and one day the duke compounded the continuing offense by making insulting remarks to the earl's face. The earl, whose sense of politeness prohibited him from reproaching his wife, felt it necessary to defend his (and her) honor by challenging the duke to a duel. The challenge was accepted, the two fought, and the earl was mortally wounded.[27] As in many duels over the centuries, the exercise of getting revenge for a personal humiliation required a risk that had destructive consequences.

Losing face is extremely aversive, and people will go to great lengths to prevent or remedy a loss of face. They will accept substantial costs to accomplish this end, costs large enough to make the response seem irrational, and even self-defeating. People really will cut off their nose to save their face.[28]

The first goal is to stop whatever is causing the loss of face. People will accept tangible, even financial losses in order to bring an embarrassing situation to an immediate close.[29] Whether these trade-offs are a good or a bad bargain may be difficult to establish, but it is nonetheless surprising that people will abandon important goals and sacrifice monetary gain in order to avoid a temporary, unpleasant feeling of embarrassment.

If another person is responsible for the loss of face, people will often look for revenge. Here, too, studies have shown that people will go to great lengths and accept tangible losses to get even.[30] The determining factor often seems to be the degree of loss of face. The irrational, self-destructive pursuit of revenge doesn't seem to occur if there is little or no loss of face. If someone has caused you trouble or cost you money, you may be angry and may try to get even, but you probably will not want to lose even more of your resources in the quest for revenge. If the person has also humiliated you in front of others, however, you are much more likely to be willing to accept losses and sacrifices for the sake of revenge. The role of aversive self-awareness in these patterns is quite obvious. Embarrassment is one prototype of a state of high self-awareness combined with unpleasant emotion. People will make whatever choices promise an immediate end to these unpleasant states, even if these choices carry significant costs.

Outside the laboratory, similar factors operate. The writer Calvin Trillin has noted, in a discussion in his book *Killings*, the element of pride that underlies long-running feuds between rival families or gangs. As Trillin puts it, it is not simply that you have murdered my brother so I must murder yours, as if it were a business transaction; rather, you murdered my brother, and so you think you are stronger than we are and can look down at us, and to show you that you are wrong in feeling superior, I will murder your brother.[31] Often such killings are not in direct retribution for other killings but occur in response to verbal insults. A member of one family makes insulting remarks to the member of the other family about his family, and the second pulls a gun and kills him, perhaps even in front of ten or twenty witnesses.

Here again, self-defeating behavior results from a desire to avoid feeling bad about the self. In this case, the public self is at issue. It is distressing to think that others are laughing at you or regarding you in some negative fashion. People will seek revenge, even at substantial material cost to themselves, in order to prevent that from happening. The cost to the self makes this behavior self-defeating, but people will do self-defeating things in order to avoid a negative view of self.

Shyness

Nearly everyone has felt shy at some point, and two people out of five describe themselves as shy people.[32] Shy people are not committed loners or contented introverts, however; most shy people strongly desire to get along with others, to have friends and lovers, and to experience intimacy, but they are afraid that they will make a bad impression and experience rejection, humiliation, ostracism, and anxiety.[33] They are painfully aware of how they might be perceived by others, and they constantly fear that others see them in a bad light.[34] They focus on avoiding anything that might produce rejection or embarrassment.[35] If required to interact with others, the shy person will nod and smile but not reveal anything very personal. If not required to interact, the shy person will often withdraw from social situations and avoid other people.[36]

Shy people do indeed end up being relatively lonely,[37] having few intimate, long-term, romantic relationships[38] and relatively little sexual experience,[39] as compared with non-shy people. Shyness often leads to self-imposed isolation, and the accompanying loneliness testifies to the self-defeating nature of the cycle. The shy person ends up destroying his or her chances to become intimate with others. The shy person fails to approach others for fear of being rejected, but the only way to get close to others is to approach them—to share oneself. It is necessary to take a chance on being hurt.

A secondary problem is that shy people often fail to develop adequate social skills. Shy people are more awkward and more often behave inappropriately in social situations. They are slower to start conversations with others than are non-shy people. When they do converse with someone, they say less than non-shy people, make less eye contact, reveal fewer emotions in their faces, and smile less.[40] All of these things reduce the message of warmth and interest that encourages people to get to know and like each other. As a result, shyness may become self-perpetuating. If a person is afraid of being rejected, he or she avoids other people, and this avoidance prevents the shy person from learning how to make friends and become intimate with others.

The trade-off in shy behavior is the sacrifice of long-term satisfactions of intimacy and friendship for the sake of short-term safety from anxiety and rejection, fitting the by now familiar pattern in self-destructive trade-offs of immediate benefits with costs that only become apparent over the long run. The causal role of the self is clear. The withdrawal is a response to the aversive emotional state (that is, anxiety), which is caused by the discrepancy between how the person wants to be regarded and how he or she expects to be regarded.[41] The large gap between the hope of acceptance and the anticipation of rejection focuses the shy person's attention painfully on his or her own inadequacies. This awareness produces anxiety, and shy withdrawal is the result. By avoiding others, the shy person can prevent that horrible, anxious feeling of self-consciousness.

A final category of self-defeating behaviors has less relevance to the present argument. Errors in judgment, whereby people overestimate their abilities and take on too much, can lead to suffering or loss. These actions are indeed self-defeating, but they seem unrelated to self-destructiveness or escapism. These people choose strategies they think will bring them success, but that backfire—to their disappointment.[42]

PAINFUL SELF-AWARENESS

A common thread among the factors discussed in this chapter is the state of feeling bad about oneself. Painful self-awareness seems, as suggested earlier, to reflect the circumstances of modern life. Concepts of self (including one's public image or reputation) are extremely important, and people have fewer alternative values to live for than previous generations did. When self-image is threatened, people fear they have nothing left to hold on to. The result may be panic or anxiety. Without their good name, what is left? Anxiety is a terribly aversive state, and people who feel it want to do whatever will make it stop, go away—and not return. In many cases, escape from self-awareness will accomplish this.

Thus our survey of self-defeating behaviors leads back to the notion of escape from the self. People don't seem to harm themselves out of a death wish, guilt-based wish for punishment, or self-hatred. The jilted lover who drowns his sorrows in alcohol isn't trying to enact some Freudian death instinct or punish himself for his failure as a lover. Rather, he's trying to turn off his view of himself as an unwanted, undesirable, unlovable person. The underachiever who doesn't study before a major exam isn't trying to ruin her life in order to punish herself for some past sins, but to protect herself from being proven stupid, on the principle that if you're going to fail, it's better not to have tried your best. The shy person who avoids dates and parties isn't trying to prove that she's worthless or to spare others the burden of her miserable companionship; she's afraid that if she approaches others they might reject her, which would be the most painful short-term experience she could imagine, partly because it would imply that she's a worthless, unattractive person.

It is thus love, not hate, that underlies self-defeating behavior. Our love of self is so great that it becomes intolerable
to let ourselves be seen in a bad light. When events do cast
the self in a bad light, the first impulse is to turn the light
off—that is, to escape from awareness of self. We shall look
next at the mechanisms whereby that escape is accomplished.

FOUR

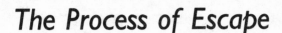

The Process of Escape

I tell you solemnly that I wanted to become an insect many times. But I was not even worthy of that. I swear to you, gentlemen, that to be hyperconscious is a disease, a real positive disease. Ordinary human consciousness would be too much for man's everyday needs.

—Fyodor Dostoyevsky, *Notes from the Underground*

How, exactly, do people manage to take their minds off their identities? The self cannot simply be turned off like a lamp. At first blush, the notion of escape from self seems logically impossible, and in practice it often remains difficult even when people learn how to manipulate their minds so as to accomplish it.

It is important to remember that there is something of a difference between escaping *to* and escaping *from*. Some people want to escape from themselves because the self has become linked with distressing thoughts and painful emotions. Others may desire to escape for the sake of benefits, such as gaining ecstasy or flow. Just as there are many escape routes, so there are many paths leading to the desire to escape. In most cases, the process of escaping the self shares some common features.

UNMAKING THE SELF

Forgetting the self would be easy if one could simply force one's mind to think about something else, but forcing one's mind to avoid any sort of unwanted thought is generally difficult and only marginally successful.[1] When it is the self that is to be suppressed, the difficulties multiply, for the self cannot monitor its own efforts to suppress these thoughts without attending to itself. You can't force your mind to forget who you are, but you can trick yourself with mental strategies that drastically diminish the scope of the self, to the point at which many elements that make up the self are removed.

Identity and Meaning

As we have seen, the self is typically a vast and multi-faceted entity—much too large and complicated to be completely present in awareness at one time.[2] When you feel self-conscious or think about yourself, you actually focus on only a part of the self. It may be the body, or part of the body, or a personality trait, or someone else's impression of you, or an occupational role, or some small aspect of the work self, such as how good you are at preparing charts in the reports you write. By shifting your focus, you can become aware of these different parts of yourself. Obviously, this doesn't get rid of the self-concept in any permanent sense, nor does it force you not to think about yourself at all. But it does shift attention away from particular aspects of the self. If your boss told you that the charts in your last report were disgraceful and sloppy, you would probably feel bad about yourself in that respect. One solution is to shift your attention to some other aspect of yourself. Thinking about being a good parent or skilled musician may enable you to escape from the bad feelings associated with your poor performance at making charts.

For many people, the different parts of the self are interconnected.³ It doesn't work simply to shift into a different role and remind yourself that you are good at other things. Or thinking about another role isn't enough to overcome the setback. In those cases, the person needs more drastic measures. The next resort involves *shrinking* the self. Instead of shifting awareness to a different part of the self, you focus very narrowly on a small aspect, ideally one unconnected with the problem. What often seems to work is to reduce the self to its most fundamental and least meaningful aspect—the body—by directing the mind to the movements and sensations of direct bodily experience, such as pain, warmth, walking, or even breathing.

This shift strips away the many layers of meaning that make up personal identity. As the web of meaning is cut away, only the body is left: The problems and worries and emotions and stresses were based on the *meanings* of the self. Whether the charts in your work reports are good or bad is a concern related to various meaningful conceptions about yourself—your job, your future and career, your view of yourself as competent, your ability to support your family financially. That whole set of concerns vanishes if you can manage to be simply, merely, exclusively aware of your body. If you can go jogging and keep your mind focused on the feelings in your legs, the other issues are left behind. You are still focusing your mind on yourself, for your legs are part of you. But they are a very small part and one that is not linked to elaborate or complex meanings. If you can keep your mind on your leg muscles, you can forget about those terrible charts in your report.

Escaping the self reverses the process of making the self. You detach additions, strip away roles, traits, and obligations. If the self is a *construct*, in the sense that it is created by attaching many things together, you escape by *deconstructing* it, which essentially means to take it apart or unmake it. That leaves you with only the irreducible core of self, namely the body. Apart from the body, the rest of the self is something that was *made*, and to escape the self, you must mentally unmake it.

If you can limit your awareness of yourself to your bodily processes and feelings, you will be free of most of the self. An extreme example of this is the beginner's exercise in Zen meditation of focusing the mind exclusively on breathing. Breathing is something everyone does all day, over and over, usually without even noticing. It is worthless as a way of defining one's identity. It is hard to imagine any context in which the question "Who are you?" would seriously be answered with "I am someone who breathes." Breathing doesn't distinguish you from any other living person (or even animal). The fact that you breathe doesn't discriminate between any possible activity, any plans or involvements, anything at all. Breathing, as the most banal of bodily processes, is perhaps the most minimal aspect of the self imaginable. So to be aware merely of your own breathing is to escape very far from the self. Past, future, symbols, meanings, possibilities are gone. The self has been taken apart, unmade, to such an extreme that almost nothing is left of it.

Mental Narrowing

The mental processes the mind goes through to escape self-awareness can be grouped under the headings of rejection of meaning, shrinkage of time span, focus on details and procedures, rigid thinking, and banality. The rejection of meaning, that is, the avoidance of meaningful thought, is the essence of mental narrowing. Identity is made of meanings; one way to rid one's mind of one's identity is to cease meaningful thought. Since meaning constructs identity by linking the physical body with many symbols, ideas, and other entities, avoiding meaningful thought cuts the body off from all those things. Without meaning, the world is a chaotic assortment of fragmented, isolated, individual, unrelated things and events.

The rejection of meaning may be particularly desirable when escapist motivations arise from a calamity. The calamity and its implications about the self are typically based on meaning. Consider the student who fails an important test. The failure is itself a matter of meanings, for failure is relative, and test responses depend on understanding and responding to specific questions. The implications of the bad grade may encompass a poor grade in the course, endangering prospects for graduation, and even impairment of opportunities for graduate or professional school or getting a good job. They may also involve the question of the student's intelligence: Am I smart enough to succeed in my chosen field? Worry, fear, anxiety, and other unpleasant emotional states may follow from this outcome and from its implications about the self. If the student can cease meaningful thought, these things will vanish from his or her mind. To be aware of the self as a body sitting in a chair (and nothing further) avoids all the questions about ability, prospects for future success, and other anxiety-filled topics.

By ceasing to think in meaningful terms, a person can avoid emotionally unpleasant conclusions. If threats and anxiety are associated with drawing the conclusion from a particular test grade that one isn't smart enough to succeed, stopping the mind from drawing any conclusions at all avoids that particular threat. Or if the sting of this failure is the implication for one's career goals and life plans, cutting off thought of broad contexts again stops anxiety.

In escaping, people will show a tendency to avoid meaningful thought at any level. We want to stop the mind from thinking about complicated or wide issues that will remind us of problems and worries and anxieties. It may be OK to think about some narrowly circumscribed topic—figuring out how to fix a leaky faucet or some other task devoid of reminders of the failure. The key is breaking conceptual links; suspending the mental activity that relates present affairs to other times, places, events, and concepts; and minimizing interest in general contexts or principles. The mind must stop seeking to learn, to draw conclusions, to invoke broad attitudes. The present must be cut off from other events and times, and experience from moment to moment left unanalyzed, uninterpreted, unelaborated. Things happen, and that's that, and there's no use in trying to figure them out. By unmaking or *deconstructing* experiences, one banishes their threatening and upsetting aspects from the mind.

It is in the escapist phenomenon of shrinking the time span that the term "mental narrowing" is most obviously appropriate. Masochistic sexual activity, drunkenness, or preparations for suicide all focus the mind very strongly on the here and now, shrinking one's time span to the immediate present, shutting out past and future. Anything outside of one's immediate sensory environment seems far away. Past and future events recede from awareness.

This short-term focus may alter a person's sense of the passage of time. It is common knowledge that time seems to pass slowly or quickly under different circumstances. As past and future are cut off, one feels the present expanding. Time will seem to pass slowly, to drag. When you look at the clock, you are surprised at how little time has passed. To understand this, consider some of the variations in the passage of time. At one extreme, when you are deeply involved in meaningful thought, such as preparing for an important event, time will seem to pass quickly. Someone deeply engrossed in meaningful, creative work, will often be surprised at how late it has suddenly become.

In contrast, meaningless activity may have the opposite effect. Time will drag, and one is surprised at how *little* time has passed. Ten or twenty minutes spent standing in line may seem like forever. The mental narrowing involved in escape will tend to make time seem to pass much more slowly, resembling the experience of young children, heroin users, or depressed people, for whom each day may seem endless.

The focus on the here and now is related to the rejection of meaning, for as a general rule, broad meanings have broad time frames.[4] Part of the enormous value of meaning for human adaptation is that it enables us to move beyond the immediate range of stimuli—to plan, anticipate, consider possibilities. Meaning enables us to think about something other than what's right in front of us. But escape involves confining our awareness to the immediate range of stimuli. To think about next week or next year requires meaning: forming concepts, envisioning possibilities, weighing options. But to be aware of the immediate present does not necessarily involve any meaning. Lower animals, for example, can be fully aware of their immediate sensory environment, but without meaning they can't do much thinking about next year.

Focusing attention on small things or processes, thereby avoiding broad and meaningful thoughts, is another mental mechanism of escape. Means are, by definition, closer than ends, so the more you focus on the immediate present, the less you think about future goals and outcomes, and the more you concentrate on procedures and details. Thinking about goals and outcomes may draw you into meaningful thought by invoking moral evaluations or measurements against performance standards. These contexts may bring the mind back to the things you are trying to forget. To focus on details and processes is to avoid those wider issues. A procedure finds its context in the immediate goal, and that is sufficient.

There is some evidence that people do try to focus their minds on details and procedures when they want to avoid meanings. When meaningful contexts and implications would be threatening, people seem to limit their thinking to details and technical issues. Criminals, for example, don't typically consider moral issues or socioeconomic implications when committing crimes. They don't wonder how people will react to being victimized or consider the implications of stealing someone's property; rather, they focus on how they can most effectively get the job done. They think about avoiding detection, preventing fingerprints, opening the window, and other immediate details and techniques.[5]

A similar point has often been made about the participants in the Nazi genocidal projects.[6] The workers, doctors, and guards at the concentration camps didn't reflect on their activities in the context of participating in atrocious mass murders. Rather, they concentrated narrowly on the immediate tasks at hand. They learned to think of their actions as checking lists, moving lines of people, following orders, and pushing buttons. By immersing their minds in technical issues and procedural details, they could avoid the overwhelming emotional threat that would accompany taking a general view of their activities.

The mental narrowing involved in escape may make a person closeminded and mentally rigid. If pushed, the person may draw on knowledge and experience, but thinking will tend to follow preset or stereotyped patterns. This rigidity particularly affects creative thought. Creativity tends to involve *divergent thinking*, that is, exploring new possibilities, implications, or meanings—precisely what the escapist is trying to avoid. An artist or creative writer may try to imagine things in different contexts or to assemble things in novel ways, and so his or her mind must be ready to play, to experiment, to shift and shuffle ideas around. Narrow, predetermined thinking is deadly to the creative mind, which probably explains the decline in creative art in the USSR during the years of totalitarian communism. Great art requires freedom of thought.

Mental narrowing reduces openness to new ideas and other new possibilities. The mind becomes inflexible. The person can still solve short-range problems or apply past lessons to present issues. The mentally narrow individual might perform well on an arithmetic test, for that is simply a matter of applying familiar rules. Creative thought, such as imagining multiple ways of using some familiar items, would be much more difficult.

Integrating new ideas into one's belief system normally requires mental flexibility. One might have to rethink assumptions about oneself and the world, and such rethinking is a very broadly meaningful activity. This is not what the escapist is trying to do. Likewise, playing with ideas, shifting contexts, or searching for insight all run contrary to the main thrust of mental narrowing.

The narrow mind of the escapist is focused on immediate stimuli, and so it is preoccupied with concrete things. It stays on the surface of things rather than delving into deeper meanings, mysteries, implications, and contexts. It is determined to remain superficial. Thus the mind's focus on immediate stimuli, on the here and now, and its avoidance of deeper meanings and contexts have the combined effect of making the stream of thought rather banal. It is empty of interesting content. Persons at an extreme of mental narrowing are likely to be boring to others, and they may themselves be bored, too.

People generally process the events of their lives in a highly meaningful fashion. They consider their actions in terms of long-term goals and consequences. They interpret their experiences in relation to moral rules and values, other experiences, lessons to be learned, and general principles. In contrast, mental narrowing reduces action and experience to their bare minimum. The least meaningful awareness of action is of the simple movement of one's muscles.[7] Imagine a biography of Abe Lincoln that described only the movements of his muscles throughout his life. That would be a very boring and superficial account, and it would miss all the profound meanings of his actions in the context of U.S. history.[8] If you can limit your awareness to the movement of your arms and legs, you have managed to escape from complex meanings. The self that just moves its arms and legs is merely the body, not the socially defined identity.

Experience can similarly be reduced to mere sensation. Experience in its full-fledged form involves a complex, meaningful integration that interprets events and relates them to each other across time and space.[9] Events have meaning and are interrelated. But mental narrowing tries to reduce experience to how things look and feel. Sexual intercourse provides a useful illustration. Sex can be a highly meaningful action and experience if it is understood in contexts such as expressing love, sharing oneself with others, forming (or breaking!) interpersonal commitments, and building or sustaining intimacy in a relationship. But sex can also be reduced to a sequence of movements (undressing, embracing), and sensations (skin contact, warmth, discomfort, pleasure, fatigue). As can be seen among rabbits, sex is possible without language, symbolism, implication, responsibility, or commitment—the hallmarks of meaning. The point is, these meanings do transform sex if they are invoked. (Although it sounds as if meaning improves sex, this is not necessarily the case, since sex depends fundamentally on a set of bodily processes, and preoccupation with meanings can interfere and prevent satisfaction—as sex therapists have long recognized.)[10]

CONSEQUENCES OF ESCAPE

Thus far, we have looked at what goes on in a person's conscious mind during the process of escape. How does this process affect the person's actions and feelings?

Passivity and Impulsivity

The first consequence is that people become passive. Taking control and exerting control form an important part of the self, and escape from the self, therefore, could be expected to involve being passive.

Taking initiative often requires the use of meaning. It involves planning and deciding, which are activities that implement meanings and are themselves based on meaning. Consider the thought that goes into planning a new project at work: evaluations of chances of success and usefulness, time schedules, selection of personnel, relation to other plans and goals, possible conflicts with other projects at the firm. The final plan becomes a blueprint for what the individuals will be doing for several months. Someone who is trying to avoid meaningful thought is not likely to want to go through all that.

Moreover, action implies responsibility. To make a decision is to expose oneself to criticism, failure, and second-guessing, not to mention such matters as moral evaluation and legal action. This is the lesson that many bureaucrats are forced to learn: It is safer to do nothing. To act is to implicate oneself. Passivity preserves one from risk, while responsibility extends the self and makes it vulnerable. If you are trying to escape yourself, added responsibility is the last thing you want. Hence escape will tend to promote passivity and avoidance of commitment, responsibility, and other possible implications of action.

Acts without meaning that do not implicate the self in any lasting way present no conflict with a desire to escape. Meaningless or irresponsible action does not invoke the self. One large category of meaningless or irresponsible action is *impulsive* action, that is, doing something without reflection, without planning, and to a substantial extent without responsibility. When people are criticized by others for something they have done, one defense is to say that it was merely an impulse.[11] Even the legal system is more forgiving of impulsive murder than of premeditated murder. Impulsive action does not implicate the self. It may even help a person escape the self by providing distraction. Engaging in actions that are unplanned and lacking in any long-term context can take the person's mind off broader and more meaningful concerns.[12] When trying to forget a recent heartbreak or failure, one may impulsively go out and drive around in the car, take a walk, putter around in one's basement, or go shopping without any specific list and simply buy whatever strikes one's fancy.

Compulsive actions represent an extreme case of acts stripped of meaning. Compulsive acts are those in which the person lacks a full conscious understanding of what they mean, as in the familiar example of a compulsive hand washer. Such people derive some satisfaction from washing their hands again and again and feel anxiety when they fail to wash often enough. But they are aware that they are not really unclean, and they usually don't know why they feel this urge to wash their hands so often. A therapist or analyst may find the deeper meaning behind the compulsive hand washers' actions, but these meanings are hidden from the persons themselves. Part of the appeal of such actions may well be that they enable the person to deal with some personal conflict in a symbolic fashion—while avoiding a conscious recognition of the troublesome meanings.

In general, escape involves passivity. Most actions make

use of the self, and shedding the self will bring inaction. The main exception is low-level, meaningless activity, done on impulse, without responsibility, without planning. It is no coincidence that alcohol and drug use are often described as irresponsible, for responsibility requires maintaining the self.

Suppression of Emotion

Emotion depends on meaning. This point has been repeated in the different theories of emotion. For example, the psychologist Stanley Schachter argued that the main difference between mere bodily arousal and full-fledged emotion is the addition of meaning: Emotion consists of arousal *plus* an interpretive label that is based on the situation.[13] Another research psychologist, James Averill, has similarly described emotions as transitory social roles based on cultural interpretations of experiences.[14] The feelings of human babies or lower animals that arise without meaning are only analogs to emotion, not full-fledged emotion.[15] That we can have strong emotional reactions to reading a book or a letter makes clear that the emotion is not simply a natural response to physical stimuli but rather culturally induced.[16] People feel emotions in response to events that are defined in terms of cultural and social values, expectations, prescriptions, and options. Anger, for example, depends on complex evaluations of the situation against a fine-tuned set of norms and expectations.[17]

The rejection of meaning, therefore, tends to reduce emotion. The cessation of meaningful thought can be an effective way to shut down one's whole emotional system. Consider the example of test anxiety. If you regard the test as something that will determine your level of ability, and thus your worth as a person, or as something that will decide your fate for the rest of your life, you are likely to have powerful feelings of fear about the test. You may panic when you see a difficult question. In contrast, if you think of the test as a mechanical exercise of reading questions and making marks on paper, you will suffer much less emotion. It's easy to get emotional when your entire life hangs in the balance, but it's hard to get emotional about making pencil marks. The evidence shows that people perform better on tests if they can keep themselves at a low level of meaning, presumably because this lessens emotional involvement and anxiety.[18]

Emotions are also linked to the self. As two writers put it, "Emotions are about what the self is about."[19] That is, emotions involve responses to and evaluations of developments in relation to the self. If your concept of yourself is based on being a successful lawyer, you will have emotional reactions to events that imply that you are a good or a bad lawyer. If being a good parent is important to your self-image, you will have emotional reactions whenever some event suggests that your children are turning out well or badly.

Another way of putting this relationship is to say that emotions are based on how the self perceives its progress toward its goals.[20] Emotions help the self regulate its own regulatory activities. That is, the self is a system that helps an organism keep on track making progress toward its goals, and self-awareness involves evaluating how one stands relative to these goals.[21] The self also regulates itself and evaluates how well it is doing at keeping on track toward these goals. Progress brings pride, satisfaction, and joy, reinforcing the process. Setbacks bring anger, frustration, and sadness, which provide energy for making changes such as trying harder or finding alternative strategies.

The connection between self and emotion has also been discussed by psychologist Tory Higgins in terms of vulnerability to negative emotions. The self is associated with numerous standards and expectations: One measures oneself against others' expectations, against moral principles, obligations, achievement levels and hierarchies, goals and ambitions. Falling short of these standards creates unpleasant affective states.[22]

This link between emotion and self is a further reason that escape from the self reduces emotion. Limiting meaning or identity reduces the causes of emotion. A self that is nothing more than a body is little to get upset (or overjoyed) about. The freedom from emotion is of course one of the central attractions of escaping the self. Escapist motivations often arise from unpleasant emotions or even the possibility of unpleasant emotions. People want to avoid feeling bad. Shedding (or stripping down) the self reduces one's vulnerability to emotional distress.

Removal of Inhibitions

Escaping the self can reduce inhibitions, or internalized barriers against behavior. Inhibitions are typically concerned with the meaning of actions, especially their meaning in relation to one's identity. Sexual inhibitions, for example, typically focus on subjective meanings of sex: Will I perform satisfactorily? Am I immoral for liking this? Will people call me names if I have sex? These are not fears about genital contact per se, but rather about what genital contact will mean and how the self will be redefined.

Consider again the difference between muscle movements and meaningful actions. As discussed earlier, muscle movements are the least meaningful way of thinking about behavior. Inhibitions are almost never based on muscle movements. Theft involves commonplace muscle movements that ordinarily evoke no thought or emotion. Few people are afraid to pick things up or put their hands in their pockets, but when these actions constitute stealing, people feel inhibited from performing them. In a certain context, picking something up and putting it in one's pocket constitutes stealing, and the inhibition is aimed at this meaningful definition.

Firing a gun also employs everyday muscle movements about which people feel little inhibition—lifting the hands, moving one's index finger. But in certain contexts, those movements can be defined at a higher level of meaning as hurting or killing another human being, and people feel strongly inhibited from doing that. In preparation for combat, soldiers learn about weapons and practice all the movements necessary to fire a weapon. Yet in battle, they often find that unexpected inhibitions arise. In the Second World War, researchers were astonished to find that about three-quarters of U.S. combat troops were unable to bring themselves to fire their weapons at the enemy![23] It was not the body movements, the aiming, the squeezing of the trigger, that bothered them—they had gone through those many times with no problem. Rather, it was the full meaning of the action, as defined by the broader context, that produced the inhibitions.

Research shows that inhibitions cease to function when identity is forgotten and meaning is rejected. Self-awareness makes people reluctant to commit immoral actions like cheating;[24] when people manage to forget themselves, their reluctance diminishes. Sexual inhibitions often involve acute self-awareness, and losing oneself is helpful in overcoming these inhibitions.[25]

Escaping the self does not, however, result in a broad pattern of uninhibited behavior. As discussed earlier, escapists are not open to trying new things or creative exploration; rather, they tend to be banal, narrow, closeminded, and rigid. Only those inhibitions are affected about which there is some inner conflict. When a person both wants to do something and feels inhibited about doing it, mental narrowing may make the person more willing to go ahead and do it. Perhaps it is most accurate to say that internal barriers are removed, so the person *would be* willing to do a much wider range of things than usual. In many cases, the person will not actually do them, because of passivity or preoccupation. But the usual inner checks and restraints aren't working. If there were to arise a reason to carry out the acts in question, the person would find there is nothing to hold him or her back.

Instability of Mentally Narrow States

Once a person starts to escape the self, can the state be sustained easily? That is, is rejection of meaning a single event, or does it require a continual struggle? These questions bear on the mind's natural tendencies. If people could effectively keep their minds focused on empty, banal, meaningless things, escape might end with the simple removal (and resulting absence) of all these meaning structures. People could turn off unpleasant thoughts and feelings and remain comfortably numb without effort or struggle. If the mind were content to remain empty, escape would be easy to sustain.

Unfortunately, it's not. Escape states are unstable. The mind is *not* content to remain focused on empty things. The human mind inevitably starts looking for broad meanings and is naturally inclined to think, seek patterns, and analyze. Children don't need to be forced to learn to think or to draw conclusions—they start to do these things on their own, and once they have started, it is often hard to get them to stop. Likewise, meditators typically discover that the mind refuses to sit still and constantly wanders, leaps, or rambles. People seem driven to want to experience their actions in meaningful terms. In reflecting on their own actions, people seem naturally inclined to seek broad, meaningful descriptions.[26] They deviate from this general upward tendency only when there is some specific reason to shift to lower levels and to stay there.

The human mind may be innately programmed to analyze and find meaning. The mind presumably evolved as an adaptive tool to help people take advantage of their environment. To do this, it had to recognize patterns and infer general principles, all of which involve moving beyond single events and drawing broad conclusions. If this is what the mind is for, it should not be surprising that it will tend to do this whenever it can.

In short, the mind will naturally tend to drift toward broader meanings. Under normal circumstances, this tendency is no problem. Indeed, it may continue to be helpful and adaptive as it was in our earlier evolution. In learning some new activity, one starts by focusing on the mechanics, but as these are mastered, one moves toward higher levels and broader meanings.[27] A novice at tennis needs to concentrate entirely on how to hold the racquet and position the feet. As these are mastered, the player can begin to focus on more meaningful aspects of the game, such as keeping score, noting which tactics succeed against which opponents, and planning strategies across successive games.

The mind's tendency to drift upward creates a major problem for the person seeking escape. Escaping the self requires the rejection of meaning, thereby creating a kind of mental vacuum. As the mind tries to fill this vacuum, it will be constantly tempted to resume meaningful thought. Staying at a low level can be difficult, requiring continuous exertion or an external damper or distraction. When the alcohol or drug wears off, you'll need another dose, or the undesired thoughts will resume.

The mind's natural tendency to think is not the only difficulty in the way of sustaining the mentally narrow state. Events may remind you of things you are trying to forget. The rejected lover may be trying to forget her pain and her faithless partner. She may strive to shut him out of her mind. But many things are associated with him in her mind, and these will remind her of their time together. A song on the radio, a few words on television about a place where they traveled together, the sight of an appliance they purchased together—these things bring back all the meanings one is trying to avoid.[28] A single reminder can start a flood of memories, implications, worries, and emotions. Constant vigilance may not be enough to maintain an empty, narrow mental state.

The mind's tendency to think can be helpful. When a major personal trauma or setback occurs, for example, the initial response may be the rejection of meaningful thought, as in denial. Then, gradually, the person copes with the crisis by finding a new way to interpret what went wrong and to put the world back together.[29] Likewise, shifts to relatively meaningless forms of awareness are often vital parts of personal change and growth. Psychotherapy often involves changing the way people view themselves and the world. The first step may require stripping away the person's old ways of thinking. Then new ones can be introduced. Research has shown that shifting people to less meaningful ways of thinking, as in mental narrowing, is an effective first step toward getting them to accept new ways of thinking about themselves.[30] As we shall see, mental narrowing can be used deliberately to that end. Meditation, for example, focuses the mind on narrow and banal things (like breathing or counting) as a first step toward giving the person a radically new and improved way of seeing the world.

Whether the mind goes backward or forward, the instability of the narrow state is the same. It is very difficult for people to remain indefinitely in the absence of meaningful thought. Either they slip back into the meanings from which they are trying to escape, or they move forward positively into new ways of thinking—a fact with important implications for understanding escapes. Escapes vary in how powerfully they narrow awareness. Drunkenness will effectively prevent meaningful thought until the effects of the alcohol wear off, at which point the person may need a new dose. Meditation, in contrast, relies on an act of will to maintain concentration, and all meditators soon discover how relentlessly the mind wanders. For someone who has just had a miserable experience and is trying to shut out waves of painful emotions and esteem-threatening thoughts, meditation is not likely to be sufficiently powerful to work.

These differences in power are presumably related to the different motivations to escape from self. In a crisis, strong and compelling manipulations of mind are needed. At the other extreme, people who are trying to clear their mind temporarily in order to permit new growth or spiritual progress will prefer a means like meditation.

Irrationality, Fantasy, Inconsistency

With the rejection of meaning and the deconstruction of the self, one's normal channels of thought and social being are disrupted. Socialization—the process that turns the helpless wild animal that is a newborn human infant into a member of human society—involves a great deal of learning *how* to think. Social intelligence is a matter of learning what the rules are, how one is expected to act, what comparisons are appropriate, how events are to be understood. One product of this process is what is known as common sense, or awareness of those things the average member of this society is expected to know, and thinking the way the average member of this society is supposed to think. With the rejection of meaning, many such rules and principles cease to function. Rules and principles, after all, are fairly broad and high-level forms of meaning, and mental narrowing tends to push them aside. In many mentally narrow states, such as presuicidal thinking or drunkenness, common sense is an early casualty. Modern identity encompasses ways of thinking about life.

Personal values, for example, are broadly meaningful standards of evaluation, and these too are swept away when the person escapes the self.

In the previous section, we noted that the mind does not naturally remain at an empty, meaningless, idle, narrow level, but strives to resume broader and more meaningful thinking. Because familiar ideas and thought patterns are suspended, however, there are far fewer restrictions on what sort of meaningful thoughts will fill the mental vacuum. We become vulnerable to bizarre, unorthodox, weird thoughts, ideas, and fantasies and novel and deviant systems or ideologies. A person in a mentally narrow state may embrace a new set of ideas much more readily than he or she would under normal circumstances. Also, significantly, people become much less sensitive to inconsistencies in their behavior. In subsequent chapters we will look in more detail at how suicidal people think in irrational terms and come up with seemingly bizarre notions. Sexual masochists are similarly open to acting out scenes that would normally be unthinkable. Under the influence of drugs or alcohol, people embrace as profound ideas that they would normally dismiss with a scoff.

Escape underlies these patterns, partly by reducing the person's acquired common sense. Without common sense, many ideas that would normally be rejected can start to seem plausible or appealing. Common sense tells you how to think; in the process it suppresses both bizarre notions and some creative insights. The philosopher Martin Heidegger and other theorists have criticized common sense as an obstacle to authentic, creative thinking for that reason.[31] Whether this suppression is good or bad is not the issue here: the point is simply that common sense keeps thoughts running in familiar, reliable pathways, and when escape takes you out of those pathways you may become receptive to notions that you would ordinarily reject.

Another factor in escape is the suppression of critical and evaluative processes. Normally, when you encounter a new suggestion or possible insight, you ask whether it fits the evidence and is consistent with accepted principles. Such critical thinking involves using the mind at a highly meaningful level, assembling multiple ideas and exploring whether their implications are compatible or contradict each other—not the sort of thing people do when they have managed to reject meaningful thought. Instead, escape from the self may cause new ideas to be accepted uncritically, with the result that people end up being more than usually receptive to new religious views, new political doctrines, creative insights, or bizarre and irrational conclusions. Again, this may be either for better or for worse.

The notion of consistency may be especially important. Consistency, by nature, involves multiple operations that use meaning. Specific actions must be translated into general principles and compared with other principles (such as those associated with past actions). Avoiding these processes, escapists may perform actions inconsistent with their normal patterns of thinking and acting. The disinhibited behavior discussed earlier can be regarded as a form of inconsistency, the reducing of inhibitions resulting in actions contrary to the individual's usual patterns.

There is a seeming contradiction here. We noted earlier that thinking tends to become rigid and stereotyped during escape; here, there seems to be the possibility for new, creative thought. Obviously, thinking cannot be both rigid and open to new ideas. There are several ways to explain this apparent contradiction. In the first place, mental rigidity refers to the person's own, spontaneously generated thinking, whereas openness refers to being vulnerable to notions introduced by others. Mentally narrow persons may be rigid in the sense of reciting clichés or firm principles to themselves when guidance is needed. Likewise, mentally rigid persons may be willing to embrace a new idea or approach suggested by someone else—but be unlikely to come up with new ideas on their own. Additionally, people may quickly become rigid about the new and strange ideas, whether they initially came up with them or not. Once the strange notion or belief or fantasy finds its way into a person's mind, it may set up shop and take over, so to speak. For example, it is hard to know exactly how masochists first develop their favorite form of sexual fantasy, but once they have it, they may become particular about following the preset script.

Finally, we can distinguish an initial escape phase (in which familiar meanings are rejected) and a reconstruction phase (in which new meanings are accepted or elaborated) in dealing with a crisis. Rigidity tends to accompany the first phase, for the person is trying not to think, but the second phase involves accepting new meanings, and here the person may go beyond rigid adherence to doctrines. This second phase differs considerably from the first, especially in the process of responding to a personal crisis. The initial response to a personal trauma is often one of denial and mental numbness.[32] Denial and numbness entail the refusal of meaningful thought, and if thought is required it is likely to be simply the rigid parroting of clichés or doctrines. Full coping, however, requires the reconstruction of the meaningful world, and for this the person does have to find new meanings. Openness to new meanings may therefore accompany this second stage.[33]

The biggest problem is faced by people who for whatever reason cannot cope normally—that is, cannot rebuild their meaningful world. They remain stuck in the mentally narrow state, unwilling to go back and unable to go forward. The mind's tendencies to seek meaning make them vulnerable to bizarre and irrational thoughts. These can be entertained safely because they are sufficiently removed from the meanings the person wants to escape, but they don't help the person to put the world back together.

These people's situation becomes increasingly desperate. Their minds automatically try to think but find no acceptable set of meanings. They suffer greatly from the instability of the mentally narrow state. They can neither move nor stay put, and so they begin to want stronger and stronger means of escape, such as drugs or alcohol in an escalating pattern or even, as we shall see in the next chapter, suicide.

FIVE

Suicide: Oblivion Beckons

The thought of suicide is a great consolation: by means of it one gets successfully through many a bad night.
—Friedrich Nietzsche, *Beyond Good and Evil*

Mary attempted suicide but failed, and when she recovered she promised her family never to do such a thing again. She tried to pull herself together. She quit drinking and went into therapy, but nothing seemed to work. She remained unhappy. Her son started to say she was not really his mother, she was a witch. She had no idea how to answer him. Everything that happened to her seemed to increase her feeling of failure. She said she felt herself "permeated with a profound sense of degradation, of helplessness and hopelessness."[1] She felt herself to be in a box, a trap, "running around inside in meaningless patterns that didn't go anywhere or produce anything,"[2] surrounded by an atmosphere of despair that grew increasingly oppressive.

Mary started saving aids to a possible suicide attempt. She had promised not to make such an attempt, and she did not actually decide that she would break that promise, but she started making preparations just in case. She found a razor blade in a sewing kit and hid it. She saved pills. A sympathetic doctor had prescribed a tranquilizer for her, and a kind pharmacist refilled it repeatedly despite the no-refill stipulation. She built up a hoard of several hundred pills of various sorts.

A particularly bad day came. She had a kidney infection, and although the physician treated her, she left his office feeling that he didn't really care about her. She felt her psychotherapist had failed her, too. She and her husband went to their family therapists, and she thought they cared more about Dave than about her. She felt rejected, unloved, superfluous, and cut off. No one really understood her or cared. Her life had reached a dead end. Overcome with despair, loneliness, self-hatred, and self-pity, she retrieved the razor blade and began slashing her wrist. In retrospect, she thought the scene took place in slow motion, permeated with horror and disgust. She saw herself moaning, crying, gasping, shrieking, overcome with ugliness and desperation. She felt pain in her wrists, but she accepted it, even embraced it, and pushed herself to continue.

"I don't think suicide was clearly in my mind at that point. What I was doing was having a temper tantrum," she wrote later.[3] Striking herself with the razor expressed waves of rage and despair.

Her husband heard the noise and came to investigate. He took the blade away and treated the razor cuts, which were not serious. She later reported feeling "calm and remote,"[4] feelings accentuated by her observation of how frantic and upset her husband was. She had broken such an important promise to him. He didn't know what to do, whether their marriage could continue. As he paced around their house, Mary gradually lost interest in him, in life. She felt she had done something unforgivable and lost any remaining chance of receiving love and sympathy from anyone. Now it would really be impossible to go on living.

If the razor blade incident had been only a tantrum, Mary now prepared for an earnest attempt at suicide, calmly focusing her mind on how to take her life. While her husband followed her around the house, she was unable to retrieve her stash of pills. Then the mail carrier came, and her husband went to answer the door. Mary quickly collected the pills from her hiding places. To avoid suspicion, she poured all of the pills into one large aspirin bottle. This was fortunate, because when Dave came to ask her what she was doing, she wasn't standing there with six different bottles of pills, but only one aspirin bottle. She told him she had a headache and was getting some aspirin.

Mary said she wanted to go upstairs and lie down, and her husband let her go. Alone upstairs, she slipped into the bathroom and began to take the pills quickly and quietly. She had already decided what sequence would be most effective: first the tranquilizers, then some of the others, finishing up with the aspirin. She had made one mistake, which was to fail to bring more than a tiny paper cup for water. That meant that she had to keep refilling it and refilling it to wash down every few pills, and she had several hundred pills to take. Mary spent a long time intensely concentrating on the task: quietly running the water into the little cup, putting a couple of pills in her mouth, drinking the water to swallow the pills, refilling the cup. As she did this over and over, she soon lost count.

She stopped when she began to feel nauseous. It would be such a waste to throw up and ruin everything, she thought. She went back into the bedroom and lay down, wondering whether she should leave a note. She composed a suicide note in her mind. Just one sentence: "Don't forget to feed the cats."[5] In her mind, she privately said goodbye to her husband, her son, and her therapist. She had to get up briefly when her husband called her, but then she returned to bed and lost consciousness. Her husband found her there later, unconscious and bathed in sweat. He realized what had happened and called an ambulance.

Mary survived this event, but for a period of hours she was intent on ending her life. Was this impulse a cry for help, or an inward turning of aggression, or an expression of status inconsistency, as some of the many theories about suicide have proposed? I shall argue that suicide is often an extreme attempt to escape from self.

The extreme and maladaptive nature of this escape is obvious in people who *succeed* in killing themselves, but it is also true for people who merely attempt suicide. Many of them risk death or serious injury, and survival is often a matter of luck. Permanent damage to the brain or other organs can further impair their chances to live a happy and fulfilled life. The desire for life, the instinct for self-preservation, is certainly one of the most universal and deeply rooted motives in all living things. What could override this and cause an intelligent, adult human being to try to take his or her own life?

Most theories about suicide have started with either Freud or the French sociologist Émile Durkheim. Freud thought the desire to kill oneself derived from the desire to kill someone else: One feels guilty about wanting to kill others and turns the aggressive impulse against oneself. Research has undermined this theory. Recent findings contradict it, suggesting suicidal individuals direct their aggression out toward others rather than inward;[6] these persons fail to exhibit feelings of personal guilt or feelings that they deserve to be punished.

Suicide rates decrease during wartime. For many years, Freudian thinkers pointed to that fact as support for their view: They argued that war directs aggression outward, leaving less aggression to direct inward, thereby causing the reduction of suicide. But recent studies show that suicide rates decrease during wartime even in neutral or occupied countries, where people are not able to direct aggression outward. Indeed, under a foreign occupation, the outward expression of aggression is especially inhibited, and if the Freudian theory were correct, suicide rates should increase. But the opposite appears to be true.[7]

Durkheim proposed that suicide increases as a result of societal processes, and that people poorly integrated into the social community are more likely than others to kill themselves. This theory appears to be correct as far as it goes, and current evidence continues to support it.[8] It is quite true that suicide rates are higher among less well integrated groups; apparently, social integration is a major deterrent to suicide. The theory also accounts for the decline in suicide rates during wartime, for war increases feelings of national unity even in neutral and occupied countries. The theory fails, however, to explain why some people kill themselves, and others in similar circumstances do not.[9]

Some recent views treat suicide as a "cry for help." Sometimes people attempt suicide to manipulate others into treating them better. This is not often an effective strategy in the long run. In a study of women who had attempted suicide, which examined their relationships with their husbands and lovers, the suicide attempts were shown to be counterproductive. The women had hoped to open up their relationships, sensitize their partners to their needs, and gain an increase in intimacy. Instead, the men tended to see their behavior as neurotic and manipulative ploys, and they typically responded by withdrawing further."[10]

Part of the enigma derives from the dual role of the suicide, who is both murderer and victim. Throughout history, this double involvement has frustrated efforts to understand and deal with suicide. Legal and religious responses to suicide have often emphasized the murderer aspect: It is wrong to kill, therefore it is wrong to kill oneself. Many theories about suicide have emphasized the murderer's role. As just noted, Freud believed that the suicide is primarily a killer and that the desire to kill oneself is derivative of the desire to murder someone else.

But in contrast to Freud's theory, the victim role may be the key to understanding suicide. Suicides seem to claim the victim's role for themselves, to see themselves as victims and convince their families and relatives that they are victims. The family of a suicide attempter might in principle become angry and hostile toward that person as someone who had tried to kill a loved one. Instead, they tend to react with pity and sympathy toward the suicidal individual, as a loved one whom someone has tried to kill. If anything, they feel guilty themselves.[11] Some societies have taken this view to an extreme, in which a woman who commits suicide is permitted to formally designate someone else as her killer (such as a husband). Her relatives then come after him as if he had murdered her.[12]

As we saw in chapter 4, passivity is a common component in the escape process. To the extent that suicide is an escape, therefore, suicidal individuals may be more likely to claim the passive role of victim than the active role of killer. In their own minds, they are not perpetrating violence, but suffering it. If they could die passively, without having to take positive action like shooting a gun, they probably would do so in many cases.

I will argue here that the need that suicide satisfies is not one for violence, help-seeking, or revenge. Rather, it is a wish for oblivion. The goal of a suicide attempt is to obliterate the self—to escape from painful emotions and distressing thoughts connected with the self.

This escape theory focuses on what makes people *attempt* suicide. Researchers have found a number of differences between people who attempt suicide but survive and people who succeed.[13] Many factors affect survival. Some persons may feel a strong wish to live alongside the wish to die; the wish to live may cause the person to back out at the last minute or to take some action that increases the chances of surviving. Another factor is the means the person chooses; guns are much more effective than pills. A third factor is luck. The suicidal wish often seems to take the form of extreme risk-taking, such as driving in a very unsafe fashion. Under such circumstances, survival may be determined by external factors. These distinctions have little bearing on the problem of escaping the self, because the difference between fatal and nonfatal suicide attempts has little to do with the need to escape.

An *unsuccessful* attempt at suicide may be a *successful* attempt at escape. Someone who survives a suicide attempt is likely to be hospitalized, removed from everyday life with its crises and problems, treated gently by family and friends, and surrounded by nurses and other professionals who exert themselves to make life pleasant and bearable.

For someone in the midst of a major life crisis, a suicide attempt is often an effective way to escape from it—at least temporarily. The problems don't really go away, but they may seem to for a while. And in the suicidal state, time perspective is sufficiently narrowed that "for a while" is almost as good as "forever."

THE CRISIS

Of the motives for escape discussed in chapter 2, suicide falls more often into the category of calamity-driven escape than the stress-relief or ecstasy patterns. The evidence says that very few people are actually chronically suicidal. People turn to suicide at particular crisis points in their lives, when things have become unusually desperate and intolerable; the vast majority of people who make suicide attempts and survive

will never make another attempt.[14] This contrasts strongly
with other forms of escape; for example, the most common
response to a first experience of masochistic sex is a desire
to do it again,[15] and alcohol is well known to be habit forming. But masochism and alcohol are escapes used on a regular basis to cope with the continuing stress of maintaining
the self. The situation with suicide, as we shall see, is different.

Disappointment: High Expectations, Poor Outcomes

We are concerned here with personal crises that *end* with
a suicide attempt. But how do they *begin*? Not surprisingly,
they begin with something major going wrong—from the suicide's point of view. What is surprising, however, is that the
circumstances don't look bad to outsiders. Suicide rates are
often higher among people who seem to be well off. It is
startling to think that the better off someone is, the more
likely that person is to commit suicide. The reason may be
that well-being fosters higher expectations: It is not the occurrence of something bad, but rather the *contrast* between
great expectations and poor outcomes, that leads to suicide.

Let us consider the evidence. More people (per capita) kill
themselves in prosperous countries than in countries with
lower standards of living. Parts of the United States that have
higher standards of living have higher suicide rates. Countries that support individual freedom also have higher suicide rates than unfree countries. Suicide rates are higher
where the climate is better. More people kill themselves in
spring and summer, when the weather seems most pleasant,
than in fall and winter. In places like southern California
where there is little seasonal variation in the weather, there
is also little seasonal variation in suicide.[16]

Studies of young people show that students have higher
suicide rates than their peers who aren't in college;[17] there

seems little question but that college students are better off
than their same-age peers who are not in college, for student
life offers a promising future and a flexible, stimulating present, in contrast to the lessened prospects of unskilled employment. Another study examined the grade point averages
of students who had attempted suicide. Perhaps surprisingly,
they were above average.[18] Suicidal students had better grades
than nonsuicidal students!

A variety of factors generally thought beneficial seem to
promote suicide. A common theme is that all of the factors
also seem likely to foster higher expectations for success and
happiness. Certainly college raises one's expectations in life,
although the stereotype of college life portrayed on television or in movies is often much more attractive than the
reality. Likewise, living in a region that has good weather and
a high standard of living seems likely to raise people's expectations. In short, the more you expect out of life, the more
vulnerable you may be to suicide.

Suicide rates also rise in connection with negative factors
like unemployment or divorce. The rule seems to be that
suicide results from favorable long-term circumstances but
unfavorable short-term ones.[19] The favorable circumstances
foster high expectations, and short-term problems or setbacks increase suicidal tendencies. People who live lives full
of suffering and oppression don't kill themselves. Rather,
suicide happens when life has been good to someone and
then, abruptly, things take a downward turn.

Kathy Love Ormsby was a woman who seemed to have
everything going her way. A relentless perfectionist, she
drove herself to be a champion runner, a devout Christian,
and a highly successful premedical student. In high school
she had been class valedictorian and set state records with
her running. In college she also excelled at both studies and
sports. In April 1986, her junior year of college, she broke
the collegiate women's record for the ten-thousand-meter

race. At the year-end NCAA meet, she was expected to become the national champion, but early in the final race, she fell behind. She struggled back into fourth place, but she couldn't catch up to the leaders. With about two miles remaining in the race, she turned off the track and ran toward the stands. Unnoticed by the crowd of spectators who were focused on the dramatic competition among the leaders, she ran out of the stadium, crossed a baseball field, climbed a fence, ran down a main thoroughfare onto a bridge and jumped off. The fall failed to kill her, but it broke her back, leaving her paralyzed from the waist down for the rest of her life.[20]

For most people, being the fourth fastest runner in the entire country would be a memorable success. But not for Kathy Ormsby. She felt that everyone expected her to win, perhaps even to break her own record again. She felt that not finishing first would mean letting everyone down, including herself. Thus, what seemed objectively a great performance was a disappointment to her. Her case is an extreme example of the tragic effect of lofty expectations.

As in the case of Kathy Ormsby, suicide attempts tend to occur in the period immediately following some personal calamity. In prison, for example, most suicide attempts occur within the first month of imprisonment. In mental hospitals, the first week of stay is the most dangerous; people who don't attempt suicide in the first week are much less likely ever to do so. Bereavement increases the risk of suicide, but mainly in the first two years. In short, suicides tend to occur very soon after things take a turn for the worse. It is not the condition of bereavement or imprisonment, but rather the shock of transition into that condition, that leads to suicide.[21]

Another indicator is the economy. Depressions and recessions tend to increase the suicide rate.[22] The fear of a drop in the long-term standard of living may be a factor. Suicide rates are highest when people are accustomed to prosperity but experience a sudden deterioration: Again it is the contrast between the favorable expectations and recent or current problems that fosters suicide. Of course, people commit suicide in response not to the national economic outlook but to developments in their own lives, such as downward social mobility. Poverty does not lead to suicide when one is accustomed to it. Rather, it is the fall from prosperity to poverty that leads to suicide.[23]

Similar patterns are found with regard to love and marriage. Married people are generally happier than single people,[24] but overall there is only a slight difference between the suicide rates of married versus single people. In contrast, the transition from being married to the less desirable state of being single—such as in divorce or bereavement—leads to a substantial increase in suicidal tendencies. One study found, for example, that recently divorced or separated people were six times more likely to commit suicide than other single people![25]

Suicide also increases when romantic or other intimate relationships deteriorate. Loss of love, increased conflict, separation, or other signs that a relationship will fall short of expectations are all associated with an increased suicide rate.[26] This is especially a problem among people who have trouble finding romantic partners, such as shy and lonely adolescents, or homosexuals. When they do finally find someone, they tend to latch on to that person desperately and develop extremely high expectations for intimacy. Often this heavy investment in one relationship is accompanied by further withdrawal from all other social contacts. If these intense expectations are not fulfilled, a suicide attempt may be the outcome.[27]

Two brothers had been inseparable companions until they fell in love with the same woman. For the younger and less attractive one, this was his first great love, and he clung to her fiercely. He was in agony when he realized she preferred his brother. He threatened to kill himself unless she chose him. Shaken, she did as he asked and married him. He was happy and felt himself at last to be a mature, attractive man, with a wife who loved him. Alas, love does not always obey resolutions and threats, and the woman found she still loved the older brother. She began a secret affair, but the guilt of deceiving her husband was too much for her. When she and the brother told the husband that they were in love and she could not continue as his wife, he went berserk, alternately threatening and pleading. For him there could be no other; indeed, her rejection signified to him that he would never find happiness because he was not lovable. One night when she was with the brother, he turned on the gas stove, wrote an angry letter blaming his death on his unfaithful wife and malicious brother, and died.[28]

It is not surprising that suicidal people are often those with problem-filled interpersonal relationships, but they do not appear to be loners or voluntary isolates. Some research suggests that these individuals have greater than normal needs for social closeness.[29] The combination of intense desires for intimacy plus interpersonal failure—a large, unfavorable contrast between expectation and outcome—is precisely the sort of situation that fosters suicide.

Other evidence confirms this pattern. Deterioration in health is associated with increased suicide rates, as is deterioration in circumstances at work.[30] The latter need not include loss of one's job: An increased workload, reduced status, or some other change for the worse may suffice. Indeed, failing to get a promotion can trigger a suicide attempt, if the person had been counting on the promotion.

The same pattern is reflected in the way the suicide rate fluctuates with the calendar. Careful research has finally demolished the clinical stereotype that people kill themselves during the Christmas season or at the approach of other major holidays. In fact, suicide rates drop with the approach of holidays, but rise again after the holiday.[31] There is actually a slight peak in the suicide rate *after* a major holiday. The implication is that as a holiday approaches, people expect good things to happen: to be together with family, to see friends, to have time off from work or school, to share gifts, and in general to feel happy. These positive feelings reduce the suicide rate. But if reality does not conform to these expectations, suicide attempts may result. For example, if the family reunion is marked more by sarcasm and quarrels than by harmony and love, or if intimates fail to show as much love as the person wanted, the disappointment may be intense. Similar patterns are found in the days of the week: Suicide rates are highest on Mondays and lowest on Fridays,[32] suggesting that people may feel happy anticipating the weekend but may kill themselves if their hopes are dashed. (A factor here may be that people who kill themselves over the weekend are not discovered until Monday.)

I mentioned earlier that suicidal college students have higher than average grades. There is another side to the story, however: In the study I cited, the conclusion about grades was based on the students' total performance since entering college. A different picture emerges if one looks only at recent performance, for grades the semester before a suicide attempt were typically *lower* than average.[33] Thus, the composite picture of the suicidal college student is someone who is generally doing well in college and presumably expects to continue to succeed, but who then receives a severely disappointing set of grades. Once again, the contrast between high expectations and less favorable outcomes is crucial. Other studies of these students confirm that scenario—the students tend to have demanding parents or to feel in other ways that they are expected to perform at a high level. When they fall short of inflated expectations, they grow desperate, and suicidal tendencies increase.

It's All My Fault

Crises and setbacks alone are not enough to produce suicide. The person must also blame the problems on himself or herself—people who can direct blame elsewhere have little need to escape from self-awareness, for they do not feel that their problems reflect badly on them. Research confirms that suicidal people do tend to see themselves as responsible for what has gone wrong in their lives. One study employed a long checklist of mental, emotional, and behavioral signs to distinguish suicidal people from others. Self-blame was found to be the single most common factor among people who had attempted suicide.[34]

More generally, suicidal people tend to have low opinions of themselves. Over and over, research reports on suicide refer to feelings of personal worthlessness and low self-esteem.[35] Suicides have acute feelings of rejection by others, and this sense of rejection shapes how they see themselves. One researcher interviewed the handful of people who by extraordinary chance survived leaps from San Francisco's Golden Gate or Bay bridges. These leaps are nearly always fatal, so it seems reasonable to regard these people as earnestly bent on killing themselves. Again, a common theme in their interviews was feeling that they were worthless individuals.[36]

A study examining suicide attempts among military personnel found a range of negative attitudes toward the self.[37] Many of the subjects simply said they disliked themselves; others reported feeling inadequate, humiliated, rejected, or guilty. In other cultures, condemnation of self is the most common impetus toward suicide.[38] People feel that they are guilty or unacceptable, or they regard something they have done as irreparably wrong, and so they take their own lives.

Obviously, many people have low self-esteem, but only a

few people kill themselves. Two important differences between those with suicidally low self-esteem and other people
who lack confidence support the escape theory of suicide.
First, suicidal tendencies mainly emerge when one's opinion
of oneself is *changing* for the worse. This fits the argument
that suicidal tendencies arise when one blames oneself for a
recent calamity. Several studies have shown that when people's concepts of themselves change for the worse, their suicidal tendencies increase.[39] Second, of the people with low
self-esteem only the suicidal ones see themselves more negatively than they see others. Many people with low self-esteem
are critical of everyone, not just of themselves;[40] in that important sense, they regard themselves similarly to the way
they regard everyone else. But suicidal people have high
opinions of others and see themselves as the only ones who
are inadequate.[41] The contrast between seeing everyone else
as successful and seeing oneself as a failure is what separates
the suicidal person from other people with low self-esteem.

In general, then, the suicidal process involves blaming
oneself for one's recent problems, with the result that one's
self-esteem suffers. If people can manage to blame their troubles on luck, fate, malicious others, unfair rules, "the system," or any other external factors, they are not likely to
become suicidal. Suicidal tendencies increase when the individual directs the blame inward.

Painful Awareness of Self

Self-blame adds another dimension to personal misfortune. It is no longer merely a matter of circumstances falling
short of expectations—you are disappointed with *yourself*. In
the earlier example of the two brothers who loved the same
woman, the woman's rejection of the younger brother meant
to him that he was a failure as a husband, that he didn't have
what it takes to win the love of a good woman.

This turning of attention toward the self is an important feature of the presuicidal process and central to escape theory, for the motive to escape from self-awareness would hardly arise for people unaware of themselves. The next question to ask of the research evidence, then, is whether suicidal people show elevated levels of self-awareness. Does suicide follow a preoccupation with self?

It is hard to get a direct look at the mental state of someone about to commit suicide. Even under laboratory conditions, it is difficult to know whether people are thinking about themselves—because once you ask them, then of course they are. The difficulties are immensely compounded in trying to discover what is transpiring in the mind of someone sitting alone in a room somewhere going through a once-in-a-lifetime experience, but researchers do have some evidence. One approach has been to look at groups of people known to have high rates of self-consciousness and ask if they also have high suicide rates. The answer appears to be yes. Researchers have established, for example, that self-consciousness is high among adolescents, and suicide rates (especially the rate of unsuccessful suicide attempts) are also high.[42] In chapter 7, we will see that alcoholics and other heavy alcohol users have high rates of self-consciousness, and their suicide rates too are much higher than in the general population.[43] Depressed people tend to be preoccupied with themselves, especially in response to a recent failure or setback,[44] and their suicide rates are also elevated (especially after a recent failure). Turning from individuals to societies, the same pattern emerges: Societies that place a premium on the individual[45] or that emphasize self-oriented emotions[46] have higher suicide rates than other societies.

These studies yield substantial indirect evidence linking self-consciousness to suicide, but is there no direct evidence? Suicide notes offer one avenue for investigation. One must be cautious in generalizing from such notes, for only a minority of suicide attempters write notes, and these people may also differ in other ways from other suicidal individuals. Still, these notes may reliably reflect the mental states of people who are ready to kill themselves, for they are free of any biases that creep into retrospective accounts of unsuccessful attempts.

Studies of suicide notes indicate that the period before a suicide attempt is indeed one of high (and unpleasant) self-awareness.[47] A quantitative approach is to count how often the note writer refers to himself or herself in the note: If you talk about yourself or refer to yourself often, that's a sign that you're on your own mind.[48] These tabulations have revealed that suicide notes are inordinately high in first-person references, much higher than a statistical baseline derived from a wide assortment of documents. It is important to recognize that this high rate of self-reference is not simply due to the expectation of death. One researcher found suicide notes to contain a higher frequency of references to self than writings by people facing involuntary death.[49] The approach of death does focus attention on the self, but an impending suicide attempt is associated with even higher self-focus.

Another relevant aspect of suicide notes concerns their portrayal of the person's social world. People facing involuntary death speak of others in ways that link them together. Writers of suicide notes rarely use such language and instead speak of significant others as cut off from them or opposing them. A person dying of an incurable disease might write to a spouse of "our life together," but someone writing a suicide note would be more likely to speak of "your life" and "my life," as if the two moved in opposite or unrelated directions.[50]

Self-awareness is typically more than simply noticing yourself. People do not take dispassionate, disinterested, casual looks at themselves; instead, they tend to be strongly evaluative when they think about themselves. They measure themselves against standards: goals, ideals, and expectations. Even the simple act of looking in a mirror is typically more than a casual noticing of one's reflection. When people see themselves in a mirror, they immediately measure their image against the way they want to look: Is my hair untidy? Are my clothes arranged properly? Do I look good? Self-awareness as a general rule compares one's view of self with these various standards.[51]

Suicidal people find themselves wanting. The theme of falling short, of personal inadequacy, is found over and over in studies of suicide. The feeling of being unable to meet parental demands is a major factor in the suicide of young, pre-teenage children. College students who commit suicide often have parents who are unusually demanding or who hold lofty expectations for the student's academic success.[52]

The sense of personal inadequacy is perhaps most dramatically shown in suicide among physicians. Physicians' notoriously high suicide rate[53] has prompted repeated efforts to understand how people who seem to have it all would want to kill themselves. But although physicians hold an esteemed position in the community, they must also bear a heavy burden of expectations. Physicians feel they are expected to be full of energy, thoroughly knowledgeable and expert, trustworthy and compassionate, always capable of finding answers and solving the most elusive puzzles. These attributes seem more appropriate for an omnipotent, omniscient god than for an ordinary human being, and many physicians find the burden stressful. The more the physician feels this pressure, and the more he or she feels unable to live up to these demands, the higher the risk of suicide. For example, suicide rates are higher in medical specialties that cast the doctor in a more omnipotent role. Another factor is the feeling of losing skill or competence and being unable to live up to the standards of past performance. This decline, which is to some degree inevitable with aging, is very distressing and may be responsible for the high suicide rates among older physicians just when they would seem to have reached a comfortable, secure, and enviable position in life.

Emotional Distress

Do suicidal people feel more unpleasant emotions than people in general? This would seem to be so obviously true that it would be trivial to point it out. Yet, surprisingly, the evidence is weaker here than for other steps in the theory. One reason may be that since the mental narrowing of the escape process is aimed at suppressing emotion, researchers find little evidence of emotion in suicidal people.[54] The main exception is depression: Suicidal people tend to be substantially depressed. For a time, researchers believed that depression caused suicide, but that view has now been discredited. Since the vast majority of depressed people never attempt suicide, the theory was at best inadequate, and if hopelessness and depression are measured separately, the predictive power of depression drops out of the range of statistical significance.[55] It is hopelessness, not depression, that predicts suicide. Probably the best general conclusion is that people who are prone to experience unhappy emotions are prone to have higher suicide rates. This doesn't mean that they actually are full of emotion when they try to kill themselves, but it is consistent with the view that they are doing their best to avoid these emotions.

Consider anxiety, for example. There is little proof that people are filled with anxiety when they are about to commit suicide. Indeed, they may often be calm. But people with anxiety-prone temperaments[56] and people who experience repeated panic attacks[57] have high rates of suicide and suicide attempts.

Anxiety seems to accompany the loss of social bonds, such as through social rejection.[58] Studies of divorce, loss of employment, and bereavement have shown that people who experience social rejection have elevated suicide rates. Suicide rates rise with the dwindling of chances for forming social bonds: If you belong to a population that is shrinking—an occupational category, an ethnic subculture, a life-style enclave—your suicide risk is increased.[59]

Similar patterns emerge from the study of other emotions. Feeling depressed is one of the most common factors associated with suicide.[60] People who seem most likely to experience a temporary depressed state—such as people who have lost a loved one or job—have increased suicide rates. There is a smattering of evidence for states of anger, sadness, worry, and guilt feelings among suicidal individuals.[61]

NARROW AND EMPTY: THE SUICIDAL STATE OF MIND

Mental narrowing is the key to understanding the state of mind of someone involved in escaping from self. As we shall examine in detail in this section, suicidal people show all the signs of this narrowing, including rejection of meaningful thought, shrinking of time perspective, and deconstruction of the world.

Rejection of Meaning

The noted suicide researcher Edwin Shneidman described the thinking process that precedes suicide as "tunnel vision"—a narrow focus on immediate concerns, avoiding meaningful, integrative thinking, and being closed to new ideas or interpretations. The suicidal person's thinking becomes inflexible and one-sided.[62] The person is unwilling to entertain new ideas or alternative ways of looking at things, to try new approaches or creative solutions to problems, or to see any other side of things. There is a loss of spontaneity in favor of clinging to fixed patterns of acting. In one study, subjects were asked to generate solutions to interpersonal problems drawn from their own personal lives. Suicidal subjects were significantly less able to do this than nonsuicidal individuals.[63]

The link between rigid thinking and suicide has long been established. For many years, researchers thought that rigidity was a personality trait that predisposed people to commit suicide, but recent evidence indicates that the rigidity of suicidal persons is temporary,[64] part of the response to personal crisis. This fits the view of suicide as an escape from the self: A person undergoing a personal crisis responds with mental narrowing, which includes the rejection of meaningful thought and a rigid adherence to preset, narrow styles of thinking.

Time Perspective

The sense of the passage of time among suicidal people resembles that of acutely bored people. The present seems an endless drag. Whenever one looks at the clock, one is surprised at how little time has passed. This has been confirmed with carefully controlled lab studies in which researchers measure out a fixed interval of time with a stopwatch and then ask subjects to estimate how much time has elapsed.[65] A five-minute interval may seem like eight or ten minutes to a suicidal person; nonsuicidal people are much more accurate.

Another sign of the restricted time perspective of suicidal persons is their inability to think about the future. They are less able than others to imagine the future. They can usually talk (with some difficulty) about the past, which they tend to remember in vague, distant, and unpleasant terms, but the future often seems a blank to them. This is apparent even in the grammatical patterns of their speech: They use the future tense less than other people.[66] It appears that this constricted sense of time derives from the desire to escape from thoughts about what might happen in the future. The recent catastrophe brings unpleasant implications about what could happen in the future, and the person avoids these distressing thoughts by focusing narrowly on the present. As one researcher put it, these people are seeking "to stop their lives at a fixed point."[67]

In general, then, the suicidal mental state involves an avoidance of past and future. The mind is narrowly focused on the immediate present, which is felt as empty and somewhat boring—but this is preferable to the acutely unpleasant feelings associated with thinking about the past and future.

Concrete and Banal

We might imagine suicide notes to be reflective, philosophical, broad, and meaningful, to explain the writer's rejection of life. Fictional suicide notes in novels and movies tend to conform to those stereotypes: "Life is no longer worth living" or "Teach my son to be a good man." But actual suicide notes are mundane and specific,[68] reminders to pay the electric bill, requests regarding one's funeral (or lack thereof). Mary Savage, whose suicide attempt was described at the beginning of this chapter, considered leaving a note reading "Don't forget to feed the cats."

This concreteness is specific to suicide notes. People facing involuntary death often write in more abstract and meaningful terms. A computerized analysis of the content of suicide notes found them lacking in "thinking words" and similar expressions of insight or mental processes compared to the writings of people facing a nonsuicidal death.[69] Suicide notes are higher than other notes in references to specific, concrete objects, places, and people, but they contain fewer references to mental processes or inner, psychological states.[70]

Case studies point to similar conclusions. The presuicidal state often includes efforts to deaden the mind by immersing it in routine, narrow, nonmeaningful concerns. This too is contrary to the way people imagine suicide. Stereotypes about suicide may be based on spectacular instances of very creative individuals, such as the writers Sylvia Plath and Ernest Hemingway. These cases seem to imply that thinking wild, creative thoughts leads to self-destructive tendencies, but the reality seems to be that people spend the time prior to a suicide attempt in empty, meaningless busywork. One researcher found a pattern in suicidal college students of immersing themselves in "dull, demanding mental labor" and "emotional deadness."[71] Instead of creative or abstract thought— writing poems or analyzing philosophical dilemmas—they occupied their minds with copying numbers, sorting files, proofreading, or simple calculations.

Another sign of banality and concreteness is preoccupation with details and short-term concerns. That suicidal people are preoccupied in this way can be concluded from the fact that many are recalled by their acquaintances as having been unusually neat, meticulous, and fastidious.[72]

All of these features may be combined in the suicide attempt. Facing death produces an intense concentration on the immediate present, and the mind can be fully absorbed in concrete, here-and-now details. In the suicide attempt described on the first pages of this chapter, Mary Savage had to gather her pills and slip away upstairs without arousing her husband's suspicion. Then she found she had nearly two hundred pills of various kinds to take with only a tiny cup for water. The tasks of planning what sequence to take the pills in and filling and refilling the water cup absorbed her fully. During such moments, one's mind can achieve a kind of peace, for all the distressing thoughts of the self's past and future are far, far away. It no longer seems to matter what events have said about the self.

EFFECTS OF ESCAPE

We have now seen how the suicidal person struggles through a process of mental escape. Four effects of this process and struggle are particularly relevant: passivity, lack of emotion, irrational thought, and the removal of certain inhibitions.

Passivity

Passivity seems key to escaping the self. Being active gets the self involved: One plans, initiates, takes responsibility, and acts as a unity, an identity. Passivity requires far less. As long as one does nothing, the self is not invoked. At least, that seems to be the principle operating in people who are trying to escape from the self. Numerous studies confirm the view of suicidal individuals as passive, adopting attitudes of withdrawal,[73] avoiding responsibility for their actions,[74] responding to challenges with passive acquiescence,[75] or waiting to see if the problem will go away.[76] Their coping strategies rely on social withdrawal rather than problem-solving.[77]

Suicide notes reflect passivity. This takes on added significance in that if any suicidal people have an active stance, it would presumably be the ones who leave notes (because at least they take the initiative to write something). But even they exhibit a passive attitude. The language of suicide notes indicates submission and resignation, in sharp contrast to writings by people who face deaths that they have not chosen. It seems ironic that people who are actively taking their own lives speak in passive terms, whereas people who are passively undergoing involuntary death speak in very active terms.[78]

There are other indications that passivity is central to the suicidal outlook. Suicidal individuals seem to see the world as something they have little influence upon, and this includes a sense that they cannot do much to alter the course of their own lives.[79] They are prone to exhibit passivity toward life in general[80] and feel helpless to exert any control over circumstances.[81]

As explained in chapter 4, the significance of passivity for escapism lies in the avoidance of *meaningful* action. Random, impulsive, meaningless activity presents no obstacle to escaping the self. There is some confirmation of this in research on suicide. Several researchers have characterized suicidal people as impulsive.[82] Other researchers have failed to find evidence that suicidal people have the personality trait of impulsiveness[83] but find the suicide attempt itself is often described as something done on impulse. Thus, while impulsiveness may not be a stable part of these individuals' personalities, it seems to be part of the mental state associated with presuicidal, escapist tendencies.

Lack of Emotion

We saw earlier that there exists surprisingly little direct evidence of unpleasant emotional states among suicidal individuals. Certainly, one would expect their circumstance to bring an abundance of painful emotions: Suicidal people tend to be depressed or anxiety-prone persons who have recently experienced major life crises or disappointments. That emotion is hard to document suggests these people were somehow managing to make themselves emotionally numb.

There is indeed evidence that suicidal people become emotionally numb. In one study particularly important in this regard, researchers asked people in a laboratory to recall memories associated with various emotional states.[84] The researcher would say "happy," and the person was to respond by describing some past experience that made him or her happy. The researchers secretly timed how long it took people to think of a memory that fit the cue, the speed presumably indicating how easy it was to think of such an incident. If it takes you ten minutes to produce a happy memory, then it seems safe to conclude that you haven't had a lot of happy feelings recently. The researchers predicted that suicidal people would respond faster than other people to words referring to unpleasant emotions, but about the same with reference to positive emotions, proving that suicidal people's minds were more attuned to negative, unpleasant emotions.

The results of this experiment were quite different from the predictions: Suicidal people had a harder time coming up with *any* emotional memories—often they couldn't produce a memory that fit the cue at all. When they did produce a memory of a bad emotion, they were no faster than nonsuicidal people, and their memories for good emotions came much more slowly.[85] These findings paint a picture of the suicide as someone who is trying to shut down his or her entire emotional system. Suicidal people seemed alienated from their past emotional experiences. They might have a few unpleasant emotional memories floating near the surface, but they had difficulty remembering themselves feeling any emotional states.

This evidence fits the view of escape theory, namely that the presuicidal mental state involves suppressing emotion. The mental narrowness in the person's response to the personal crisis is at least partly effective in shutting down feelings and cutting the person off from direct experience.

Irrationality

There is some evidence that suicidal people become reluctant to think about their lives in rational, meaningful terms.[86] In many cases, these individuals live in social worlds that are profoundly unsatisfying, their lives characterized by social isolation, rejection, and withdrawal from human contact. Others have relationships full of problems and conflicts or live with aloof, withdrawn, or abusive partners. Many suicidal people compensate for their deficiencies with fantasy,[87] imagining happy, close relationships that provide them the intimacy they lack in real life.

Research suggests that people who reach the point of suicide have tended to think about their lives and their problems in unrealistic, irrational ways and hold irrational beliefs. The suicide attempt itself may be contemplated with fantasy or irrational thinking.[88] Some people indulge in suicidal fantasies. They think about killing themselves, about their final acts and deeds, the coming of peaceful death, and then the discovery by others of the death. They may dwell on the thought of how sorry everyone will be when they are dead.

Other people seem not to fully grasp the fact that they will be dead. They contemplate their suicide yet maintain an interest in what will happen afterwards. Some people imagine themselves looking down on their family or friends from their place in heaven, ignoring the fact that their religious faith denies any place in heaven to suicides. Some researchers place special emphasis on the anticipation of heaven as a sign of the irrationality and inconsistency in suicidal thinking.[89] But only a minority of suicidal people seem to engage in this sort of fantasy or irrationality, and there is little evidence of fantasy or irrationality in presuicidal thinking, which seems marked more by narrowness or absence than by errors.

One last fantasy deserves mention because of its special relevance to escape. In an extensive survey a large number of people, including a group identified as suicidal, were asked what they would like to change about themselves.[90] To the surprise of the interviewers, 20 percent of the suicidal people expressed a wish to be someone else. None of the normal control subjects expressed any such wish. Becoming somebody else is as complete an escape from self as could be imagined. The fact that it is such a strong element in suicidal thinking is an important sign that escaping from oneself is indeed a guiding theme in the motivation to kill oneself.

Disinhibition

Long-range, meaningful constructs such as laws against suicide, desires for self-preservation, internalized social norms, and feelings of obligation and responsibility toward others, as well as expectations of future happiness, inhibit people from self-destruction, and those must be overcome if the person is to attempt suicide. Thus, attempted suicide is itself a sign of disinhibition. But it is clear that many people end up dead without forming the specific plan of killing themselves. Rather, they simply take substantial risks which bring about their deaths. Suicide researchers debate what proportion of single-car traffic fatalities are really suicides, although officially the vast majority of them are classified as accidents. In reality, it may be almost impossible to draw the line. A person may not deliberately decide to drive off a bridge, but may simply take a greater chance than usual— something akin to playing Russian roulette. This gambling with death could result from the loss of normal inhibitions against taking dangerous, life-threatening risks,[91] and there is direct evidence for increased risk-taking among suicidal persons. On personality measures, suicidal people are no more risk-taking than the average person, but in the mental state that surrounds the suicide attempt, they do seem to have a willingness to take greater risks.[92]

More ominous evidence comes from studies of murder-suicide, where people kill themselves immediately after killing someone else, usually a lover or family member.[93] The typical murder-suicide is perpetrated by a white adult middle-class male with no prior criminal record; he kills his wife or girlfriend and then kills himself. These murders of intimate partners would normally be extremely off limits, but something has overcome the person's inhibitions: The implication is that the presuicidal mental state involves a strong enough reduction of one's ordinary inhibitions that such actions become thinkable.

An alternative explanation—the standard Freudian view of such incidents—is that people first commit the murder of the spouse or lover and then, overcome with guilt, kill themselves as punishment.[94] The evidence contradicts this interpretation. Close examination of individual cases consistently shows that the suicide was primary and the murder secondary. Typically, the man was extremely upset at the spouse or lover and viewed her as responsible for his problems. Although he committed the murder first (any other sequence would have been impossible), it appears that usually he first decided to kill himself. Once that had been determined, he then might decide to kill his wife or lover as a kind of revenge for his own death.[95] This fits the picture of the suicidal state as characterized by a removal of inner restraints.

MAKING THE LEAP

We have seen the evidence showing suicide to be in the category of escapes from the self. How does it lead to a suicide attempt? The picture that emerges is as follows: A person undergoes a personal crisis that is blamed on the self, with the result that the person is acutely aware of self as incompetent, undesirable, guilty, or otherwise inadequate. This self-awareness is accompanied by painful states of emotional distress, which the person wants to stop. That's the basis for the desire to escape.

In an effort to suppress meaningful thought, avoid evaluative self-awareness, and shut down his or her emotions, the person narrows his or her mental focus. The resulting state is a kind of numbness, characterized by rigid and concrete thinking, focus on the here and now, banality, and lack of insight. As we saw in the previous chapter—crucial to understanding how the person comes to take his or her own life—this mental state tends to be unstable. The numb and narrow state of mind, already vaguely unpleasant in itself, is difficult to sustain indefinitely. The mind begins to try to resume meaningful thought.

In many cases, people will come out of their crisis, find new sources of meaning or new ways of making sense of recent problems and losses, and resume a normal life. These people are not the suicidal ones. Suicidal feelings arise in the people who find themselves stuck in the narrow, numb state. The world won't stay deconstructed, but they find themselves unable to put it back together in a satisfactory way. Returning to meaningful thought brings a resumption of the aversive self-awareness and the emotional distress that the person has been struggling to suppress. Daily life oscillates between these unpleasant states. One is alternately bored, empty, numb, and acutely aware of personal failure and inadequacy, filled with anxiety, sadness, and other intensely unhappy emotions. Choosing the lesser of two evils is an extremely stressful position to be in.[96] The numb state is the lesser of these particular two evils, but the person can't manage to sustain it.

The person begins looking around for escape. Having lost

hope of ever feeling good or happy, he or she wants something that will at least block out those moments of acute emotional distress and assure a neutral state—something akin to restful sleep, utter removal from all these troubles and circumstances, some form of oblivion. The notion of suicide takes shape as a promise of oblivion.

Normally, people have no positive desire to kill themselves[97] and do have many inhibitions against taking or even risking their lives. This must change for a suicide attempt to take place. When the personal crisis is far enough along, it does change. The future seems blocked or blank or an endless continuation of current suffering. Missing out on such a future does not seem like any great loss.

A factor that normally holds people back from suicide is self-love. Most people hold a favorable view of themselves and are reluctant to let anything jeopardize it. But for the suicidal person, recent events have shaken this positive view of themselves: The self has been shown to be incompetent, unlovable, guilty, or inadequate in some other way. The reservoir of self-love that protects against suicide is quite low. To a person in this state, the future is no precious treasure, and neither is the self.

A last reason to shun suicide is responsibility to family and others: Out of obligation or fear of disapproval, people feel they cannot kill themselves. For example, a man with a wife and family depending on him would not normally feel entitled to take or even to risk his own life. But these obligations are often weakened or removed by the crisis that provokes the suicide attempt. As already noted, suicide rates increase among people whose family lives have been disrupted, and one reason may be that these disruptions remove the responsibility and family obligations to remain alive. If a man's wife divorces him and takes the children with her, suddenly he has fewer external reasons to stay alive. Additionally, because the mental state during the crisis rejects meaningful thought and overcomes inhibitions, a person may cease to think in terms of responsibility to others and obligation to live. In any event, once the ordinary restraints that prevent people from endangering their own lives have been weakened or removed, if a positive desire to die arises, there is less to oppose it than there would be under normal circumstances.

The suicidal impulse, according to escape theory, is less a desire to kill or to be dead than simply a desire for oblivion. The person is looking for peace, freedom from suffering. If someone were to come along and magically offer a wholly new life, one without the troubles and problems the person is suffering, the person would presumably accept this offer rather than kill himself or herself. As we saw earlier, many suicidal people express the wish to be someone else if they could. Unfortunately, there can be no magical transformation into a new identity and new life, but death remains an alternative to the present.

In a sense, then, suicide is simply an escalation in a person's efforts to escape. The person tries to shut thoughts and feelings out of the mind by sheer mental effort, but this doesn't succeed well enough. The person may then turn to alcohol or drugs as allies in the effort to numb the mind, but perhaps these don't work either. Suicide promises to be a stronger, more effective ally. Suicide promises to make it all go away. Answers given in interviews about how people had thought about drug overdoses they had taken confirm this view.[98] They hadn't thought of taking an overdose as a violent act of self-poisoning or of doing permanent, possibly fatal, damage to their internal organs. Rather, they likened the overdose to getting extremely drunk or falling into a deep sleep. It was a way to forget their troubles and find relief from their personal misery.

Suicide is a desperate and extreme form of escape, occurring when awareness of oneself has become intolerable, and yet no solution or improvement is in sight. Obviously, suicide is extremely maladaptive, even in the case of people who survive suicide attempts (as argued earlier, unsuccessful suicide attempts can still be very successful escapes), for it leaves problems unsolved while often causing lasting harm. Viewed objectively, it is a poor solution to personal problems. But to suicidal individuals, desperate and irrational, it may appear as the most powerful, or only, solution available.

SIX

Masochism:
The Pleasure-Pain Paradox

O tried to figure out why there was so much sweetness mingled with the terror in her, or why the terror seemed itself so sweet.
—Pauline Reage, *The Story of O*

Unlike suicide, masochism does not appear to be harmful. Masochists are typically very careful in their practices and choice of partners, engaging in their unusual sexual activities with little danger of experiencing harm. And whereas suicide is usually attempted only once even if the person survives the attempt, masochism tends to become part of a person's way of life.

Masochism illuminates several key features of escape,[1] particularly the reduction of self from identity to body. Masochism is a pattern of sexual response, and it seems to be effective in boosting sexual responses because it puts its emphasis on the body. Clinicians long thought that masochists were frigid, impotent, or otherwise incapable of sexual pleasure, but it has become clear that many masochists enjoy a great deal of sexual pleasure. The possibility remains that people are drawn to masochism because it boosts their sexual responses. People with high thresholds for sexual stimulation, who need a lot to get them going, may be attracted to it. An underlying factor may be that ego and identity simply get in the way when it comes to sex.

The detrimental effects of ego on sex can take various forms. When sex is based on the self, it often seems to lose a great deal. The conquest mentality, for example, uses the number of one's sexual partners to boost one's self-esteem. Groupies seek egotistical boosts from sleeping with famous people. Some people see sex as a test of their skills and techniques; for them, intercourse is a way of showing off. All of these tend to interfere with sexual pleasure. Sex therapists have found banishing the ego from the bedroom helpful in boosting the sexual response. Worrying about the quality of your erection, or about whether you're pleasing your partner, or about whether you're having enough orgasms of the right kind and neither too soon nor too late all detract from sexual enjoyment.

Sex therapists' advice is usually aimed at people with inadequate sexual response, but it seems likely that the same factors work for intensifying sexual response among normal people. Some people are probably attracted to masochism because it gives them intense sexual pleasure. Masochists often claim their activities provide them with intense, memorable orgasms. Such claims may attract thrill seekers and others looking for powerful sexual experiences.

WHAT IS MASOCHISM?

Masochism can be defined as a pattern of sexual behavior involving submission to pain, loss of control, or humiliation and embarrassment. Masochists derive sexual stimulation from a wide range of specific practices, but most masochists seem to have fairly precise preferences. In most cases, the masochistic activity functions as a prelude to sex.

There is a fair amount of evidence available on what masochists like to do. Most masochists wish to experience some degree of pain, although the threat or hint of pain, or a token amount of pain, may be enough. A light spanking or paddling on the buttocks is common—painful but tolerable. Many couples apparently develop codes by which the masochist can signal the partner to stop if the pain becomes too strong.

The giving up of control takes different forms. Perhaps the most common involves bondage, in which the masochist submits to being tied up or blindfolded. Probably more people have experienced blindfolding during sex than any other masochistic practice, for it seems likely that most people who take an adventurous attitude toward sex have tried blindfolding at one time or another. Some couples use stockings or neckties, while others purchase handcuffs. The dominant partner may also issue arbitrary commands or rules that the masochist has to obey. Permission may be required for speaking, going to the bathroom, or having an orgasm. These practices symbolize the masochist's submission to the dominant partner.

Humiliation plays a part in numerous practices, ranging from verbal insults, to public display, to symbolic transformation into a lesser being. Many masochists like to define themselves as slaves. Some masochists, mainly males, like more extreme degradations, such as being treated as a baby (with diapers and all) or as a dog (with leash). Other masochists, mainly females, like to be displayed nude in a deliberate contradiction of our cultural conventions of feminine modesty. To be naked in the presence of people who are fully dressed is arousing to these masochists.

There is no one typical script for a masochistic experience, but these practices make up the set from which most masochists choose their own fantasy. Typically, the masochist and his or her partner will act out a "scene" or "game" (these are their most favored terms for these activities, and they aptly capture the separation of masochistic activity from ordinary reality). During or after the culmination of these acts, they typically have some form of sexual intercourse.

Consider this scene described (probably with some exaggeration) by a man as his favorite masochistic experience. He arrived home from work one evening and, as arranged, undressed and waited quietly for his wife. When she came for him, he looked briefly at her face, which was against their rules, so she slapped him. Next, she took him down to their basement, chained him up to a hook in the ceiling, dressed him in a brassiere, stockings, and panties, and gave him a mild whipping on his buttocks.[2] She invited some other people over. The man was embarrassed to be seen tied up and dressed in lingerie. He submitted to a severe spanking while everyone watched. One of the guests was an attractive woman, and he was told to beg for the privilege of serving her. He was allowed to kiss and lick her feet and perform cunnilingus on her. After a while, the guests departed, except for one man who was the wife's lover. The wife and her lover took the husband to the bedroom, tied him to the wall, and attached a vibrator to his penis with masking tape. They got into the bed and had sex while the husband watched.

This example, although probably composed more of fantasy than of actual experience, combines many different features of masochism. The man experienced pain from being spanked and whipped. Loss of control was implicit in being bound and gagged and subjected to arbitrary rules and commands. Humiliation was achieved by dressing him in women's underwear, requiring him to beg, having him kiss a woman's feet, displaying him in front of an audience, and making him observe himself being cuckolded.

Is masochism always sexual? The term *masochism* was coined by the German neurologist Richard Krafft-Ebing to refer explicitly to a pattern of sexual behavior, and he took the name from an Austrian novelist, Leopold von Sacher-Masoch, whose activities were unmistakably sexual.[3] Beginning with Freud, however, the term has been used to refer to nonsexual behavior as well, most commonly self-defeating behavior. The presumed but false analogy unfortunately persists due to psychology's primitive and misguided understanding of sexual masochism. The broader usages of the term primarily mislead and anger people without shedding any light on their behavior, and it seems best to restrict the term to its original meaning, namely sexual masochism. As discussed in chapter 3, since there is reason to question whether people seek satisfaction from suffering, explaining self-defeating behavior on the basis of masochistic motivations seems dubious.

Who Does It?

Recent evidence discredits the stereotype of a highly deviant individual with serious emotional problems or low self-esteem, or someone full of guilt and resultant self-destructive urges. Masochism does not appear to be associated with mental illness or emotional disturbance. All signs indicate that masochists are surprisingly normal people apart from their admittedly deviant sex lives. Nor does masochism appear to be part of a deviant or maladaptive life-style; instead, it tends to go with an otherwise normal and healthy psyche.

Another stereotype associates masochism with females. This too appears to be false. Masochism occurs in both men and women, though only in a minority of either. As such, it is typical of neither men nor women. If anything, there appear to be more men then women who engage in masochism or admit to having masochistic fantasies. Some have concluded from this that men are more masochistic than women, but more men are reported in nearly every unusual form of sexual practice, so perhaps this pattern simply reflects general trends in behavior or reporting. Although interest in masochism may have no relation to gender, it would be wrong to suggest that gender is irrelevant to masochistic styles. Men and women practice masochism in slightly different ways, presumably reflecting gender differences in roles, expectations, sexuality, and ego.[4] But there are broad similarities as well, and the incidence of masochism is certainly not confined to women.

Probably the most important point is that sexual masochism appears to be more common among successful, individualistic people. The distribution of masochism supports the view that masochism is a form of escape from the self, for the people who seem most vulnerable to the stressful burden of the self have the highest rates of masochism. Consider some of the factors:

First, there is the socioeconomic distribution. The evidence points toward there being more masochists at the top of the socioeconomic hierarchy than at the bottom. Prostitutes catering to lower-class clients rarely receive requests for domination, whereas those who cater to the rich and powerful get many. A group of researchers who set out to study the call girls who work in Washington, D.C., serving the politicians, federal judges, and other influential men in that city, soon shifted their focus from the women to their clients, for the men proved much more interesting. And one of the biggest surprises was the large quantity of S&M services the women were asked to provide. Apparently, many of our congressmen, senators, and federal judges hire prostitutes to spank them and dominate them in other ways—among these elite clients, requests to be spanked or beaten outnumbered requests to deliver a spanking or beating by a ratio of eight to one![5]

Other evidence of the relationship between masochism and the burden of the self is the historical spread of masochism. Most sexual practices have been documented since ancient times, but masochism is a significant exception: It appears to have emerged in our society only during the early modern period (1500–1800). This coincides with our culture's shift toward greater emphasis on individuality.[6] Just when our culture started to increase the stressful burden of the self by insisting that each person cultivate a unique, autonomous, individually responsible and authentic identity, the appetite for sexual masochism spread through the society. It would appear that masochism emerged historically as a response to the spread of individuality—exactly what one would expect if masochism is an escape from the self.

Cross-cultural comparisons also show that masochism is linked to cultural emphasis on individuality. Researchers have found most sexual practices all over the globe, but masochism seems limited to the West. (I refer here to full-fledged masochism. Biting and scratching during sexual intercourse are found in other cultures and may indeed be more common in some of them than in our own; biting and scratching during sex are not the same as masochism.)[7]

The bigger the burden of the ego, the more likely people seem to be to turn to masochism. Masochistic desire is apparently a response to the requirement of sustaining an inflated image of the self. Politicians furnish an excellent example, for they are constantly required to present a superhuman image—competent, virtuous, energetic, and decisive. Moreover, they must sustain this image in the face of forces constantly trying to discredit it, such as hostile news media which love to embarrass them, or political opponents whose success depends on making them look bad. The politician's burden of self is one of the heaviest, and a high frequency of masochism would not be surprising if masochism is indeed a means of providing temporary relief from the stress of the self.

When Do They Do It?

In chapter 5, we saw that most suicide attempters make only one attempt, even if they survive. Suicide is a rare and extreme response to an unusually desperate crisis. Masochism is quite different. All signs suggest that masochists prefer to indulge their sexual desires on a regular basis. Masochism becomes a way of life, or at least a regular part of one's way of life. In one study people were asked how they responded to their first masochistic experience, and the most common report was of a strong desire to do it again.[8] Of the many people who write in to magazines to describe their first experiences with masochism, only a tiny minority indicate that this was their only experience.[9]

Several years ago a masochist and his partner were engaged by an adventure club in the San Francisco Bay area to stage an experience for the group. Members of the club were certainly not masochists, and most had never tried S&M. They belonged to the club out of a spirit of adventure, for the club offered a variety of novel experiences such as hang gliding and motorcycle trips. The S&M experience was approached in the same spirit. The couple arranged for the group to get an initial taste of S&M through exercises such as mild spankings and having the men undress and don pantyhose and submit to verbal mockery by the women. After this episode, a significant number of the club members became active in the local S&M scene.[10] This is as close to a controlled experiment as there is likely to be. A sample of people without prior S&M experience and without any specific interest in such activities was given a taste of the activity. As a result, many of them began to engage in these activities on a regular basis.

Of course, people cannot necessarily engage in masochism whenever they want. It can be difficult to find partners. Many people with masochistic desires find themselves in marriages or relationships with people who have no inclination to try such forms of sexual activity. There is also the need for time, privacy, and energy—S&M "scenes" can require a substantial investment of all three.

The available evidence fits the view that masochism is used fairly regularly, if possible. In describing the stress of self, I said that stress research suggests that it doesn't matter *when* one finds a period of safety and relief, as long as these occur periodically. That seems to be the model for masochism, and these regular patterns provide further evidence that masochism is a form of escape from the continuing stress of maintaining the self.

THE STATE OF MIND

We have seen the basic masochistic practices; let us consider the effect these have on a person's state of mind—how masochism works as an escape.

Pain and Awareness

The central enigma of masochism is pain. Why would people desire pain? The notions that the pain becomes pleasure or that masochists desire pain as punishment appear to be wrong. Pain is for them an unpleasant sensation without a great deal of symbolic baggage: It is not what the pain means, but the way it feels, that is important to the masochist.

The key to understanding the appeal of pain is its effect on meaningful thought. In the insightful account of pain's effect on the mind in her book *The Body in Pain*, Elaine Scarry concludes that pain deconstructs the self and world.[11] In pain, the person is reduced to the body, and the world is shrunk to one's immediate surroundings. Considerable evidence supports Scarry's argument. Pain and meaningful thought don't easily coexist. Pain is difficult to communicate, and as pain increases, people find it hard to engage in abstract thought on any subject. People who suffer from chronic pain experience it as an absence of meaning and often spend much time and energy searching for an explanation, even if that does nothing to alleviate their pain.[12]

Scarry's most detailed evidence comes from torture. Under torture, people act in ways that contradict every aspect of their identities: They renounce deeply held beliefs and values, betray relationships to colleagues and loved ones, abandon loyalties to people and causes, or sacrifice personal commitments. If pain is sufficient, all those other aspects of the self cease to seem real. Torture deconstructs the individual's identity, leaving only a poor broken body wanting physical comfort. To end pain, actions completely contradictory to one's definitions of self will be taken. This inconsistency has already been mentioned as a consequence of the cognitive narrowness of the state of escape. When the self has been taken apart, people cease to be reluctant to perform actions inconsistent with the self.

The implication arises that pain might have great potential as a narcotic, except for the fact that it is so very unpleasant. By finding ways of keeping the unpleasantness of pain within reasonable bounds, masochists are able to benefit from its narcotic effects. Pain is a way of grabbing the mind and focusing it on the here and now. One woman who has had extensive experience with S&M expressed the usage of pain in this way: "A whip is a great way to get someone to be here now. They can't look away from it, and they can't think about anything else."[13] As the comment implies, the actual administration of pain is not even necessary; the threat of pain may be enough to focus the person's mind on the immediate present. When she ties up one of her girlfriends and takes out her whip, the other woman's attention is completely absorbed in what she is doing, even before the whip touches her—and even if it never does.

Removing the Self

In itself, pain is already a powerful means of accomplishing escape, preventing thoughts about long-range concerns or other meaningful issues. Masochism extends this assault on the self through two aspects emphasized in chapter 1: esteem and control. The self seeks to maintain and even enhance its esteem, and it seeks to gain and maintain control over the environment. Masochistic practices undermine both of these functions.

Esteem

Identity depends to some extent upon respect and dignity, but masochists systematically deprive themselves of these. Some masochists desire to be treated like dogs—put on leashes, made to walk on all fours. Others wish to be treated like human infants, another substantial loss of status. Still others seek out verbal abuse and humiliation. Male masochists often refuse to have sexual intercourse with their dominant partners, because they feel that to penetrate the partner would be inconsistent with their proper inferior status.[14] To express their degradation in their sexual activities, they may service their partner orally or masturbate while being watched.

A common male humiliation fantasy goes something like this. The dominant female partner invites one or more female friends over, who sit around and have drinks while the man is ordered to strip naked and put on a show by masturbating for them. Depending on the man's specific preferences, his humiliation is extended by having the women make derogatory comments during his performance, by being required to kiss their feet, by being required to clean up his semen, or by having to perform cunnilingus on each of them.

Female masochists seem less oriented toward degrading practices, but some loss of dignity is implicit for them. A popular form of humiliation among female masochists involves being displayed nude in a revealing pose.[15] Being naked in the presence of fully dressed other people is likely to be embarrassing and jeopardizes one's dignity. One woman described posing nude during a small cocktail party. She lay on a table with the hors d'oeuvres, and the guests viewed and touched her body while getting snacks for themselves. She recalled the exquisite embarrassment of being naked and exposed in a group of well-dressed people. Her body, including its most intimate parts, was available to anyone who was interested, just like the chips and crackers.

In such instances, the ordinary identity is stripped away, for it is impossible to maintain a normal self when engaged in activities that radically contradict it. A modest and respectable woman does not lie naked on a serving table at a cocktail party. A successful professional man does not permit others to watch him masturbate or to make insulting remarks about him, nor does he crawl around on hands and knees wearing a leash. These humiliating practices counteract one of the self's most basic and pervasive functions, namely the pursuit of esteem. Masochists purposely deprive themselves of the dignity required for sustaining their normal identity. Nor are these side effects: They are the goal and purpose of the masochistic practices. Humiliation and embarrassment make it impossible to continue being yourself.

Control

Masochists also seek to be deprived of control, most commonly by bondage. The masochist is tied up and rendered helpless and vulnerable, incapable of decision, activity, or even initiative. Often the loss of control is carried further into arrangements that require the masochist to submit to the partner's commands or rules, and these may be quite arbitrary, because their purpose is simply to demonstrate that the masochist is fully in the partner's power.

The irony is that often the couple's activities are guided by a script that the masochist has written. Typically the masochist initiates the activity, often needing to persuade the partner to take the dominant role. In a sense, therefore, the masochist remains in control, although the scene is designed to give every indication that the masochist is powerless. This contradiction parallels the problems of suicide, in which the person must commit a murder in order to claim the desired role of victim.

Becoming Someone Else

The masochistic assault on the self is most obvious in practices and fantasies involving wholesale identity change. We saw that a significant minority of suicidal individuals express a desire to become someone new. A parallel desire is reflected in masochistic practices that transform the person into an entirely different person.

One form of identity change involves altering one's gender. Being male or female is one of the earliest and most basic components of identity,[16] and so changing one's gender is a fundamental and far-reaching change. Yet many male masochists seem to desire precisely that. In one sample, 40 percent of accounts by male masochists (including fantasies) involved some degree of symbolic feminization.[17] Most common is dressing in women's clothes, especially lingerie. A man might wear a woman's brassiere, panties, and stockings. Some men add makeup and a dress, going out in public wearing feminine clothes, or engaging in sex acts as a woman.

They may take female names or perform tasks connoting "women's work," such as housework.

There is little evidence that female masochists desire to be converted symbolically into males. One possible reason is that our culture associates maleness with higher status; to masculinize a female would not reduce her status. This argument suggests that the feminization of male masochists is one form of embarrassment and humiliation, which seems very likely to be the case. Another explanation is that the female role, as envisioned in our culture, is closer to some notions of masochism (that is, passivity, submissiveness, orientation toward pleasing others) than the male role. Another related factor may be that our culture allows women to wear pants more readily than it allows men to wear dresses. Regardless of why female masochists don't seem to use gender change, the fact remains that gender change is a significant form of identity change in masochism. Being converted into a new person with a new gender, new role, and new name is a thorough alteration of one's identity: One escapes from the self so thoroughly that one becomes someone else.

Another popular fantasy among masochists is to become a full-time sex slave. A significant number of masochistic fantasies end up with the person quitting his or her job, moving into the dominant partner's home, and taking on an entirely new life as that person's slave. This new role may involve catering to the person's sexual needs as well as doing housework and other chores. In some cases, the dominant partner may maintain an active sex life with others, while the submissive masochist waits on them or helps out in other ways.

There is some evidence that full-time sexual slavery is impractical as a real way of life.[18] Masochists don't really want to devote their whole lives to someone else. Few people really like to do all the washing and cleaning all the time. But the importance of the fantasy is not diminished by its failure to work in reality. That masochists are stimulated by the idea of becoming a full-time sex slave indicates the appeal of the idea of a thoroughgoing identity change.

This impracticality is consistent with the view of masochism as an occasional escape from the self. Masochists like to imagine a complete change, but they don't really need one. Relieving the stress of maintaining the self requires only an occasional escape. But if the masochist admitted the practice was only occasional, the ordinary identity would not be effectively suspended. Hence it is necessary to pretend to change completely.

Slavery as an image of masochism is revealing in other ways. Being a slave or a sexual servant is the most common designation used by masochists to refer to their role in their sex games, and indeed it is in general a common metaphor for masochistic submission. Why is this appealing? The meaning of slavery is loss of identity. Slavery originated as a substitute for being killed in war, and slavery has always involved some degree of social death and symbolic substitution for physical death.[19] Slaves are treated as if they lacked family ties, honor, civil rights, and opinions. On becoming a slave, a person loses his or her name, possessions, social status, all claim on esteem, and all right to control his or her life. A slave, in short, is a nonperson, a being without any place in society. The fact that masochists like to imagine themselves as slaves is a naked indication of the desire to shed one's identity.

Merging with the Partner

In a broader sense, all masochistic practice involves becoming someone else. By eradicating his or her will, individuality, and esteem, and accepting the partner's will and individuality and esteem in their place, the masochist throws out his or her own self and replaces it with the partner's.

Masochists seek to transform themselves into extensions

of their partners. They do whatever the partner wants (or at least that is the game). They worship and admire the partner. The exaltation of the partner goes hand in hand with their own debasement, just as attending to the partner's every whim is linked to denying their own pleasure and comfort. To put it in terms of the self, masochists give up their own esteem and control and become exclusively concerned, instead, with the esteem and control of their partners.

Masochists, therefore, are strongly oriented toward relationships. Masochistic fantasies are much more likely than other sexual fantasies to involve continuing, long-term relationships.[20] The relationships are important for several reasons, but one of them is the need to know the partner well in order to make oneself into a part of that person. It is not easy to submerge one's will to that of a total stranger, because one can't readily anticipate what the stranger wants. Fleeting encounters allow little opportunity for an intimate merger of souls.

Concrete and Rigid

Rigidity is apparent in the masochist's desire to follow a predetermined script very closely. Because the masochist is supposed to be submitting to the dominant partner's will, rigid insistence on a plan preset by the masochist can seem contradictory, even, on occasion, comical. The anthropologist Gini Graham Scott describes cases in which couples ended up in fights because the masochist insisted on being dominated in precisely a certain way and complained about some of the things that the dominant partner wanted.[21] The masochist would say, "I'm completely in your power, and I'll do anything you want"—but when the partner would give a command, the masochist would refuse or make an excuse.

Likewise, prostitutes who cater to masochistic clients report them to be very particular. Describing how exasperating this can be, one prostitute said many clients desired to be abused and insulted and would pay her well to do this.[22] However, she had to follow a precise series of insults. If she deviated from the list in any way, such as by adding different insults or changing the sequence, the masochist would get upset, insist she start over, or refuse to pay!

It is uncertain whether all masochists are so narrowly specific in their desires. It seems likely that specific interests in particular forms of submission would conflict with desires to do anything the dominant partner wants. Still, the tendency for rigidity is apparent, consistent with what was described earlier as typical of the mentally narrow state involved in escape.

Another feature of the mental shift involved in escaping the self is increased concreteness. In masochism, concreteness is reflected in the emphasis on sexuality and sensation. The masochist's interest is in bodies. The elaborate symbolism of submission comes down repeatedly to bodies. The kneeling, the kissing of feet or buttocks, the acceptance of spanking or whipping, and similar practices give a concrete, physical expression to the exchanges. Extremes of submission continue to take physical form, as described in Pauline Reage's famous masochistic novel *The Story of O*: having sex with someone other than the dominant partner, making one's body into a gift to be given away by someone else, or having one's body marked by branding or piercing. The masochist wants to relinquish his or her own will, individuality, and identity, and this renunciation is accomplished and expressed with the body.

The masochist's world is one of physical pain and pleasure. To some extent this is true for everyone. But for most people, pain and pleasure take abstract, delayed, vicarious, and complex forms; the masochist lives for pain and pleasure directly and immediately.

EFFECTS OF ESCAPE

For the masochist, the escape appears to be an end in itself. The masochistic activity is not a means to another end, except as submissive activities per se are a means of achieving sexual pleasure. It seems that the masochist desires the combination of submission and sex as a way of effecting an escape from selfhood. The masochist finds satisfaction in that cycle and that release, and nothing further is needed. Still, the mentally narrow state of escape has additional consequences that affect the feelings and actions of the masochist and shed further light on the general processes and effects of escaping from self.

Fantasy and Irrationality

As suggested in chapter 4, the escape from the self involves a rejection of meaning that can leave a kind of mental vacuum. The suspension of normal, critical thinking resulting from the narrow state of mental escape makes the individual vulnerable to new ideas, including bizarre ones. Bizarre fantasy is central to masochism. When normal adults imagine themselves transformed into sex slaves, infants, or members of the opposite sex, it is clear that they have departed from the realm of ordinary common sense. Pain deconstructs the masochist's everyday world, and in its place the elaborate fantasies crucial to masochism can develop.

The influential theorist Theodor Reik proposed that a highly active imagination is a prerequisite for masochism.[23] Unimaginative people will have to find some other form of escape! We have already seen that the fantasy of becoming someone else is popular among some masochists. During the S&M scene, the masochist often takes on a new identity.

Masochists describe their sexual activities as games, and the adoption of the masochistic role resembles the way a child becomes a cowboy, princess, or astronaut during play.

For many persons, the fantasy alone is enough to satisfy the masochistic desire. Prostitutes who cater to masochistic clients report a high rate of no-shows. As many as 95 percent of the men who make appointments to be sexually dominated by a professional mistress fail to appear for their appointments.[24] This rate is sufficiently high that many of the women in this line of work cease to take first-time calls seriously, insisting that the person call back to confirm the appointment on the scheduled day, and they rely heavily on repeat customers to make their work profitable. The point here is that for many of these men, the act of calling and arranging to be dominated seems to be enough to satisfy their masochistic desires.

Passivity

Passivity, a central feature of the escape process, is abundantly clear in masochism. Masochists seek to be made passive. Their attitude toward their partners is one of submission and yielding. They relinquish the right to make their own decisions. Passivity was implicit in the earlier discussion of control: Taking control of circumstances is active, and yielding control is passive. Masochism is centrally concerned with yielding control and so passivity is a major part of it. In many cases the passivity extends beyond symbolic submission and encompasses an enforced inability to do anything. People who are tied up so as to make movement difficult are thoroughly, blatantly passive. They can simply lie there helplessly and submit to whatever their partner wants to do with them. This passivity is often precisely what is exciting to them.

The extremes of masochistic passivity can pose a problem

for the partner, especially in living out a full-time S&M relationship. The negation of the masochist's identity leaves
the dominant partner alone in an important sense. Imagine
having a romantic partner who left all the decisions up to
you, never initiated conversation, and simply did whatever
you said. Although that might appeal to certain authoritarian
individuals, in fact many report it to be boring. A theme
that emerges repeatedly in research about masochists is the
gradual loss of interest by their partners, perhaps especially
just as the relationship reaches its full potential for submission, because the masochist has ceased to be a stimulating
partner.[25]

Emotion

Although escape from unpleasant emotions was a central
part of the appeal of suicide, it does not appear to be significant in masochism. Indeed, some masochistic activities seem
designed to engender the ordinarily unpleasant emotional
states of fear and embarrassment. These states are created
and played out within the unreal world of the masochistic
scene, however. Emotional concerns from everyday life are
blotted out, and part of the appeal of masochism may be
replacing anxieties and insecurities from everyday life with
the manufactured fears and embarrassments of the playacted
scene. Again, the analogy to children's games and other forms
of play is useful: People may develop emotional feelings
within the game context, but these reactions primarily reflect
their absorption in the game—and the accompanying removal from the affairs of everyday life.

One area in which masochism does seem to remove unpleasant emotion concerns sex itself. As already suggested, a
variety of emotions can interfere with sexual pleasure, particularly emotions that are based on the self. Possessiveness,
fear of inadequacy, and performance anxiety are known to

impair sexual response.[26] In masochism, these feelings are swept away, reportedly enhancing sexual response and increasing enjoyment.

What about love? Elsewhere I have suggested that masochism be regarded as an "alternative intimacy"—a form of relating to others that can provide some effects similar to love but does not require love.[27] Clearly, many masochists prefer to be in love with their partners, but love seems to be neither necessary nor sufficient for masochistic pleasure. S&M brings people close to each other and enables them to feel things together much as love does. Even without love, two people can merge and become one in the same sense that lovers do. In this way, masochism can replace love. This is not to say that masochism and love result in precisely the same outcome. In love, two people become one, and that one is some new totality of the slightly idealized versions of the two people. In S&M, two people become one, and that one is the dominant partner (hence the tendency for the dominant partner to become disenchanted and lonely, for in a sense this person is alone after having absorbed the other's self). The important point is that both love and masochism offer the peculiar fulfillment of allowing the individual to lose his or her self through merger with another human being.

Disinhibition

The mere participation in masochism seems to indicate the overcoming of certain inhibitions, for few people would normally be willing to allow someone to tie them up and spank them. Disinhibition seems to be a factor in the escalation of masochism. Research indicates that people often begin with tentative, mild scenes. A first experience might involve little more than being blindfolded, or having one's arms held over one's head during sex. This might progress to a little spanking. Later, the bondage may become more complete, or the pain more severe and protracted.

This argument becomes circular: Masochistic experiences produce a willingness to engage in masochistic experiences. If masochism really does remove inhibitions, it should make people willing to do things other than those directly involved in masochism, such as participation in new sexual acts. Masochists report engaging in actions they have never done before, including oral or anal sex. Others report a first instance of homosexual intercourse occurring during a scene of masochistic submission. Often the dominant partner presides, sometimes bringing in a third person and instructing the subject to have sexual contact with this person.

One might wonder if the masochist surreptitiously desired these forbidden sexual activities and used the masochistic episode as an excuse to engage in them. For example, one man described how his mistress dressed him up in lingerie and then had a male friend have sex with him.[28] In another example, a woman reported in a diary of her life as a masochistic lesbian that her attraction to bondage was that it freed her from responsibility for her homosexuality: "It gives you a chance to be sexual without any responsibility for your sexual feelings, without any control over what happens. You were being 'forced' to submit, 'It's not my fault, Mommy.' "[29] Such long-standing desires on the part of the masochist for homosexual experience are fully consistent with the escape theory. Escape removes inner barriers that prevent people from doing things they might otherwise want to do. This is not the same as creating new desires. These people may have felt inner conflict—both desire and reluctance to engage in these forbidden forms of sex. The escape state removed the inhibitions, allowing them to go forward with the experience. The fact that the S&M scene absolved them of responsibility for their actions merely facilitated their participation.

Masochism is a powerful form of escape from the self. That it is linked to sexuality has two important effects. First, it means that the desire for it will recur. Sexual desire is renewed on a regular basis, and once masochism is associated with sex, masochistic desires will be felt on a regular basis. This is most compatible with the type of escape associated with avoiding the continuing stress of maintaining the self, for such escapes need—by definition—to be repeated periodically. In contrast to the calamity-linked motivations for escape (such as underlie suicide), a single escape experience cannot satisfy the ongoing, perennial need for relief from the normal burden of identity. In other words, a single suicide attempt is often enough, but a single masochistic experience is apparently not enough at all.

The second effect of linking escape with sexuality is that the activity will be reinforcing. Sexual pleasure strengthens a person's desire to do it again. The fact that the ending of the masochistic episode is a powerful, intense orgasm—and as we have seen, there is some support for the masochists' claim that their practices provide unusually intense sexual experiences—means that the person is likely to recall masochism as desirable and pleasant. Even the problem of pain is solved. Although wanting pain's narcotic, attention-grabbing effect, the masochist does not want the unpleasant aspect of pain to predominate. But the use of pain is rendered acceptable in the context of an intensely pleasant experience. By linking pain to sexuality, masochists make a peculiar use of that general willingness to tolerate a certain amount of unpleasantness if the outcome is pleasant and desirable. Pain becomes a price that they pay for intense sexual pleasure.

Of course, the bargain is absurd. There is no need to suffer pain in order to enjoy sex. Masochists do not really have to accept pain as a necessary price for sexual pleasure. Rather, they use the pain as a means of seizing their attention and removing self-awareness. But this is taking an objective, detached, rational view of the matter, which is not to see it from the inside. To the masochist, the pain may seem like a necessary prerequisite or accompaniment to sexual enjoyment.

The point is, pain ceases to be a deterrent to masochism, because the sexual pleasure renders it a good bargain. In reality, the masochist wants pain, not because of sex, but in order to escape the self. Sexual pleasure is a fortuitous by-product of the procedure, but it makes the whole package much more enjoyable and probably increases the masochist's interest in doing it all again—and again.

SEVEN

Floating Away with the Bottle: Alcohol Use and Abuse

God made only water, but man made wine.
—Victor Hugo, *Les Contemplations*

I t was a miserable week at the hospital. Bob's supervisor was bothering him and a couple of co-workers had quit, which put a burden of extra duties and overtime on those who remained. Then Bob's wife called him at work. She said she was leaving him, going home to mother, and taking their son with her.

She and he had had many fights and arguments; on several occasions they had briefly separated. Each time, he thought it was the end of the world. This time seemed final, for she had taken the furniture with her. She had run home to mother before, but this was the first time she had rented a truck. It was 4:30 in the afternoon. He had been at work since 7:00 A.M. and was due back at the hospital at 7:00 the next morning. He had planned on seeing his family and grabbing some food and a few hours' sleep, but now his life was suddenly torn apart. No child, no wife waiting for him, just an empty run-down house, with hardly any place to lie down.

He knew he was partly to blame—his wife warned him that she would leave because of his drug use, of which she disapproved, and yesterday he had lied to her and taken drugs. But she wasn't being honest or straight with him either. Her frequent bouts of drunkenness were surely a greater risk to their son than his occasional indulgence in cocaine. And it was unfair of her to take all the furniture, since he'd paid for it. Between self-blame, mixed feelings of love and hate toward her, and not knowing what he was going to do about any of the immediate or long-range practical problems that had suddenly appeared, Bob was overwhelmed with unhappy feelings and unwanted thoughts. He was angry at his wife and angry at himself. He felt rejected, betrayed, sad, worried, threatened, annoyed. Soon his mind focused on one thing he was sure of: an overwhelming urge to get drunk. It was the only sensible and appealing thing to do. And it called for an immediate start.

Bob stopped at a store on the way home and bought a twelve-pack of Stroh's beer. He drank the first couple of cans rapidly, while he drove in the rush-hour traffic. There came no feeling of intoxication, of pleasure, of peace. Instead, he simply felt more and more angry. His unpleasant feelings coalesced in pulses of intense rage at that stupid woman, alternating with moments of simple frustration with life and with himself. By the time he arrived home, most of the twelve-pack was gone, and he was madder than hell at his selfish, petty, unreliable wife.

Bob and his wife had been friends with another couple who lived nearby. They knew she had left him, and they called to say they were coming over. Fine with him, but he'd need more beer. A quick trip to the corner store yielded another twelve-pack. He didn't even care what brand it was—just something cheap and cold. The other couple arrived while he was drinking the first can. With his friends there, Bob's rage melted away. They drank together, quickly, talking about football, car repairs, events in the distant past—anything but his wife and child. There was scarcely any furniture left in the house, so they sat at the old table in the kitchen. The radio played, and they talked over it and drank. Jokes began; soon they were laughing and joshing each other.

When Bob's anger subsided, the effects of the alcohol hit him abruptly, and he found himself quite drunk. He felt warm, sluggish, content. The beer tasted fine, the laughter felt good. The second twelve-pack disappeared, and someone fetched another. As they worked their way through it, one of his friends made a disparaging joke about Bob's wife, and then another, and Bob was laughing about her, at her. He remembered being mad at her, but it no longer mattered much. Cutting her down felt good. Vaguely, Bob knew his life had been screwed up, but it was nothing to worry about, nothing he couldn't handle, nothing urgent, nothing too bad. The problems were far away. His friends and his beer were right here.

The end of the evening was a blur. The radio kept playing. Clumsy hands knocked over a glass; a halfhearted effort was made to sop up the beer with a towel. With later spills, the cleanup efforts became increasingly ineffectual. The hour grew late, and Bob felt drowsy and nauseous from all the alcohol. The sofa was still there in the living room, and it seemed preferable to negotiating the stairway up to the bedroom. He spent the night on his own sofa. He woke up once to vomit, after which he felt much better, and he returned to the sofa and slept. Then at six, his alarm went off, and it was time to head for work. He would need multiple doses of aspirin and coffee.

Bob's story is fairly typical of a calamity-induced drinking binge.[1] Alcohol is a chemical that acts as a physiological depressant on the human body, but Bob, like nearly all other drinkers, did not consume it intending to become depressed.

Bob wanted the beer to blot out the distressing thoughts and feelings associated with this particular, sudden crisis in his personal life. For him as for many others, alcohol offered an escape from self-awareness.

Alcohol holds a favored place in Western society. Indeed, as the United States became increasingly obsessed with the dangers of drugs throughout the 1980s and into the 1990s, relatively few people expressed alarm about alcohol, which in this country causes more harm, misery, financial loss, and death than all illegal drugs combined. One reason for this apparent unconcern may be our society's past unsuccessful attempts to rid itself of alcohol. Despite decades of campaigns against drinking, leading finally to a constitutional amendment prohibiting alcohol, alcohol use continued to be widespread, and the side effects of illegality were so drastic that a second amendment was passed to repeal the earlier prohibition. Alcohol is clearly here to stay—the "drug of choice" for the United States and other Western countries. Efforts to limit alcohol use continue to fall far short of success. For example, 77 percent of college students—who are mostly below the minimum drinking age of twenty-one— admitted in a national survey in 1988 to consuming alcohol on a regular basis, and an astonishing 43 percent said that at least once in the previous two weeks they had had five or more drinks in a row.[2]

The power of alcohol to provide desirable experiences can be roughly inferred from the amount of trouble people, and society at large, are willing to accept for its sake. By this measure, alcohol's appeal must be extremely powerful, for its cost is high. "When the cost of lost production, crime, and accidents due to alcohol are totaled, and added to the cost of treating alcohol addiction . . . the ticket comes to over $50 billion a year."[3] Alcohol is involved in a wide range of antisocial behaviors. It is implicated in about two-thirds of the murders that occur each year in the United States, as well as

88 percent of knifings and 65 percent of spouse batterings.[4] Alcohol abuse causes severe health problems as well as injuries resulting from accidents, and the combination is responsible for around 125,000 deaths each year in the United States.[5] Alcohol addiction, also known as alcoholism, can blight an individual's life and devastate his or her family well into the next generation or even two generations. One scholar, comparing alcohol withdrawal to heroin withdrawal, concluded that by that measure at least, alcohol was the more dangerous form of addiction; alcohol withdrawal can be fatal, whereas heroin withdrawal never is.[6]

What does alcohol offer to make it worth this cost? A basic feature of alcohol's appeal is its power to facilitate escape from the self. Alcohol reduces self-awareness.[7] The consumption of alcohol decreases the drinker's ability to process information relevant to the self. The drunk is aware of things happening but doesn't think through the implications. After a setback or failure, you drink, and intoxication helps you avoid drawing the conclusion that you're a worthless, incompetent human being. Or, when drunk, you're more willing to do something wild, crazy, or risky, because you don't worry about your reputation.

Can we generalize from alcohol to other drugs? No. After all, if other drugs provided only the same effects as alcohol, there would hardly be so much interest in them, given, at a minimum, the inconvenience of their illegal status. Different drugs do have different effects, and escape from self may be facilitated or inhibited by these drugs.

Heroin may be alcohol's closest relative, in that the escape it offers may be similar to (although perhaps more intense than) that of alcohol. In contrast, while LSD deconstructs part of the self, in the process it also promotes insight and encounter with the self, making it a signally poor drug for escapist purposes.[8] Its use in psychotherapy reveals its potential for stimulating insight into self, which is precisely the opposite of what escapists are seeking. Cocaine is typically described as producing an intensified sense of self. Cocaine users report feeling a rush of egotism, as if they can accomplish great things or are likely to be admired by other people.

This feature of cocaine makes it in a sense the opposite of an escape from the self. Cocaine gives people an enhanced sense of who they are—brilliant, glamorous, successful, larger than life. Ironically, though, its use serves some of the same purposes as escape. Remember, the problem is that the self does not measure up to its own standards, so you feel inadequate, unhappy. Alcohol makes you forget the self, its standards, and your shortcomings; you feel good. I know of no direct evidence on the point, but it seems reasonable to speculate that cocaine makes you feel as if you are measuring up to the high standards after all, and again you feel good. Thus, although the psychological effects of cocaine may carry attention toward the self rather than away from it, its use may turn up in the same places and patterns as other escapist activities.

CAUSAL FACTORS

The use of alcohol is unusual as an escape from the self in that it seems to fit all three of the paths into escape. Some alcohol use follows the calamity pattern, like suicide; some follows the stress-relief pattern, like masochism; and some seems to pursue ecstasy.

Calamity

The essence of the calamity pattern of escape is a major personal setback, problem, or trauma, resulting in a strong desire to stop thinking about oneself. The case of Bob, described at the beginning of this chapter, illustrates this pattern: Upon finding that his wife had left him and taken their son and their furniture with her, Bob's immediate reaction was a strong desire to consume alcohol. He indulged his desire and, in fact, succeeded in blotting out his painful thoughts and feelings—for a short while.

Laboratory studies find this same pattern of binge drinking after a personal setback that makes self-awareness unpleasant. (One advantage of alcohol over other drugs is the availability of information; scientists have enormous difficulty conducting studies with illegal drugs, but it is relatively easy to conduct research on alcohol.)[9] People who tend to be highly self-aware show a clear inclination to consume more alcohol after failure than after success. People with low self-awareness show no such pattern.[10] Thus, the greatest amount of drinking results from the combination of experiencing a recent failure with a tendency to focus attention on oneself.

Similar findings emerged from an ambitious study of alcoholic relapse. As a group of alcoholics neared the completion of an alcoholism detoxification program, they were tested for major current life events and for tendencies to focus attention on themselves. The researchers predicted that the combination of high self-consciousness and stressful or unpleasant life events would foster binge drinking, with the result that these individuals would be most likely to relapse soon after completing their treatment. And that is exactly what happened. Within three months after successfully being cured of alcohol addiction, three out of every four individuals who met the criteria of high self-consciousness plus stressful life events were back to heavy drinking—drinking at least as much as before the detox program. Only a minority of individuals who did not meet those criteria had relapsed.[11]

Does stress play a role? It has long been thought that stress—referring to any sort of problems, pressures, or troubles—leads to alcohol abuse. The evidence doesn't fit this broad view. Some forms of stress do not lead to increased drinking. For example, one of the most stressful experiences in life is a death in the family, but studies have shown that death of a family member does *not* increase alcohol abuse.[12] Only when the stress includes unflattering implications about the self does alcohol use rise.[13] Personal problems that are too much to handle, or setbacks that make you feel like a failure (as we shall see in the next section) lead to increased drinking.

Stressful Burden of the Self

Obviously, many people use alcohol on many occasions that do not follow a personal or professional catastrophe. Not every alcoholic drink is consumed in response to a setback, failure, or rejection—in fact, many people drink alcohol especially on occasions of celebration. The stress-relief model of escape holds that people periodically need to lose or lessen their awareness of themselves, simply to ease the stressful burden of selfhood. It may not matter a great deal when these escapes occur, as long as they occur with some regularity. Many people do clearly consume alcohol in such a pattern. People come home from work and have a drink. Such casual alcohol use is widely thought an appropriate way to relax, helping one enjoy life. These attitudes confirm the notion that one feels better if one can periodically escape one's normal identity.

The use of alcohol in celebrations calls for special comment, for there are several interpretations of the attraction of serving drinks at parties. The first is that when one feels good, alcohol can help enhance these feelings. This interpretation has little to do with escape, since according to this view, alcohol narrows one's scope of attention and reduces the number of things one can think about.[14] Self-awareness might even increase. If you are feeling bad about yourself, your bad feelings may increase if you drink, unless you find something else to focus attention on. For this reason, depressed people may be better off not drinking alone; instead, they should drink while talking to other people or while engaged in some absorbing activity. Many patterns of alcohol use do in fact emphasize combining it with some other activity. If you are feeling good about yourself, however, then alcohol may intensify this elation by blotting out distracting thoughts.

A second view looks at alcohol's effacing of self-awareness. This view holds that in celebrations one wants to shed one's inhibitions in order to have a good time. The normal ego identity can be compared to one's best set of formal clothes, and for having fun one may want to change into something more casual. The silly antics characteristic of many celebrations (such as wearing funny costumes) might be hard to reconcile with one's carefully cultivated dignity, but alcohol use removes concern about dignity and reputation, allowing one to join in the merrymaking with enthusiasm. Parties and social functions often rely on this effect: A fair number of slightly nervous strangers get together in a large room and begin, awkwardly, to talk among themselves. After a couple of drinks, they are relaxed, feeling good, and speaking loudly.

In any case, it is clear that some uses of alcohol do fit the pattern of supplying temporary respite from the stressful burden of selfhood. Many people use small doses of alcohol on a regular basis and report that it affords them relaxation and pleasure or helps them forget the worries that attend the image of self that they cultivate at work. Other people use alcohol as a coping mechanism that blends the stress-relief and calamity models. For people who feel chronically vulnerable and exposed, minor problems or setbacks can revive these larger worries and unpleasant feelings. The setback itself may not qualify as a major catastrophe, but it can be enough to make the burden of self especially aversive. Thus, a hard day at the office may induce a person to drink an extra martini, beer, or glass of wine upon arriving home.

Ecstasy

The third model of escape from the self emphasizes the intrinsic appeal of states that are based on loss of self. A vivid, if controversial, example of the cultivation of ecstasy through alcohol use is the Bacchae.[15] Dionysus (whose Roman name was Bacchus) was a late Greek divinity, whose father was a god and whose mother was a mortal woman. His worship prefigured the salvation systems that soon dominated religion everywhere; significantly for our purposes, he was also the god of wine. Dionysian rites were celebrated at night, and participants attained states of frenzy that led to a variety of wild actions. Some accounts speak of upper-class women losing control to the point of killing wild animals with their bare hands and devouring the flesh raw. Alcohol use—specifically, wine drinking—was part of these ceremonies, although it would be unwarranted to infer that wine alone would cause such extreme behaviors.[16] The participants surrendered themselves to a form of religious mania that made extraordinary actions possible; wine probably helped this along, but it was not likely the only factor.

Certainly the Dionysiac frenzy involved a form of ecstasy that was highly appealing, perhaps especially to women. "The Dionysiac ecstasy means, above all, surpassing the human condition, the discovery of total deliverance, obtaining a freedom and spontaneity inaccessible to human beings," according to Mircea Eliade.[17] This renowned scholar goes on to speak of "deliverance from prohibitions, rules, and conventions of an ethical and social order" and "a communion with vital and cosmic forces"[18] similar to divine possession. As chapter 9 will explore in some detail, many religious experiences involve loss of self or surrender of individuality for the sake of communion with the divine, and alcohol can play an important part in this. It is probably no accident that Christian ritual has a long tradition of using alcohol in connection with communion, although nowadays the doses are typically kept so small as to have minimal direct effect. All the same, this use of alcohol derives from its potential for causing spiritually important effects, such as the reduction of self-awareness.

THE STATE OF MIND

Alcohol affects the drinker's state of mind in ways that seem consistent with those we have seen for other escapes from the self. First and foremost, alcohol is an effective means of accomplishing the mental narrowing central to escape and the rejection of meaning. The mental narrowing caused by alcohol has been termed *alcohol myopia* by some eminent researchers.[19] Of course, alcohol does not affect the eyes or literally make people shortsighted, but it does restrict their mental field. Alcohol intoxication impairs the mind's capacity for processing large and diverse sets of information. The intoxicated person doesn't notice as many things as the sober person.

In addition, the mind loses its ability to elaborate on the information that comes in—the drunken mind is less able to draw conclusions, make connections, and infer implications. It may still take in information, but it doesn't make full use of this information and doesn't effectively fit information into what it already knows. New information lacks its full context, and the intoxicated mind ends up appreciating only part of the meaning of what it perceives.

The odd and sometimes humorous behavior of intoxicated people is often attributable to this mental narrowing. For example, a young man was drinking with a friend at the friend's house, and after many drinks he became nauseous, went to the bathroom, and vomited. He remembered that he was a guest, so he did his best to take care of the mess he had made. After sponging off the floor, he felt that he had successfully cleaned up the room except for one small rug, which still bore blatant witness to his loss of control. To his clouded mind, the important thing was to finish the job of cleaning up the room, which required doing something about the presence of the rug. With some difficulty, he managed to open the bathroom window and hurl the rug down into the backyard! It was not until the next day that he realized the inadequacy of this solution.[20]

Loss of meaning is accompanied by a restricted time perspective. The intoxicated individual loses any tendency to think about the future or past, dwelling instead on the feelings and sensations in the immediate present. This shrinking of the time perspective is closely linked to the removal of inhibitions, since inhibitions often depend on considering what one's action might mean tomorrow. The researchers Claude Steele and Robert Josephs offer the example of the impulse to vent anger at a landlord after one has had a few drinks.[21] Normally, one might hold one's tongue, because today's rude behavior might lead to tomorrow's eviction notice. Under the influence of alcohol, however, a person fails to think about tomorrow and may express displeasure or indignation, quite possibly with regrettable results.

There is some evidence that thinking becomes concrete, rigid, and banal under the influence of alcohol. Anyone who has overheard drunken conversations can testify that these rarely involve thoughtful treatment of profound issues; more often, they feature dogmatic assertions of opinion and graphic discussion of physical cravings or experiences. Alcohol is not known for stimulating creative thinking. The drunk is not given to reflecting on subtle implications or probing for deeper insights; instead, "superficially understood, immediate aspects of experience have a disproportionate influence on behavior and emotions."[22]

Thus, alcohol intoxication produces a state of mind that conforms to the pattern we have seen for escape from the self: a narrow, immediate focus on events combined with a tendency to ignore broader meanings and implications.

EFFECTS OF ESCAPE

Escape from unpleasant emotion is one goal of escaping oneself. Alcohol use can accomplish this, but it does not necessarily do so—alcohol can instead increase unpleasant emotional states, such as anxiety or depression. The effect depends on how alcohol is used as well as external factors and distractions. Alcohol essentially limits the mind to one set of thoughts or cues; it accomplishes mental narrowing by intensifying the mind's focus on this set, making the person increasingly oblivious to everything else. The mind may become so thoroughly immersed in one aspect of an issue that the person ignores all other implications. My uncle described watching a football game on television while drinking. He was an ardent supporter of one team, and his favorites were not performing well. He became increasingly upset, angry, and depressed as the game went on, and when it ended with a defeat for his team he was in a thoroughly foul mood. After sulking for more than an hour, he realized that the total points scored in the game exactly matched what he had predicted in the office pool, so that he had won nearly two hundred dollars! His drunkenness had prevented him from realizing one very important and personally relevant aspect of the game he was watching.

Generally, the emotional effects of alcohol depend on whether one focuses the mind on things connected with feeling bad—or on other things. Drinking and brooding can make people feel worse and worse, as the troubles they brood over gradually engulf their entire outlook. Drinking and watching television can erase one's bad mood, for as the mind becomes preoccupied with the television program, it ceases to think about its own troubles. For this very reason, alcohol is often used in connection with other stimuli—beer and a ball game, or cocktails and conversation.[23]

For purposes of escape, then, it is essential to add some distractor to alcohol. But alcohol use can backfire and leave a person wallowing in misery, intensifying the painful emotions that it was supposed to remove. Studies have shown that alcohol can increase anxiety and depression—yet it is also clear that people turn to alcohol when they feel anxious or depressed.[24] These people are not completely mistaken, but if they use alcohol incorrectly, such as by failing to provide additional distractions, the alcohol may increase their emotional suffering. A cycle can develop in which the depressed person turns to alcohol for solace but ends up feeling even more depressed, leading to further alcohol use.[25] The escalating depression and alcohol use can have very harmful consequences.

Passivity has been noted as a consequence of escape, insofar as people try to avoid implicating the self or taking responsibility. Although there is little direct evidence about passivity in connection with alcohol use, it is clear that people use alcohol to avoid responsibility for their actions. A particular form of this avoidance is self-handicapping,[26] whereby people use alcohol to furnish themselves with an excuse for possible failure or misbehavior. If they perform badly, they can attribute this to the alcohol rather than to their own incompetence, weakness, or character flaws.

Familiar examples of alcoholic self-handicappers are people who achieve spectacular success early in their career, gaining the reputation for brilliance, but secretly feeling insecure about their ability to live up to this reputation. Alcohol abuse offers a way to preserve their reputation by not putting it to the test. If the people fail to turn in outstanding work, others will attribute it to the alcohol. (And if they happen to do well, others think they must be exceptionally gifted to be able to perform effectively despite a drinking problem.)

This pattern is illustrated by the case of Gordon. While working on his Ph.D., Gordon published several outstanding papers. His adviser, an internationally famous scientist, became convinced that Gordon was exceptionally brilliant and destined for greatness, a view that Gordon was happy to share. When Gordon finished his degree, his adviser wrote letters all over the country extolling Gordon's talents and predicting an extraordinary future for him. The best universities in the United States competed to offer Gordon a position on their faculty, and he was able to choose among them.

Living up to such high expectations is not easy. Gordon felt great pressure to come up with extraordinary, creative discoveries, but also felt that he was far too brilliant to devote his time to the tedious spade work required in laying the foundation for scientific research. He tried one or two very ambitious projects that didn't turn out well. He did have some success with conventional, run-of-the-mill projects, but these were too mundane to satisfy the exalted expectations that surrounded him.

Gordon began to withdraw. He became reluctant to tell colleagues what he was working on. When he met others in his field, he alluded vaguely to dynamic new theories and grand research projects, but he refused to share any details. He began to keep odd hours, working at his office in the middle of the night, sleeping during the daytime. Students found it increasingly difficult to find him, and he became all the more isolated. He began drinking heavily, and rumors about his drinking problem spread around his campus.

His tenure deadline approached. Everyone knew that to earn tenure at such a top-notch university, one had to have an exceptional record of publishing excellent work. When friends asked how he was doing, Gordon continued to express confidence that he would receive tenure, especially if this great work he was doing could be completed in time. He convinced the university to extend his deadline, saying that his research had been held up by federal funding problems through no fault of his own.

The great work never materialized, and Gordon was denied tenure. But instead of being regarded as an overrated mediocrity, Gordon was widely considered to be an extremely intelligent and promising scientist who had gone off the track because of alcohol (and, it was also rumored, cocaine) abuse. He left with his career in shambles, but his reputation for brilliance intact. Many colleagues felt that if he could simply get clean and sober he would still do great work.

It would be too easy to read self-destructive motivations into Gordon's story. He *did* destroy himself, but to conclude he was driven by a death wish or some other need for destruction would be a mistake. Gordon wanted to be a great success, not a failure—if he had really wanted failure he could have achieved that aim by avoiding alcohol and simply turning out poor work. It is more likely that he used alcohol as a tool of self-protection than of self-destruction: Alcohol represented the best available excuse for not living up to expectations—and, hence, of preserving his aura of potential (even if troubled) genius. By accomplishing this separation between self and performance, alcohol use ensures that the treasured image of competence is not jeopardized by any possible outcome.

Disinhibition is another consequence of mental narrowing, and alcohol has long been recognized as an important means of removing inhibitions. People serve alcohol at parties to make them wilder. Alcohol is a popular aid in sexual seduction, on the assumption that it makes the target more likely to comply. And throughout history, soldiers have been given alcohol before battles to make them more willing both to risk their lives and to inflict harm and death on the enemy.[27]

Recent studies have clarified the disinhibiting effects of alcohol.[28] Alcohol does not simply make people do things they normally would not want to do, but primarily affects behavior about which a person feels internal conflict. Where people feel both a positive impulse to act and an inhibition against acting, alcohol weakens the inhibition and tips the balance in favor of action. For example, alcohol does not simply make people more aggressive or violent. But if they have a reason to act aggressively, alcohol can weaken the inner restraints that normally keep aggressive action to a minimum, with the result that aggressive behavior ensues. Alcohol won't make people go looking for a fight, but the same provocation can elicit a more violent response from someone who has been drinking than from a sober person.[29]

The range of behaviors potentially affected by alcohol is wide. Alcohol makes people more willing to respond aggressively, more willing to disclose intimate and personal information to others, more willing to gamble for high stakes, more willing to take action in romantic or sexual ways.[30] It can even make us more willing to help others. Tipping, for example, is often marked by inner conflict, for people want to be generous but also want to inhibit this impulse in order to conserve their money. Restaurant patrons who drink leave larger tips (in proportion to the bill) than patrons who do not drink,[31] and the more you drink, the more you tip. Laboratory studies show that alcohol consumption makes people more willing to cooperate with requests to perform unpleasant tasks.[32]

Humility can be considered a form of inhibition: People

want to believe themselves to be terrific, and they want others to share this high regard for them, but norms of modesty inhibit bragging or showing off. Under the influence of alcohol, these inhibitions too are weakened, and humility is gradually abandoned. People are more likely to brag after drinking and to describe themselves in more positive terms.[33]

And here we return to a central goal of escape: to shake off awareness of one's faults and flaws. Alcohol apparently helps people forget their bad qualities. If they do think about themselves, they are more positive when intoxicated than when sober. These effects on self-awareness are sufficient to induce millions of people in the United States to drink. As we shall see in the next chapter, other people in distress turn to eating.

EIGHT

Binge Eating:
Vanishing Bite by Bite

The moment I become aware of the hole opening inside I'm terrified. I want to fill it. I have to. So I start to eat, I eat and eat—everything, anything I can find to put in my mouth. It doesn't matter what it is, so long as it's food and can be swallowed. It's as if I'm in a race with the emptiness. As it grows, so does my hunger. But it's not really hunger, you see. It's a frenzy, a fit, something automatic and uncontrollable.

—Robert Lindner, *The Fifty-Minute Hour*

Turning from drinking to eating, we find in binge eating many features we have seen linked to escaping the self. In a recent survey of college students asking what they do when they are in a bad mood and want to make themselves feel better, the results broke down along the lines of sex: Men drink, women eat.[1] To be sure, both problem drinking and overeating can be found in either gender, but there seems to be a general tendency for males to turn to alcohol to escape from bad feelings, while women turn to food.

Binge eating occurs primarily in two forms. One is the pathological pattern of bulimia, most typically found among young adult women, who alternate between periods of self-starvation and periods of massive, frenzied consumption of food. A far more common, although less dramatic, pattern is that of the dieter whose efforts to restrict eating are thwarted by periodic overindulgences. In both patterns, we find a tension between a general desire to restrict and restrain eating, and an occasional binge in which all these ordinary rules and patterns are suspended.

It seems ironic that dieters would eat more than nondieters, but on certain occasions this is exactly what happens. Dieters live surrounded by food that they strive to ignore, and their bodies have desires and appetites that they likewise strive to ignore. When their blinders fall off, they seem to find themselves overcome with cravings for food. Unlike nondieters, who stop eating when they are full, a binge eater may keep eating long past the point at which the body has had enough. Part of the reason for this is that dieters have learned to ignore their body's signals about food—not just signals of wanting something to eat, but also signals about having had enough.

Although few dieters would admit it, they often act as if once their diet is blown for the day, they might as well eat as much as they can. Careful studies support this conclusion. In one experiment, people were invited to come to the laboratory and then randomly assigned to be given nothing to eat, or an ordinary milkshake, or a huge double-size milkshake. Afterward, each person was allowed to eat as many crackers as he or she wanted in a "taste test." The researchers secretly kept track of the number of crackers eaten by each.

Nondieters did just what one would expect. They ate the fewest crackers if they had had the double-size milkshake, and they ate the most if they had not received any milkshake at all. No surprises there. But the dieters behaved in exactly the opposite fashion. If they had not received any milkshake, they ate very few crackers; if they had had a milkshake, they ate more crackers; and after a double-size milkshake, they ate the largest number of crackers. For them, apparently, the milkshake ruined their diet for the day, and all rules were off. They felt free to indulge themselves by eating all the crackers they could.[2]

It is precisely such binges that this chapter is concerned with. Many people normally monitor their eating carefully, but under certain circumstances they simply abandon all their rules and eat in an uninhibited fashion.

Other instances of heavy eating, such as holiday meals at which many people will eat so much they become uncomfortable, may or may not involve loss of self. The focus of the present chapter is on dieters, bulimics, and others who are torn between strong desires to eat and strong resolutions to avoid eating—and whose behavior fits the patterns we have seen for escape.

CAUSAL FACTORS

Betsy was at home with her boyfriend, Mike. She was feeling pretty good. She hadn't eaten much today—just a salad—and she had spent an hour on her exercise bike. The only sour note was Mike, who was having one of his periodic fits of paranoid jealousy. While he talked, she picked up a cold piece of pizza and began to nibble at it.

He was questioning her about where she had been earlier, when he had tried to call. He thought she was out seeing somebody else. She wasn't, but she couldn't convince him of her innocence. "Don't do this to me," Betsy whined as she picked up a second piece of pizza.

Mike turned his attention to the pizza. He began to criticize her eating habits, reminding her of her past tendency to overeat and then regret it. She defiantly took another bite, but his disgusted and critical expression induced her to drop the rest of the slice into its box. At his insistence, she put the box away in the refrigerator.

The pizza stayed on her mind. Betsy divided her attention between listening to Mike and thinking about the pizza. As soon as he left, she could finish it in peace. He stayed and kept talking. She felt increasingly annoyed with him, although she gave no outward sign. Why didn't he go? She was tired of him watching her all the time, monitoring her actions, telling her what to do, controlling her life. She deserved to be treated better. If only he were more considerate, more thoughtful, nicer to her.

Finally he left—without a kiss—and she felt simply relieved. She hurried to the refrigerator, retrieved that slice of pizza, and wolfed it down. It wasn't enough. She ate another piece, and another, until the entire pizza was gone. Instead of diminishing, her craving for food grew. She ate faster and faster, scarcely bothering to chew. She took large bites and swallowed them whole. After she finished the last slice of pizza, she hunted frantically for something else to eat. The freezer yielded a carton of chocolate chip ice cream. She ate it all while sitting on the floor in front of the open refrigerator. The combination of an entire pizza and all that ice cream made her feel stuffed and bloated, but she felt driven to eat more. She found some cold macaroni and cheese and gulped it down. In her haste, she dropped some on the floor, but she ignored it, seeing some leftover meatloaf and mashed potatoes. Finally, as she finished the mashed potatoes, she slowed eating. She felt stuffed to the point of nausea.

Betsy ran to the bathroom and thrust her finger down her throat, forcing herself to vomit several times. She felt sweaty and shaky as she stood up from the toilet, but still had that driven feeling that she couldn't get enough to eat. She went back to the kitchen to look for more.

The cupboard was full of boxes. Triscuits—no. Wheat Thins—no. Pretzels—no. Captain Crunch—yes! She sat on the kitchen counter and began eating handfuls of the sweet, sticky breakfast cereal right out of the box. Some of it spilled on the floor, but she didn't care. When her fingers touched the bottom of the box, she felt a wave of panic—what next? Back to the cupboard. This time she found a large, unopened package of sandwich cookies with double stuffing. She tore open the package and ate all of the cookies, washing them down with milk she drank out of the carton. Again that stuffed feeling came over her, but she couldn't stop eating. She forced herself to continue consuming food, put another bite in her mouth, chew, swallow, another, another, despite her body's incipient rebellion. After finishing a second box of snack food, she finally felt she couldn't eat any more. Even her jaw ached. She raced to the bathroom to vomit again.

By now Betsy felt thoroughly exhausted. Her frenzy subsided into a weak, ill feeling. She walked back to the kitchen and just looked around. Empty boxes and torn cartons scattered everywhere. Food spilled on the floor. Dirty plates, crumbs. Realization of what she had done—*again*—hit her. She started to feel guilty. Mike—ah yes, Mike, she had forgotten about him—would be angry and unsympathetic. She'd need to decide what to tell him. But she felt too depleted physically to think about that now.[3]

What Is Binge Eating?

Binge eating is a pattern of food consumption in which people who normally restrict their food intake at intervals suspend the restrictions and consume large quantities of food in a relatively short period of time. An eating binge can last from a few minutes to several hours. Betsy's binge, in the example just given, took a little over an hour.

A severe form of binge eating is *bulimia nervosa*, often called simply *bulimia*, a word that means "ox hunger." It is classified as an eating disorder[4] and diagnosed by the following criteria: recurrent episodes of binge eating, with at least two episodes per week for at least three months; a feeling of having lost control over one's eating; drastic measures to prevent weight gain from these eating binges (including self-induced vomiting, using laxatives, or fasting); and chronically excessive preoccupation with body weight and shape.

Although this chapter will talk about both dieters and bulimics, the two are not the same or even related on a continuum. Ordinary dieters who occasionally binge are not simply small-scale bulimics. Bulimia is a pathological pattern that may require professional help, and bulimics often show signs of other mental and emotional problems.

Who Engages in Binge Eating?

Dieting to lose weight has become extremely common in modern society, especially among females. For Betsy, the binge eater described earlier in this chapter, dieting was a way of life, and the same is true for many women and girls. One survey found that 80 percent of girls reported having already been on a diet by the age of thirteen; only 10 percent of boys reported having dieted by that age.[5] By the age of twenty, most women have settled into patterns of frequent dieting. A survey of college students in the 1970s found that three-quarters of the women described themselves as dieters.[6] Estimates of the prevalence of binge eating vary widely, depending on the determination of what constitutes a binge. Different studies have concluded that the number of U.S. women who engage in binge eating is anywhere from 3 percent to 90 percent of the population; for males the estimates run from 1 percent to 64 percent.[7]

Bulimia is likewise more common among females than males, although part of the reason may be that males simply do not admit to problems of this sort. Nationally, it appears that somewhat fewer than 10 percent of females are bulimics—perhaps 4 percent to 8 percent—and less than 2 percent of males.[8] If especially stringent criteria are used, the prevalence is less than 1 percent of the total (male and female) U.S. population.[9]

Still, some groups have higher rates of bulimia. The typical bulimic has been described as a white, single, college-educated, middle- or upper-class woman in her early or mid-twenties.[10] Rates are especially high among women starting professional careers in law, business, or medicine.[11]

It also appears that bulimia is characteristic of modern society. References to bulimic patterns of eating go back in history as far as A.D. 130, but the condition appears to have been extremely uncommon until recent centuries. Only around 1800 were reports of bulimia sufficiently common that the disease became recognized and well known. Many experts believe that the frequency of bulimia has risen in recent decades[12] and spread to include women lower on the socioeconomic scale.

Likewise, there are some signs of cultural relativity. One study compared Arab women in London, England, to other Arab women in Cairo, Egypt; far more bulimia was found among the former.[13] Among women from similar racial backgrounds, those living in a Western culture had a significant rate of bulimia (12 percent), whereas those living in a different culture had no significant incidence of bulimia.

The historical and cross-cultural patterns resemble those for masochism: Bulimia appears to be characteristic of modern Western culture. This evidence is consistent with the view that the modern construction of the self is a source of the problem and that the burden of modern selfhood impels some people to use powerful techniques for escaping from self.

When and Why?

Binge eaters generally live in a condition of inner tension. They want both to eat and to refrain from eating. Normally, they manage to stifle their desire to eat and keep their food intake under control. Under some circumstances, however, this mechanism breaks down.

At present, it is hard to say whether binge eating corresponds to the calamity or the stress-relief model of escape. People may go on eating binges in response to personal crises and setbacks, or they may have a binge now and then to get relief from the pervasive burden of self. Binge eating may resemble alcohol in deriving from either motive.

The calamity model is supported by evidence that people eat more when they are led to feel bad about themselves. Several studies show that an experience of failure or embarrassment can set off an eating binge.[14] Ironically, nondieters eat *less* than normal when they feel upset with themselves (such as over a recent failure), but dieters eat more. The period preceding a bulimic eating binge is usually associated with an increase in unpleasant emotional states, but these do not necessarily involve major catastrophes. Betsy's binge, in the earlier example, was set off by a minor squabble with her boyfriend.

Not all forms of emotional distress trigger eating binges.[15] Carefully controlled studies have shown that emotions like fear, which are unpleasant but do not cast the self in a bad light, fail to increase the eating of dieters or bulimics. In contrast, bad feelings that reflect on the self, such as feeling like a failure or feeling humiliated, do lead to increased eating. The threat of pain does not increase eating, but the threat of losing self-esteem does. It would seem that an acute and unpleasant awareness of the self underlies the eating binge. Overeating is not just a way of escaping from any sort of problem or distress, but rather it is specifically associated with escape from the self.

Other research portrays binge eating as more akin to the vulnerability stress pattern of escaping the self than the calamity pattern. Binge eating responds to chronic or typical conditions. The clinical criteria for diagnosing bulimia include a pattern of at least two binges per week, but it seems unlikely that two wholly new personal catastrophes hit anyone every week. Several studies have linked chronic emotional distress with binge eating, with bulimics showing high rates of depression and chronic anxiety.[16]

It could be that the two causal pathways generally merge in binge eating. For a person who feels vulnerable, with some stress of self, the event that precipitates a binge need not be a major crisis, but simply enough to remind the person of her or his major feelings of guilt or inadequacy and other worries about the self.

The stress-relief and calamity patterns of escape from the self share several features, including high standards and expectations. Present-day standards of personal attractiveness place an increasing premium on being thin, and eating disorders are most common among groups with high expectations for being thin (especially women), such as ballerinas, other dancers, and cheerleaders.[17] Dieters and bulimics are both motivated by the desire to be thin, and bulimics in particular have been found to suffer intense fear of being overweight; many bulimics report believing they are fat even though they are underweight according to statistical norms.[18]

Expectations regarding body shape are not the only relevant standards. Research suggests that any group, especially of women, that is systematically evaluated against demanding expectations is prone to binge eating. In our society, it is the high-achieving women who are most vulnerable to bulimia.[19] Women in medical school, law school, and business school have roughly double the rates of bulimia as the general population.[20] Likewise, studies that have looked at bulimics have typically found that as a group they suffer from unrealistic expectations for achieving success, irrational needs for external approval, and in general unrealistically high standards.[21] Two researchers recently summarized the bulimic attitude as "I must do everything perfectly or what I do is worthless."[22] Bulimics set higher expectations for themselves than they do for other people, and regardless of how well they do, they think they could have done better. These same researchers also noted that bulimic women tend to think that it is very important for a woman today to satisfy both the traditional values for women plus the demanding career standards traditionally associated with men—in short, they see and subject themselves to a double pressure.

Feelings About the Self

Central to the theory of escape from the self is the notion that people are motivated by an acute and unpleasant awareness of self, as in feeling embarrassed or humiliated. Do binge eaters feel this way? This question can be divided into two parts: Are binge eaters very self-conscious, and is their awareness of self unfavorable?

The answer to the question about their level of self-consciousness is a definite yes, with one qualification: Dieters and bulimics are indeed preoccupied with themselves and how they look, but primarily with respect to how they appear to others.[23] They are not particularly self-aware in the sense of being introspective or attentive to their inner processes or needs. Indeed, dieting is often sustained by learning to ignore one's inner processes, at least those that signal a desire for food, so it is not surprising that restrained eaters are insensitive to any inner dimension. Binge eaters are acutely self-conscious about public self-presentation. Betsy, in the example given earlier this chapter, was fastidious about her weight, her appearance, and her clothing. She cared a great deal about being attractive and shapely. No doubt some of her boyfriend's jealousy was stimulated by her frequent need to attract attention from other males as proof of her desirability.

The second question concerns how the self is evaluated. Binge eaters tend to focus on their faults and shortcomings, to have low self-esteem, and to regard their bodies as unattractive. Obese people in general tend to feel bad about being overweight, and many women who mistakenly believe themselves to be overweight share those feelings. Bulimics especially have low self-esteem, but even ordinary dieters tend to have lower self-esteem than nondieters. Moreover, among dieters, those with low self-esteem are more prone to binge-eating patterns.[24]

It is important to recognize that the unpleasant self-consciousness from which binge eaters suffer contributes to their restraint in eating. When they feel attention focused on them, they eat less. Eating binges are associated with *escape* from this unpleasant state of self-consciousness.

One experimental study made this point especially clear.[25] Dieters were given a problem to solve and told they should be able to solve it in about five minutes. In fact the problem was extremely difficult; none of them was able to solve it, and they felt they had failed miserably on an important task. Some people were then shown a nature program on bighorn sheep, while the rest viewed videotapes of themselves failing to solve the assigned problem. Afterward, the researchers secretly recorded how much ice cream the people ate during a supposed taste test in which they could eat as much as they wanted. Dieters who saw the nature film ate relatively large quantities of ice cream, but those who saw the tape of their own failure ate very little afterward. All of the people had failed, but some were distracted from their failure (and themselves), while others were reminded of it and of them-

selves. Escaping the awareness of oneself as a failure was associated with a high amount of eating; maintaining this state
led to limited eating.

THE STATE OF MIND

The state of mind during an eating binge is partly a reaction
to the state of mind the person has *prior* to the binge. Typically, as described in the preceding section, the person is
acutely aware of how he or she appears to others, holds high,
often unrealistically high, standards and expectations, and is
acutely aware of personal deficiencies or shortcomings, especially being overweight. When an incident involving rejection or failure brings these self-doubts to the fore, the binge
eater becomes preoccupied with unpleasant thoughts about
himself or herself. This awareness of the self's bad points is
associated with various unpleasant emotions, such as anxiety
and depressed feelings.

During the binge, the individual experiences a process that
appears to resemble the mental narrowing we have seen in
other escapes. Meaningful thought is largely abandoned for
a narrow focus on immediate sensations and short-term activities. The troubled, unloved self disappears from awareness, and instead one is preoccupied with one cookie after
another.

The evidence of mental narrowing among binge eaters is
not extensive, but what there is, is consistent. Binge eaters
avoid meaningful thought about broad personal issues, such
as what life is all about.[26] In particular, they avoid thinking
about their problems—avoidance is their characteristic way
of dealing with personal troubles.[27] Some bulimics occupy
their minds in repetitive activities with low levels of meaning, such as compulsive or obsessive patterns. Indeed, obses-

sive/compulsive patterns are far more common among bulimics than among the general population.[28]

Eating is a concrete, immediate, short-term activity. It provides the physical sensations of biting, chewing, tasting, and swallowing, and binge eaters focus on these intensely. In this context, it is important to recall that most binge eaters have tried to adopt a longer-range perspective on eating. That is what a diet is: controlling what one eats today, in order that one can reach future goals of slimness. Dieters ordinarily watch what they eat very carefully, calculating how many calories they consume and measuring this against their preset allowance. During an eating binge, however, people appear to lose this broad perspective and limit awareness to the process of eating. One study showed that people almost completely lost track of their eating during a binge, and their retrospective estimates of how much they had eaten were mistaken by amounts that were fifty times as large as the errors made by dieters under normal circumstances (or by nondieters).[29]

Bulimics in general seem to have attitudes about time similar to those of suicidal persons. The future looks bleak, full of further misfortunes and disasters, and the past is clouded with catastrophes and problems that cannot be overcome.[30] The only solace is to escape into a narrowly defined present.[31]

Studies of bulimics have concluded that the binge occurs during an altered mental state. Bulimics describe this state as "spacing out" or "letting go" and use other metaphors of depersonalization and derealization (that is, loss of ordinary sense of oneself, and loss of sense of reality).[32] Others note that the state resembles a trance in its severe narrowing of the mental field.[33] The state is accompanied by feelings of being out of control and, in some cases, by sexual feelings. The combination of mental narrowing, loss of control, and eroticism parallels sexual masochism.

The rejection of meaning makes thinking rigid and inflexible. Binge eaters have been found to think in rigid terms, and this mental rigidity increases in the period preceding a binge. Rigidity can appear in attitudes toward food:[34] Some foods are good, others are bad, according to strict guidelines. A salad may be good, even if it is loaded with salad dressing that contains more calories than a milkshake, which is bad. During a binge, these rules are inverted, and the binge eater seems to focus especially on forbidden foods, often pastry, chocolate, potato chips, and ice cream. This may be partly explained by the immersion in physical sensation, pleasant tastes enhanced by certain physiological reactions of dieters. Some binge eaters seem to be less interested in taste than in the process of chewing and swallowing, and their search for interesting sensations may lead them to eat bizarre items like frozen breaded fish sticks, raw meat or eggs, or sticks of butter.

Many of these features are captured in a famous account of an eating binge described by the psychiatrist Robert Lindner in *The Fifty-Minute Hour*.[35] A woman was upset about unhappy and conflicted relationships in her life. She felt pressured, torn, and inadequate at living up to the demands on her. One day she got carried way with an especially severe binge. During the binge, her awareness of herself vanished, replaced by "an immense, drumming vacuum."[36] The craving for food and the frenzied consumption of it filled her mind. After she had eaten everything in the house, she grabbed the telephone book and ordered food to be delivered. She felt desperate with need, shaking with fear, even though she had already consumed more than a normal meal. When the ordered food arrived, she devoured it "like someone who's been starved for weeks."[37] She ate until she vomited and then resumed eating until the muscles in her mouth were tired and sore. She forced herself to continue. Eventually she reached a state that she described as similar to drunkenness. She passed out and slept for more than thirty hours, sleep that was filled with wretched dreams and nightmares. She finally got up feeling miserable, bloated, disgusted with herself.

In this example, the eating binge was accompanied by extreme narrowing of attention. She forgot her identity and the problems in her personal relationships. All that mattered was the overriding need to consume food. While eating, she experienced an unearthly tranquility. Whenever the food ran out, she felt a period of panic, followed by intense concentration on getting something else to eat. Of course, to realize what she was doing was to invite distress—after all, she was ruining her diet, making a mess, and not helping any of her problems. She couldn't permit herself to stop to reflect. The binge continued until she reached a state similar to intoxication (which would make reflective thought impossible) and passed out. During the binge she lost contact with her normal self and ordinary reality, and she managed to postpone returning to her normal world for as long as possible.

CONSEQUENCES

The mental narrowing that occurs during an eating binge has the same effects as in other escape routes. One central feature is the removal of normal inhibitions, rendering the person willing to do things that he or she would not ordinarily do. The eating binge itself is of course the most obvious example. Binge eaters are usually very careful to keep their food intake under careful scrutiny and control. In an eating binge, they experience a strong feeling of losing control over their eating.[38] As already mentioned, ordinary dieters also cease to monitor what they're eating when they go on a minor binge. Calorie counting goes out the window.

Some people think that binges are prompted by a physical reaction—some chemical change in the body makes the dieter or bulimic start to binge. Although bodily changes do occur, such theories seem inadequate. What matters is not what the body actually eats, but rather what the person thinks he or she has eaten. In one study, people were given an identical snack and then took part in an ice cream "taste test" where the researchers secretly kept track of how much people ate. The initial meal was the same for all participants in the study, but half of them were told that it was low in calories, while the others were led to believe it was high in calories. Dieters ate more ice cream when they thought their diet was already broken by a high-calorie snack than when they thought the snack was low in calories. The bodies received the same food, but its effect depended on whether the person thought that food was high or low in calories. It is the subjective belief, not the objective physical content of the food, that is decisive.[39]

Loss of inhibition may extend beyond eating. Bulimics are prone to a variety of disinhibited behavior patterns. They are more likely than other people to engage in drug or alcohol abuse, attempt suicide, steal, and engage in promiscuous sexual activity.[40] They appear, in other words, to be impulsive in many areas. They seem willing, at times, to act without reflecting on the meanings and implications of their actions, and so they do things that run counter to prevailing social norms and standards.

An important consequence of mental narrowing is the escape from emotion, especially the unpleasant emotions that gave rise to the desire to escape. After all, if the painful emotional states continued, the escape would have to be considered a failure. It appears that eating binges are associated with a reduction in these painful emotions. Anxiety in particular seems to go away during an eating binge and to remain at bay for some time afterward. Bulimics find eating an effective way to bury anger, block out feelings of depression, and avoid worries.[41]

Researchers have drawn different conclusions about what part of the eating binge is associated with the removal of unpleasant emotions. Based largely on retrospective reports by bulimics, which are of questionable reliability, some researchers suggest bulimics experience the emotional escape only during the vomiting phase. Many bulimics never engage in vomiting or other forms of purging, however, and those who do purge seldom start until they have been having eating binges for a year. Thus, purging seems only part of the story. There may be several stages involved. If unpleasant or painful emotions are always there in the background, the binge eater may constantly struggle to suppress them. When some trigger makes them well up out of control, an eating binge may succeed at pushing the unpleasant emotions away. By focusing on seeking, chewing, tasting, and swallowing food, the person can avoid thinking about all the things that make him or her feel terrible. The binge brings a kind of emotional peace, even though the consumption of food may appear driven or frenzied. As the binge comes to an end, however, and the person realizes he or she has broken rules and resolutions about dieting, new unpleasant emotions arise. To atone for the sin of eating, and perhaps to minimize the weight gain from the binge, the person may try to get rid of what has been eaten, such as by vomiting—which brings a second escape.

In another consequence of mental narrowing, many researchers have found that bulimics tend to have irrational beliefs. Bulimics are prone to excessive, unrealistic anticipations of future misfortunes and to seeing past problems as impossible to overcome.[42] They magnify events out of proportion, interpret them in irrational and distorted ways, take everything personally whether appropriate or not, overgeneralize from problems and misfortunes, and sometimes engage in magical thinking. For example, if bulimics notice that other people are talking, they may immediately assume that they are always talking about them and how fat they are.[43]

Dieters, too, have irrational beliefs, although their distortions are less extreme than those of bulimics. On some common measures of rational approaches to life, dieters score lower than nondieters.[44] Their ideas about food, in particular, contain distortions and irrationalities. For example, they may react negatively to a four-hundred-calorie milkshake, but not to a four-hundred-calorie chef's salad.[45]

Passivity is evident in the attitudes of dieters and bulimics. The feeling of losing control, which characterizes an eating binge, is itself a kind of passivity. To be active is to exert control, and to be passive is to give up control. Giving up control is what a binge is all about. It might seem that an eating binge is an active undertaking, but people tend to describe it in passive terms, emphasizing aspects such as the sense of losing control. An eating binge is an experience of being dominated by external cues and inner desires, with the conscious ego reduced to a mere pawn. Further evidence of the passivity of binge eaters comes from studies of their coping styles. They rarely adopt active, problem-solving approaches; rather, they incline toward the passive responses of avoidance and withdrawal.[46]

EATING RELATED TO OTHER ESCAPES

The theory that binge eating is an escape from the self is supported by evidence of its links to other escapes. There is a high rate of alcohol and drug abuse among bulimics—

higher than in the general population. Researchers have suggested that binge eating is itself a form of substance abuse: Some people turn to eating binges rather than drugs because food is legal and lacks the moral, legal, and medical complications that accompany drug abuse.[47] Others suggest that alcohol is less effective at producing escape in females than in males, and binge eating takes its place.[48] This could help explain the difference noted at the start of this chapter, namely that men consume alcohol while women consume food to escape from a bad mood.

Suicide rates are likewise very high among bulimics—many times higher than in the general population.[49] Bulimics who stop short of suicide sometimes inflict injuries on themselves, and self-inflicted injury rates are also surprisingly high among bulimics.[50] Such injuries are very poorly understood; as in masochism, the appeal may be the pain rather than the harm.

Perhaps the ultimate form of escape from the self is reflected in the wish to become someone else. This wish was noted as a common aspect of masochistic fantasy and one expressed by many suicidal persons. Bulimics and other people with eating disorders report similar wishes, and people who want to become someone else tend to have eating disorders.[51] Bulimics and dieters tend to regard the desired weight loss as a significant transformation of self.[52] Many seem to think that if they could successfully lose a great deal of weight, all their problems would vanish, as if by magic.[53]

Certainly, modern Western culture encourages people to be slim—perhaps slimmer than warranted by nature and health. The demand for an attractively slim physique falls most heavily on women, and women learn early in life that they should maintain strict control over what they eat. Binge eating frustrates this strict control and can lead to significant weight gain, ruining all the woman's efforts to count calories and stay slim. Binge eating is thus a paradoxical pattern in which the person's actions prevent her from reaching her overriding goals. Escape from the self is a useful way to understand this pattern: The goals are associated with the self, and escaping the self enables the person to abandon them temporarily.

NINE

≈≈≈≈≈≈≈

Religious Exercise and Spirituality

Zen student: *I feel myself a prisoner of my ego and want to escape.*
Yasutani-Roshi: *Intrinsically there is no ego—it is something that we ourselves create.* —Roshi Philip Kapleau, *The Three Pillars of Zen*

Spirituality is the pursuit of the highest potentialities in the human being. The seeker uses religion to attempt to realize the ultimate nature of things, to understand how the Creator designed us and what the Creator endowed us with, to encounter God directly, and to achieve a major, lasting transformation in his or her own psyche.

Escaping the self is centrally important in spiritual exercise. Religious disciplines from all over the world differ radically from each other in fundamental doctrines, techniques, promised results, and theoretical context, but all tend to agree on the importance of shedding the self. We shall see this message repeated over and over: The self is a barrier to spiritual advancement.

Part—but only part—of the problem with selfhood is that spiritual techniques are designed to produce states of ecstasy.

One plausible explanation of religion is that it grew up around the pursuit of ecstatic states, which people have always valued and cherished. Religion enabled people to place these extraordinary and wonderful experiences in a context that made sense of them, and many religions developed techniques for achieving them. This is somewhat difficult to realize here in the United States today, where religion is often equated with the Protestant and Puritan traditions that emphasize sober Christian piety. But the Christian church made a political decision to move away from mystical experience early in its history, and so the Christian establishment has opposed the direct pursuit of ecstatic experiences for many centuries. Other religions have been very different. One scholarly authority traces the origin of Indian religion to the loss of the plant soma.[1] Yoga, asceticism, and other early forms of Indian spirituality were concerned with creating the marvelous experiences that people had earlier obtained from ingesting soma. Buddhism was explicitly designed to furnish these powerful personal experiences, and Hinduism has long been centrally concerned with them.

The concern with ecstatic experiences has also been apparent in many Western religions. The later forms of Greek paganism reflected the early development of mystical techniques, especially in Orphism and possibly in the Eleusinian mysteries. Some Roman pagan cults involved ecstatic experiences. Judaism had a small but important mystical legacy in Kabbalah. Early Christianity had a strong gnostic side, which was aimed at achieving ecstatic experiences. Islam, which considered itself a further development of the Judeo-Christian religious tradition, had an influential mystical aspect in Sufism. Meanwhile, in the Western Hemisphere, other religions also emphasized the pursuit of ecstatic experiences. Even today, the Native American Church uses peyote to provide powerful spiritual experiences to its members. In an ideal regimen, seekers use peyote once or twice a year to obtain personal visions that help them understand their lives and orient themselves for their next tasks.

What sort of escape from oneself is involved in religious or spiritual exercise? The answer is that people want to get away from a life seen as painful, unsatisfying, or meaningless, and to reach a better state of mind that may include ecstatic experiences. They also seek to gain wisdom, insight, or understanding that will enable them to lead their lives in an improved and more satisfying way. To accomplish all this, people engage in various exercises, often involving meditation, which share many features with the techniques for escaping the self that we have seen in previous chapters: narrow focus on the immediate present, rejection of meaningful thought, and reduction of self-awareness to body.

THE PROBLEM OF SELF

Many religions take a dim view of the self. The self is treated as an illusion, a source of trouble and suffering, or even a curse. It is blamed for a variety of ills. Consider this Christian perspective. The Oxford English Dictionary, a major authority on the English language, cites this 1680 usage of the word "self": "Self is the great Anti-Christ and Anti-God in the World."[2] Such negative references to the self were ubiquitous at that time.[3] Self was the supreme enemy of religion. The corollary that spiritual progress requires overcoming the self was widely accepted. Nor is this view obsolete in the modern Age of the Self: The Christian fundamentalist preacher Billy Graham makes clear in his account of heaven that individual selfhood will be transcended. Selfless, self-sacrificing love like that of Jesus is what everyone will feel all the time in heaven.[4]

The Islamic mystics called Sufis have been equally insistent about the self being an obstacle to spiritual progress. The goal of Sufi practice is to reach the ecstatic state of *fana*, or freedom from the self.[5] This is understood as giving up one's own, limited, conditioned self and merging with God, or the totality of all being, through intense love. The literal meaning of *fana* is "annihilation," "vanishing," or "nothingness," and its usage by mystics refers to the obliteration of selfhood.[6] The need to get rid of the self is a common theme in just about all mystical disciplines. Among British Christian mystics, it became known as "self-naughting," that is, making nothing, "naught," of the self.[7]

Eastern religions often insist that there are no separate selves and that belief in ego or individual selfhood is an illusion. The concept is difficult for Westerners to grasp.[8] For the spiritually sophisticated of the East, however, it is no abstract argument but direct personal experience. The goal of meditation and other practices is to obtain direct personal understanding of the unity of being and the truth that there are no separate selves. One's attention is controlled and concentrated so intensely that one loses all sense of personal, individual self-awareness.[9]

Of course, this doesn't mean that the spiritual wise men and women of the East lose all sense of self in practical terms. It's not as if they wake up in the morning and don't know whose face to wash or whose feet to put shoes on. As Thomas Merton wrote in *Mystics and Zen Masters*, the denial of self in Zen is not a denial of the experiential reality of the self, but rather a denial of its relevance.[10]

The lesson that there are no separate selves has two main implications. First, all people are interrelated; my self does not exist in isolation but rather in relation to you or to other people, and likewise your identity depends in part on me. Selves are constructed by the group and do not exist independently. Second, one learns not to use the separate self as a basis for action and tries to avoid selfish, self-centered, or self-oriented motives for acting. Self-interest is not a valid basis for action,[11] and self-ishness is a major obstacle to spiritual progress. By ceasing to base one's actions and reactions on self-interested thinking, one can escape the burden of self. Radical changes in one's subjective experience then become possible.

Once the loss of the self is understood in those terms, it becomes more comprehensible. Indeed, there is otherwise a very confusing paradox in many mystical writings, for they speak of gaining insight into one's true self at the same time that they speak of getting rid of the self. The gain they refer to is far more than mere improvement in the details of self-knowledge; it is a substantial change in perspective as to what the self is.

In the words of the great U.S. Zen master Philip Kapleau: "[Enlightenment involves] the 'swallowing up' of the universe, the obliteration of every feeling of opposition and separateness. In this state of unconditioned subjectivity, I, *selfless* I, am supreme." He goes on to quote Dogen, one of the founders of Japanese Zen Buddhism: "To learn about oneself is to forget oneself."[12] Taken literally in their conventional meanings, these statements seem senseless and contradictory. How can learning about oneself be the same as forgetting oneself? How can there be a "selfless I"? But such statements do make sense if one accepts the psychological interconnectedness of all beings and the removal of self-interest as one's overriding concern. Then, the self continues to exist as a point of consciousness, an experiencing agent, although it ceases to see itself as separate from the world it experiences.[13] It ends up feeling as if it has ceased to exist. That, of course, would seem to be another paradox, for how can the experiencing self experience its nonexistence? But the meaning is probably just that selfhood feels quite different once one has abandoned self-interest and other preoccupations with the self. (For example, just try to imagine how it would feel not to care how people evaluate you.) The self that is left feels quite different from the previous self. Large parts of it are indeed gone—the most obvious and overriding parts—and hence the impression that the self is completely gone.

Pride and Self-Love

In this book I have emphasized that people want to escape the self when the self is seen as bad. This line of argument is consistent with what the religious saints and mystics say, with one important alteration: They stress that even positive views of self are a detriment to spiritual progress. In religious views, self is always bad, even when it feels good, and in fact the self may be most troublesome when it feels good. Pride and self-love are major obstacles to spiritual progress.

The Christian list of the seven deadly sins includes pride and vanity.[14] That is, people concerned about admiring themselves or wanting others to admire them are unlikely to achieve spiritual advancement. To achieve exalted spiritual states, such as ecstatic communion with God, one needs to transcend these self-oriented feelings. In 1125, the famous monastic Bernard of Clairvaux wrote in *On the Steps of Humility and Pride* that humility leads one closer to God, while the steps of pride lead in the opposite direction. Other religions similarly condemn pride[15] as the root of such problems and dangers as animosity, prejudice, disharmony, and divisiveness.[16] Indeed, each success or advancement by the spiritual seeker brings a new danger of pride. The Sufis came to see pride as the greatest continuing obstacle on the path to enlightenment, or fana,[17] because pride over one's progress could prevent further progress. Likewise, the Buddha reproached religious elders of his time for congratulating themselves on their asceticism and forming an exaggerated view of their spiritual accomplishments.[18]

What is so bad about pride? One key factor is that pride and self-love make the person vulnerable to suffering, as argued in an earlier chapter. Pride can give rise to immoral or aggressive acts and produce aversive emotions. (These can readily be seen in social groups that make pride a central principle, such as aristocrats in medieval or early modern Europe: Intense sensitivity to slight affronts produced endless conflicts and sustained the institution of dueling for centuries.)[19] The higher the value you set on yourself, the more you are exposed to threats to self-value when events cast the self in a less exalted light, and so the more vulnerable you are to unhappiness.

Spiritual exercise may be the ultimate solution to the problem of the stress of maintaining the self. Be humble, and you will not suffer from wounded pride. Humility will safeguard you from many of the temptations that go with asserting your egotism. (Modern psychology is in agreement here, finding egotism a factor causing aggression, together with high but insecure self-esteem.)[20] The early stages of mysticism involve an assault on one's pride and egotism, similar in some ways to masochism. Spiritual novices also submit to degrading and insulting treatment. They may be required to shave their heads as a check to personal vanity. Some spiritual traditions require the novice to beg for food, not so much to obtain sustenance, but for the humiliation of begging as an antidote to egotism. Likewise, spiritual novices prostrate themselves, bow, kneel, and perform other gestures that connote humility.

What Motivates the Spiritual Quest?

How does the turn to religion, especially spiritual exercises like meditation, fit the escape theory? Probably the calamity pattern is the least common as a motivation for meditation. Personal crises or disasters do make people religious, but their desire is for consoling promises, compensations for their suffering, or uplifting doctrines, not escape from a short-term awareness of self as unpleasant.

Indeed, people who respond to a personal crisis by enlisting in a spiritual discipline turn out to be poor prospects. A person recovering from a personal crisis is typically in a distracted and emotionally vulnerable state of mind and lacks the strength and discipline required for a long-term commitment to spiritual exercise. When things start to get better, the person may feel better and lose enthusiasm for the monastic life. Many of today's popular religious cults have a high membership turnover because they recruit people in vulnerable states of mind resulting from recent crises. In contrast, other spiritual communities or organizations discourage people from signing up in a burst of enthusiasm or while recovering from a personal crisis, and mystics throughout history have been legendary for discouraging potential novices. During a visit to a Zen monastery in New York, for example, several dozen of us were provided with an introduction to meditation techniques and ideas, but the monastery refused to let anyone sign up for anything. A monk got up in front of the group and said that he knew that many people were excited and wanted to make a commitment, but no one would be permitted to do so. Go home, he said, wait until your enthusiasm dies down, and if in six months or a year you still want to get more involved, then get in touch and we'll see if we have an opening.

Likewise, the treatment of a would-be monk in traditional Japanese Zen monasteries was full of obstacles and discouragement. A young man would give up all his belongings except what he could carry and travel many days to the monastery, sleeping in fields because he had no money. When the young man arrived and asked to be admitted, he was invariably turned away, usually with rough or insulting treatment. At best, he was told there was no room for him and he would have to go elsewhere. Only after waiting outside for a long time—hours, even days—would he be permitted to come inside, and then only to sleep. Being accepted for study as a novice required further steps.

Meditative escapes do seem to bring relief from stress. By abandoning egotism and adopting a pervasive attitude of modesty, one can avoid the burden of keeping an overgrown, overpriced self up to inflated standards. Meditation is often used as a stress reducer; a few years back, Transcendental Meditation was popular among U.S. business executives primarily for its stress-reducing qualities.[21] Sufi meditation practices likewise seem to aid recovery from stress. "After a short time, the individual returns to the self, feeling refreshed and alert. It is as if the mind has been cleared from distracting thoughts and disturbing noises. The person is now more receptive and responsive."[22]

A broader context for the view that meditation and spirituality provide relief from stress can be found in the idea that life is suffering. Many religions are based on the notion that human life on earth is pervasively unpleasant; indeed, this hostility toward life in the flesh is fundamental to these religions and to their concept of salvation. To appreciate this attitude, it is necessary to understand how drastically world religion changed over a relatively short time. Between 600 B.C. and A.D. 400, a wave of radically new religions swept the world. They shared the assumption that ordinary human life is painful and unpleasant. The message brought by the Buddha, Jesus, and other great religious figures was that life here on earth is full of sadness, disappointment, and unhappiness, and that only religion holds the promise of salvation (for example, Buddhist nirvana and Christian grace and heaven). In India, post-Upanishadic religious thought has agreed with the Buddha that "All is suffering, all is transitory."[23] Indeed, the assertion that all life is suffering was the first of the Buddha's Four Noble Truths. The goal of Indian philosophies and meditation techniques was to liberate the person from suffering.[24] Likewise, Christianity emphasized hostility toward this world of pain and suffering, in the doctrine that Original Sin condemned humankind to toil and suffering here on earth, and a denigration of sexuality that greatly exceeded the views of other religions at that time.[25] Islam too adopted a negative view of life on earth. "The Sufis ... perceive life as suffering," as one scholar summed up their attitude.[26]

Some of the same attitudes operate today. The process of meditation and spiritual progress can be accompanied by an increasing disenchantment with ordinary strivings and daily life. The psychologist Daniel Goleman's account of meditation, based on a synthesis of techniques from around the world, explicates how the meditator comes to feel unsatisfied with the world and to perceive suffering and misery everywhere.[27]

Our third and final motive for escaping the self is the achievement of ecstasy, which is clearly central to spiritual techniques. Many religions emphasize that bliss and ecstasy follow from their practices, and there is little doubt that these religious experiences are often powerfully pleasant. The Buddha described nirvana as bliss and "unshakable happiness."[28] Modern Buddhists describe enlightenment in similar glowing terms, such as "a delicious, unspeakable delight."[29] Christian mystics have described their experiences in terms of direct, ecstatic enjoyment of God's love, even using explicitly sexual metaphors.[30] The Sufis link loss of self to joy and ecstasy, which they interpret as contact with God.[31] Written accounts of meditation techniques are filled with references to bliss, rapture, and ecstasy.[32]

Emotional Distress

In earlier chapters we have seen that escape from the self is motivated in part by a desire to escape from unpleasant emotional states. In the case of spiritual escapes, a parallel notion is that life is suffering and that religion offers the solution to this suffering.

Escape theory also emphasizes that the unhappy feelings are often associated with the self. Not just suffering in general, but feeling bad about yourself motivates us to escape ourselves. This view is at least implicit in some spiritual discussions. Christian mysticism started with escaping from sin: Medieval Christian writings typically emphasized that awareness of oneself as a sinner was the motivating force behind a desire to climb the spiritual ladder. The first steps toward realizing God's love involved incipient feelings of strong remorse for having sinned.[33] The same desire to escape from and repudiate one's sinful past appears in religious conversion experiences of modern and recent times, typically in adolescence, although in recent decades in the United States fundamentalist Christianity has made these experiences popular at all stages of adult life. As a rule, a person slowly sinks into sin, indulges selfish and pleasure-seeking desires, and acknowledges in himself or herself a set of feelings starkly inconsistent with Christian virtue.[34] The feeling of being a bad person increases, and one is suffused with guilt and self-loathing. One comes to regard oneself as a hopeless sinner, a degenerate. Self-respect becomes almost impossible. Then comes the conversion experience, in which one feels accepted and forgiven by God. The person breaks with his or her sinful past and resolves to live a new, virtuous life.

One can readily see why such experiences accompany adolescence, perhaps especially in past eras. During childhood one learns religious lessons almost as abstractions, and the rules are easy to follow objectively. Adolescence, however, is marked by serious psychological changes, including a much increased self-awareness that enables a person to scrutinize the inner self and therefore feel bad about objectionable desires even if they are not expressed in overt action. It also includes a great increase in sexual and perhaps other instinctual impulses that may be at odds with social norms and religious virtues. As the young person has not yet developed self-control or other techniques for managing these feelings, the self-conscious adolescent is not entirely incorrect in seeing himself or herself as a hopeless sinner. But with maturity and increasing ego strength, a person finds ways to integrate sexual and other desires into a socially acceptable life-style and can put this period of sinful desire behind. A religious conversion experience could be a powerfully appealing means of doing this.

It is important to realize that a first spiritual awakening or the beginning of religious activity does not entail an end to unpleasant emotions. Indeed, many spiritual and mystical writings emphasize that the ecstatic experience is often preceded by profound feelings of unhappiness, confusion, and self-doubt. Christian mystics describe this period of trouble and turmoil as "the cloud of unknowing" and "the dark night of the soul." (Both those phrases formed titles of important works that sought to guide and advise the Christian mystic.) Zen writings emphasize the accumulating "doubt-mass" as a crucial factor in achieving enlightenment. The struggling Zen novice who is on the verge of enlightenment may often feel overcome by doubts and unhappiness.

Underneath many of these feelings is the basic point that unpleasant emotional states are often based on the self. Anger, passion, frustrated desire, and other feelings are linked to conceptions of self, and by renouncing egotism one supposedly becomes free from these sources of emotional turmoil.[35] Both sin and regret are linked to selfhood, and therefore transcending selfhood holds the promise of permanent escape from feeling bad about oneself. But one makes the renunciation of self long before one enjoys the benefits; many additional periods of doubt, worry, and emotional confusion come before the ecstasies or enlightenments.

THE STATE OF MIND

Rejection of Meaning

Obviously, the context for spiritual exercises differs from that in which people get drunk, engage in masochistic sex, go on an eating binge, or contemplate killing themselves. Yet the steps involved in fostering the proper state of mind share elements with those behaviors. The rejection of ordinary, meaningful thought is important to all escapes from the self.

The techniques of meditation have usually been based on a perceived need to disrupt the mind's tendency to jabber on about everything that happens and to analyze and fit it into familiar patterns. Normally, anything that crosses one's mind is elaborated, that is, one stops and thinks about it. Meditation involves learning to let these thoughts come and go without interfering with them. There is a false stereotype that meditation aims at achieving a blank mind; it would be more accurate to say that meditation aims at fostering an awareness that is not disturbed by the helter-skelter of little thoughts.[36] Television watching offers an analogy: The normal mind can be compared to the viewer whose awareness is fully absorbed in the television program and commercials, paying close attention to every word and image and noticing nothing else. The accomplished meditator is like someone who sits peacefully in a large room with a small television off in a corner. Images flit across the screen but the person's mind is not at their mercy.

Spiritual disciplines tend to regard ordinary thought processes and conventional rationality as the enemy. The Christian emphasis on faith rather than rational thought was never stronger than among its mystics. Gnosis, not theological discussion, provided the ultimate certainty. This rejection of rational analysis is indicative of the rejection of meaningful thought.

The objections to rational thought can be found in other religions as well. The Sufis perceive a need to overcome one's intellectual and rational tendencies.[37] Some of the sternest and most creative techniques for conquering rational or intellectual tendencies are to be found in Zen. Zen seems to acknowledge that ordinary minds inevitably try to figure everything out and come up with verbal explanations: Instead of trying to force the mind into stopping, Zen lets it run wild until it finds its rationality helpless.

The device used to accomplish this effect in Zen is the koan, typically an unsolvable riddle. Novices are asked to solve the problem of what face they had before they were born, or what is the sound of one hand clapping, or what is the meaning of the nonsense syllable "Mu!" spoken in reply to the question of whether a dog has spiritual potentialities. Nor are novices simply told to think about one of these problems for a while. Instead, they are required to come up with an answer every day and to present it to the master. During periods of intense meditation, the requirement may be increased to several times per day. The master rejects all solutions, but intensifies the pressure to come up with the correct answer. The novices gradually come to feel that their minds are in an impossible situation, driven by an urgent need to solve the problem but recognizing it as unsolvable. Zen koans are designed to exhaust and frustrate the intellect, forcing the individual to solve the problem another way.[38] Instead of analyzing experience and thinking about it, the mind learns to experience and respond in a new way. Sometimes this is described as a more direct form of experience, because it is not mediated by one's conventional modes of thinking and understanding.[39] One learns to stop mistaking one's own concepts for reality itself.

Concreteness and Banality

Spiritual exercises explicitly aim to overcome the normal mental habits that underlie "the social construction of reality"[40] and to *de*construct reality. Meditation techniques focus the mind on concrete, immediate, and banal phenomena, rather than on abstract analysis or detailed thought. The epitome of such meditative exercises is the simple form of meditation taught to beginners in Zen even before they study koans. The novice is told to count his or her breaths without controlling the breathing in any way. Thus, the person passively allows the breathing to happen as it naturally does, attends carefully to the process, and counts each exhalation. When the count reaches ten, the person starts over again at one. If the mind loses count or becomes distracted, it starts over again at one. This exercise is performed for perhaps twenty minutes, or with practice slightly longer. Similar exercises are found in other spiritual disciplines.

Breath meditation is a good illustration of concreteness, banality, and the rejection of meaning. Breathing is a simple, physical, concrete activity, one that the body performs automatically and constantly. It is an uncomplicated physical activity that requires no reflection. But the meditation is not simply mechanical; rather, the person tries to maintain an intense concentration on breathing.[41] To elevate breathing to the focus of attention is thus to place emphasis on one of nature's most common and least inherently meaningful activities.

This focus on the body reflects the concreteness and banality that spiritual disciplines cultivate in their attempt to break the mind of its bad habits. This attempt typically goes beyond the breath meditation. Zen, for example, places great emphasis on other physical states. The importance of maintaining a rigidly erect spine is stressed, and indeed the erect spine is regarded as a prerequisite for a clear mind. Details of posture, such as the careful positioning of the hands, are made a focus of the meditator's attention.[42] Immobility is stressed during meditation periods, as it helps force the mind to remain focused on immediate, concrete, physical concerns. It is quite difficult to remain completely motionless for half an hour. However uncomfortable one becomes, no squirming is permitted. If one starts to itch, no scratching is allowed. The lotus position is commonly used for sitting, and many people find their legs grow numb or painful. Despite these distractions, one is not allowed to move. U.S. Zen instructors repeat the "No pain, no gain" phrase popular among sports coaches. This use of pain is similar to that in masochism, that is, as an effective way to seize the mind and direct it to immediate physical facts.

The emphasis on physical concerns goes beyond the counting of breaths. In Zen, periods of sitting motionless in meditation are interspersed with brief periods of walking meditation. The novices walk in a circle, rapidly, with hands carefully clasped and attention directly immediately in front of them. They are supposed to concentrate intensely on the activity of walking. Obviously, walking is almost as banal as breathing—it is another simple physical activity that is easily done without paying attention to it, and so directing attention to it helps remove the mind from its conceptualizing and elaborating.

Yoga furnishes another good example of the use of the body to occupy and purify the mind. Concentration on physical postures and movements is central to yoga. Likewise, the yogi gradually learns to perform each physical activity consciously and deliberately rather than automatically. Intense attention is invested in moving, eating, breathing, digesting, speaking, keeping silent.[43]

Another type of meditation uses a mantra, a syllable that the person recites mentally over and over, with similar effects.[44] In Transcendental Meditation, for example, one is assigned a special mantra by a teacher and mentally repeats this mantra for a twenty-minute period twice a day. During this time, the person is encouraged to let thoughts and feelings come and go without attempting to direct or control them in any way. Likewise, Sufism uses a syllable called a *zikr*, which the person inhales and exhales with normal breathing.[45] Again, the person passively lets thoughts, feelings, fantasies, and other mental events flow on of their own accord. Sufism also may instruct the meditator to focus attention on some point in the body.[46]

A final point about the mystics' spiritual usage of physical activity is articulated in Zen,[47] where all activity is described as purposeless and as a potential form of meditation. A person is to maintain an attitude that focuses entirely on the current process and activity—whatever it may be—rather than the outcome. This is especially relevant to the physical labor that nearly all monasteries require their inhabitants to do. When raking the leaves or washing the floor, one is not supposed to be thinking about how nice things will look when the job is done, or how much is left to do, or how proud one will be. You're not supposed to daydream, whistle, or think about what you'll do later on. Rather, your mind should be immersed in the physical movements of raking or washing. When the time allotted for working is up, one ceases the activity and moves on to the next, rather than pursuing the activity until completed. This mental approach to work (and other activities) exemplifies the immersion of the mind in concrete and immediate physical activities, as opposed to rationalistic planning and working toward goals.

Early Christianity, as is well known, held a rather pejorative view of work and regarded many forms of work as an obstacle to spiritual fulfillment, especially work motivated by concern with results—like greedily getting money.[48] Hermits and others recognized the potential spiritual value of work as an exercise, however, and sought to perform work in a way that would reap its benefits but be free of its sinful connotations and harmful effects. To accomplish this, they made sure that no material benefits ensued from their work. Several famous hermits developed a working meditation consisting of moving loads of sand around in the desert. Another famous hermit wove baskets with intense concentration month after month, and at the end of each year he burned them all and started over.[49]

Time Span

As is implicit in much of what has already been discussed, the focus of meditation is on the here and now. In breath meditation, the individual strives to fulfill the instruction, "Be present at every breath."[50] Breathing, obviously, is performed in the immediate present; past and future have little relevance. One does not plan future breathing, nor does one reminisce about breathing in the past. As the Sufis say, "The Sufi lives in the moment and is one with the moment. Rumi states, 'Oh friend, the Sufi is the child of the moment. Talking about tomorrow is not a condition of the Path.' "[51] Likewise, when inspired by his experiences with psychedelic drugs to give up his Harvard professorship and travel to India to seek enlightenment, Richard Alpert titled the book in which he reported what he learned *Be Here Now*, a phrase that became something of a slogan of the spiritual movement among hippies in the Unites States.

≈

CONSEQUENCES

The consequences of spiritual exercise share some features with other forms of escape from the self. First, these escapes tend to be transitory. Religious doctrines promise eternal salvation, but in fact ecstasies come and go. One can gain a change in perspective, new knowledge, and understanding, but the state of selflessness—or at least its intense, ecstatic, pleasant aspect—generally dissipates. This temporary nature of ecstatic states has been remarked by many researchers. The scholar Mohammed Shafii observed of the Sufis, "The experience of loss of self-awareness is frequently short-lived, but may last for days, months, or years. It may occur a number of times."[52] Historian William Clebsch concluded that medieval Christian mystics achieved "no lasting escape from the world"; rather, they returned to the world, often dedicating themselves to working to improve it."[53] Similarly, Buddhist practice encompasses the vow of the Bodhisattva, which is not to attain final enlightenment until all beings can enter into that state together. Thus, the seeker is prepared in advance for a *temporary* experience of satori.

Passivity

Passivity is one of the goals of spiritual exercise, as well as one of its methods. A properly passive attitude is conducive, if not indispensable, to the ego's ceasing its grasping activity, that is, its constant attempts to seize control of phenomena and impose itself on them.[54] As Thomas Merton explained in *Mystics and Zen Masters*, self is desire, so mystics aspire to desirelessness.

The passivity should not be overstated. Spirituality does not aim to free the individual from responsibility for his or her actions, and so escaping from responsibility is not one of the motives for engaging in meditation, unlike the use of alcohol and other escape-inducing methods. Moreover, action does not cease entirely: The Buddha included Right Activity as part of the eightfold path.[55]

Passivity is often used as one exercise to help the individual overcome the self. This is readily evident in Zen and other meditations that insist on motionless sitting. In a summer practice of some Zen monasteries, the windows are opened at the start of meditation, allowing clouds of mosquitoes in. They sit on the heads and bodies of meditators, who dare not brush them away or twitch. Sitting motionless while being bitten by mosquitoes can be considered an extraordinary exercise in passivity training.

Escape from Emotion

The goals of spiritual striving are not states of emotion. Although ecstasy and bliss are impermanent, the result of spiritual training is a profound and stable state of mind, which is quite different from the short-term fluctuations involved in emotion. Spirituality seeks not just an emotional high but a state of peace, tranquility, and understanding. Freedom from emotion is similar to what mystics speak of as freedom from desire. For them, the self is an entity full of wants and needs, and emotions occur in connection with these wants and needs. Pleasant emotions arise when the self's projects are facilitated, and unpleasant emotions arise when they are thwarted or threatened. Getting rid of the self gets rid of these desires, so the basis for emotion is removed. Without self-interest as the basic criterion for evaluating everything that happens, many emotions cease to arise.

A well-known story about a famous Zen master illustrates the seeming indifference that results.[56] According to the legend, a girl in a small village became pregnant and refused to name the father. Under intense pressure from kin and neighbors to identify the guilty male, she finally broke down and said that the father was Hakuin, a noted Zen master who lived nearby. This created a scandal. When the baby was born, the parents took it to Hakuin and told him that the child was his responsibility. "Is that so?" was his only reply. He accepted the child and cared for its needs as best he could. Of course, his reputation as a great spiritual leader was ruined by this disgraceful tale of his lustful activity. But this was of no consequence to him, for he did not care about fame, reputation, or other forms of self-aggrandizement.

After a time, the girl was overcome with guilt and confessed that she had not in fact had relations with Hakuin. She said the true father was a young man in her village, and he confessed his paternity. The parents went back to Hakuin to retrieve the child from him. They said that there had been a mistake and he was not at fault. "Is that so?" he said, as he returned the child to them.

Whether the story is truth or legend is not important. What matters is the equanimity displayed by Hakuin, who functions in the story as a representative of the ideal of being above emotional turmoil. Suffering occupational disgrace, being abruptly burdened with the care of a child, and then abruptly relinquishing the child are all events that would normally cause a great deal of emotion. The point of the story is the Zen master's freedom from such feelings.

Disinhibition

The disinhibition that often accompanies escaping the self seems less important in spiritual exercise: Saints and seekers are not known for their wild or uninhibited actions. The reason may be that overcoming their desires has removed the impetus behind many potential actions. We noted in connection with alcohol that people act bizarrely only where they had felt inhibitory conflict—that is, the person both wanted to perform the action and felt inhibited from acting that way. Alcohol removed the inhibitions but left the desire intact, with the result that the person would act on the desire. Spiritual mysticism, however, undertakes to overcome the desire as well as the inhibition. Since loss of desire removes the inhibitory conflict, no untoward behavior occurs.

Another factor may be the frequent emphasis on morality

and virtue in spiritual disciplines. They typically stress social and personal responsibility, consideration of others, ethical awareness, proper action, and other socially desirable virtues, either as means to the end of spiritual advancement or as ends in themselves.[57]

Some danger of disinhibition remains, however, or at least a sensitivity to it. Kapleau derogated misperceptions of Zen as resulting in a "Zen libertine," who supposedly feels free to pursue whims, desires, or other selfish impulses.[58] The very existence of this stereotype indicates an awareness of disinhibitions. Merton also observed that some Westerners regarded Zen as indulgence of all one's inclinations and impulses—a view he believed accurately recognized that Zen training overcomes certain inhibitions, but mistakenly overlooked the moral and ethical awareness and the strong discipline that Zen training instills.

Irrationality

The irrationality that we have seen as a feature of other forms of escape from the self has its parallel in spirituality. Indeed, rationality is often recognized as an enemy. Christian mystics emphasized faith because of the inadequacy of reason to achieve their aim. Faith, not intellectual analysis, was the best way to deal with seeming paradoxes such as the Trinity or the Virgin Birth.

Zen koans and Sufi stories are often deliberately cryptic. They defy rational or intellectual analysis, and that may well be their function: to challenge the mind in ways that force it to abandon its normal habits of thinking. A curious feature of some of these exercises in irrationality is that they too seem to swallow up the self, thus helping the person achieve the escape from self. Some observers have remarked that the Zen novice struggling with a koan gradually comes to experience his or her own entire being as a riddle without an answer.[59] With the exhaustion and defeat of the intellectual, rational mind, self-awareness merges with the riddle. Kapleau's account of his own first taste of enlightenment indicates that the days preceding the breakthrough involved precisely this loss of self in the koan. He felt that all his actions were performed by the riddle rather than by his ordinary self: "I didn't eat breakfast, Mu did. I didn't sweep and wash the floors after breakfast, Mu did."[60]

Thus, in spiritual exercise, irrationality is not simply a by-product of fortuitous consequence but is often central to overcoming the self. Westerners, at least, tend to equate the rational, thinking mind with selfhood, and so the deliberate attack on rationality is crucial to the project of freeing the person from self.

Spiritual progress and advancement seem intimately connected with escaping the self. These disciplines hold great promise of inner peace and happiness and blissful, ecstatic experiences. They demand, however, that a person relinquish many aspects of the self, some of them permanently. The person ceases to use self-interest as a basis for action or even for thought and feeling.

As a result, many spiritual disciplines regard the self as the primary enemy that is to be overcome. One's level of spiritual advancement can be roughly gauged by one's lack of pride, egotism, and similar patterns of self-oriented feeling or action.[61] One may feel a continuing tension, for spiritual attainments create a new basis for pride that can be reflected in overt signs of respect from others, with such tributes furnishing a new temptation for pride and egotism. It is no wonder that many people who do make real spiritual progress eventually fall victim to egotism.

Spiritual exercise is a very important form of escaping the self, particularly because it is generally deliberately positive and life-enhancing. In contrast to such destructive forms of escape as suicide, alcohol and drug abuse, and binge eating, meditation and spiritual exercise appear to help people become better adjusted, to be more considerate and helpful to others, and to feel better and think more clearly. Escaping excesses of the self can thus become an important part of the human striving for fulfillment and realizing the highest human potential.

TEN

Other Factors, Other Routes

When one has become an individual, one stands alone and faces the world in all its perilous and overpowering aspects.
—Erich Fromm, *Escape from Freedom*

T his book has found common elements in a wide range of human behaviors associated with escaping the self. Under different circumstances, people switch from self-seeking to self-avoiding. The desire to escape the self takes many forms—from the most pathetically self-destructive to the spiritually exalted, all sharing three basic motivations and one common process.

WHAT ABOUT OTHER FACTORS?

It would be reckless to try to explain all forms of behavior, or even all instances of suicide or binge eating, by the notion of escaping the self. Escape offers a broad pattern that covers a great deal of human activity, but it remains important to avoid overgeneralizing. Any particular case of suicide may

have a host of causes and influences, and some suicides probably do not fit the mold of escaping the self.

The notion of escape has been most commonly applied to
drug use, which is also linked to physiological factors. Could
there be physiological bases for the behaviors we have ana-
lyzed here as escapes from the self? Might a fluke of brain
chemistry explain masochism, alcoholism, or suicide? To answer these questions, we must first consider what we mean
by *explain*. Physiological explanation may point to bodily
processes that accompany psychological events, but a full and
adequate explanation would have to provide a causal account of all facets of the phenomenon. By the latter criterion, I doubt that a physiological explanation of escape is
feasible. Physiological processes may indeed operate in escapes from the self, and research may discover that brain
chemicals or hormonal patterns predispose certain individuals toward alcoholism, bulimia, or other escapist behavior.
But it is important to realize that physiology is often only a
partial or inadequate explanation.

Masochism provides a good illustration. There is little information available about the physiology of masochism, but
it seems plausible that masochists may have some special
physiological trait that distinguishes them from other people. Their tolerance for pain could be greater than that of
other people or their threshold for sexual arousal higher (requiring greater and more prolonged stimulation to enable
them to reach sexual satisfaction). Possibly their nervous systems link pain and sexual pleasure in some unusual way.
Undoubtedly, important physiological processes occur during a masochistic experience that mediate what the person
feels and desires. Even if future research should discover such
a physiological basis for masochism, however, it will be inadequate as an explanation. Individual experience, cultural
conditioning, and socialization are vitally important aspects
of masochism. To leave them out of the explanation is to
ignore a crucial part of the story.

Perhaps the easiest way to appreciate the role of such non-physical factors is in the cultural relativity of masochism. One has to assume that the human body is put together in approximately the same way that it has been for thousands of years. Masochism, however, exists mainly in the modern Western world, and unlike other sexual practices, it appears to have been unknown in past eras.[1] Masochistic activity increased greatly in our culture around the seventeenth century—but human physiology seems unlikely to have changed. People's brains were probably the same in the year 1800 as they were in 1600.

No physiological explanation can fully account for escapist patterns or rival the sort of psychological analysis that this book has pursued. But the two may be quite compatible. It seems highly plausible that emotional distress, the radical refocusing of attention, and the attainment of bliss have physiological aspects, and these are an important area for further study. The body is centrally involved in the escape from the self, but the goal of escape, as well as its precipitating cause and ultimate outcome, involves psychological effects.

Suicide also illustrates the multiplicity of causes that may be involved in some patterns this work has considered. A majority of cases of suicide appears to fit the pattern of escaping the self. But some suicides undoubtedly occur for other reasons. The Buddhist monks who set fire to themselves to protest the Vietnam war, for example, were not trying to escape from the self but to make a dramatic and powerful statement about political issues.

OTHER ESCAPES

Individual chapters of this book have featured five major escape routes: suicide, masochism, alcohol use, binge eating, and spiritual exercise. Although these are particularly important forms of escape, they are not the only ones. Any strenuous, absorbing activity can, in principle, furnish an effective means of escape. Mental narrowing can be accomplished by focusing the mind on intense sensations or muscular movements. Jogging and swimming, for example, seem capable of producing the kind of trance in which the mind ceases to engage in abstract, meaningful thought and focuses instead on the repetitive exertions involved in the exercise. These activities also produce muscular fatigue that can border on pain. Like the pain in masochism, the pain in strenuous exercise may preoccupy the mind and prevent distracting thoughts connected with the more far-reaching definitions of self.

Long-distance runners appear to experience trance or ecstasy states that arise from the repetitious activity of running combined with pain. In a recent runner's magazine, one author described his experience during a long-distance run: "I kept feeling better and better and just floated around the track for a two or three hour 'experience,' so strong that it seemed like there was a coil of energy going from my heart to my head. I felt like I could run forever."[2] The inability to tell whether this altered state lasted for two or three hours is telling. Another runner summed up his philosophy of running: "Pain is inevitable, suffering is optional" and went on to describe the spiritual benefits of running. After a detailed and graphic catalog of the multiple sources of pain and bodily trauma that afflict the distance runner, he concluded, "The spirit draws energy from the body's slow crash and burn." The deconstruction of the world is reflected in this runner's characterization of his mental state as "experiencing ... the absolute nitty-gritty of living."[3]

One medical researcher noted similarities between runners and women with eating disorders, including high expectations about the self, preoccupation with the body (including lean body mass), and high tolerance of physical discomfort.[4] The comparison of running to masochism, especially the central role of pain in both, has become a cliché. The so-called runner's high has been widely misunderstood, for many runners describe it in terms of a sense of relaxation rather than euphoria.[5] Runner's high is most commonly experienced by runners whose mental dispositions allow them to slip into trancelike states most easily.[6] As a group, marathon runners score high on hypnotizability.[7] All of these factors suggest that the mental state of the distance runner is similar in important respects to the state experienced in meditation and other forms of escape from the self.

We have also seen that masochists do not necessarily use actual pain; sometimes the threat of pain is sufficient to focus the mind. Danger is an effective means of keeping the mind from wandering, and many escapist hobbies contain an element of danger. Mountain climbing, hang gliding, horseback riding, and car racing combine intense sensory experiences with an element of danger, and this combination is probably effective in stripping away one's ordinary, meaningful self-awareness.

Even if the actual danger is minimal, the chance of falling or losing control makes certain activities absorbing. Water skiing, snow skiing, surfing, windsurfing, and similar activities require the person to pay close attention to maintain control and avoid falling. It seems likely that such activities provide an effective escape for those who pursue them, because the span of attention is necessarily restricted to one's immediate movements and sensations.

What about games? Playing a game may provide escape in the sense that one abandons consideration of one's normal identity and submerges awareness in the game. Contrary to patterns that we have seen in the escapist activities covered in this book, many games require active exertion, rational planning, and decision making. One could argue that the decisions don't really matter—after all, it's a game. Games may be more effective at providing a temporary substitute identity than at removing awareness of one's old identity. Of course, for professional players the game is not an escape at all but a primary way of defining the self.

A different question may arise for sports spectators. Do people escape themselves through emotional involvement in the fortunes of a favorite sports team or star? The study of the psychology of the sports fan is in its infancy, but we can note escapist patterns in sports spectatorship: The fan narrows his or her awareness to one small, circumscribed domain of activity. The fan, unlike the players, is essentially passive, so the individual self is not implicated. Identification with a favorite team can replace one's everyday sense of self and divert attention from one's personal affairs.

Moreover, the sports fan's individuality is submerged in the community of fans. The loss of individuality through anonymous participation in groups is an important escape from the self. We have already spoken of the deindividuation that occurs in religious communities, where people may relinquish personal styles of dress and hairstyle to look like others—and in the process experience a merging of selves. Even anonymous sexual experience can be an escape. A brief, relatively meaningless but physically pleasurable episode of sex with someone else can be a powerful way of taking the mind off other things. Surveys taken at the height of the popularity of gay bathhouses, where within a single evening a man might have sexual contacts with several or even a dozen strangers, found a majority of participants indicating that they used "anonymous sex as a way of relieving tension."[8] They also admitted that their feelings in these bathhouses tended to cloud their rational judgment and overcome their inhibitions, leading them to do things they felt they ordinarily wouldn't or shouldn't do.

Irrationality and disinhibition have long been associated with sports fans, too. As I write this, recent news stories have focused on the excesses of sports fans around the world. Detroit's recent basketball championship was followed by a local celebration that involved knifings, looting and vandalism, and even firing guns randomly into crowds of people. In Italy, the world soccer championship has been marred by rioting and streetfighting, and hundreds of fans have been arrested, jailed, or deported. Hockey fans are legendary fighters, and during this past year several large-scale brawls pitted fans against players. Less destructively, football fans paint their bodies with team colors and cavort half-naked in freezing temperatures during play-off games in northern cities like Cleveland and Chicago.

One characteristic of escape seemingly absent from the sports fan is the lack of emotion. Mental narrowing is often aimed at getting rid of unpleasant emotional states, but fans do become emotionally involved in the games they watch. Still, these emotions are far removed from the fans' personal lives, and so they may be compatible with the goal of escape.

Being a fan is probably insufficient escape for someone in the midst of a personal crisis. The sort of person who resorts to a suicide attempt would probably not find watching sports an adequate substitute. Fan activities may provide the sort of frequent, moderate escape that relieves the stressful burden of vulnerability that accompanies the modern self, and the same may be said for other vicarious pleasures, such as watching movies or television. These activities restrict attention to a limited sphere, effectively removing the individual from the issues and concerns of his or her daily life.

The escapes motivated by calamity and vulnerability to stress receive the most attention, but ecstasy may also take a variety of forms. A major theme in aesthetic theory is that of the spectator abandoning self-awareness to achieve full appreciation of a great work of art. Total immersion in the aesthetic experience is thus the optimum circumstance for maximum enjoyment. The pleasure derived from experiencing beauty may be a form of ecstasy.

This view of aesthetic pleasure derives from a long history of philosophical analysis, but it also finds support in experimental research. In one study, people were shown slides of great paintings. Half of the people were told that they were being filmed. Although they were not really being filmed, the belief that they were "on camera" made them self-conscious, and these people reported less enjoyment of the paintings than people who did not think they were being filmed. This experiment is hardly conclusive, but it does fit the view that loss of self-awareness is important to aesthetic pleasure.[9]

We might also consider an important form of escaping the self that can involve an entire society, or large parts of it.[10] In *Escape from Freedom*, the psychoanalyst Erich Fromm suggested many years ago that mere participation in groups can be a means of escape. He argued that modern individuals can find their freedom uncomfortable and that conversion to fascism, especially Nazism, can be understood as a regressive desire to merge with a compelling group.

Many cultures in the history of the world have enacted what the anthropologist Victor Turner described as "status reversal rituals,"[11] large-scale celebrations in which people abandon their normal selves as the social order is turned upside down. For a day or two, the lowliest members of society are treated as aristocrats or kings, while the rulers receive a variety of degrading and disrespectful treatments. In Turner's view, these rituals, in which people lose their personal identities and merge into the mass of people, help preserve the social structure by allowing people to discharge accumulated unhappy feelings. He cites an Ashanti ritual that allows each member of the society to speak out about any topic once a year.

In Western history, the most dramatic form of status reversal ritual was known as the Feast of Fools.[12] This practice flourished in Europe in the later Middle Ages as a distortion and parody of Christian ritual. Blasphemous and sacrilegious acts accepted during the confines of the feast included burning old shoes for incense, singing gibberish instead of the usual Latin hymns, appointing a child or the village idiot to be the bishop for a day, giving choirboys spectacles with orange peels for lenses, playing dice on the altar, dressing the clergy in women's clothes or beast masks, running around in church, and singing obscene songs. The "bishop of fools" who presided over the feast was often given a mock baptism, such as being drenched with five buckets of water. Participation in the Feast of Fools was predicated on escape from the self: People were freed from responsibility for blasphemous acts that would normally have brought dire consequences.

Other social rituals are also based on escape from the self. Turner points out that rituals for many status transitions, such as the transition from adolescence to adulthood or the elevation to tribal chief, begin by stripping away the former identity and thus contain a period in which the person has no identity at all. These "liminal" stages of rituals hold the participants in a suspended state of selflessness that violates the normal terms of social life and relationship. Many rituals include features we have seen associated with escaping the self, such as symbolic degradation. Rituals that promote an eminent man to chief can involve a phase in which he is insulted or even physically abused by everyone else in the tribe. Passivity is often enforced, such as by requiring the initiate to remain silent for a long time. Even such basic identity elements as gender are sometimes denied during these rituals; initiates may be treated as if they were sexless.

The rejection of meaning in these rituals is readily apparent. The normal rules that govern social intercourse are suspended, and ritual seems to take place outside everyday time and space. People's attributes are rendered ambiguous, and many actions can be performed without the consequences that would usually attach to them. The attributes of the key participants are stripped away. Turner speaks of symbolically converting the initiate into a tabula rasa in preparation for the new identity.[13] The image of reducing the individual to a blank slate epitomizes the notion of escape from the self.

The benefits of these rituals correspond to those we have seen for individual escapes. Turner's analysis emphasizes both stress relief and ecstasy. On the one hand, he says, these rituals allow people to say or do things that they have been repressing all year and that would be incompatible with their normal roles and identities. This practice, he feels, functions as a safety valve for discontent, similar in some ways to the relief of negative affect and stress. On the other hand, he describes the experience of shedding one's everyday self as an ecstatic merger into the mass of people.[14] The participant abandons his or her sense of self, to be carried away in the activities and good feelings of the group.

Clearly, escape from the self is not uniquely a modern phenomenon. Many societies throughout history have followed practices that periodically enabled everyone together to escape the self. The individuality of modern life, and the increased burden of selfhood, may have created the need for the forms of individual escape we have discussed in this book, but certainly they have antecedents in earlier cultural forms.

CONCLUSION

What, then, does the behavior of escaping the self tell us about modern life? It says that despite our culture's overriding fascination with self and identity, there are costs as well as benefits. The human being can't necessarily tolerate being aware of itself—*being* itself—all the time.

Identity is not a product of nature. Our notions of ourselves are imposed on us, to a great extent, by our culture and society. As such, they are constraining and artificial. To be a stockbroker, a housewife, a congressman, or an attorney, for example, is to define the self in a way that seems to rule out much of what is personal and subjective. It forces the self into a mold and places a host of demands on it. Periodically, we may rebel against this mold and these demands, especially when these bring us grief, or when we want to experience something far outside the mold. And simply the wear and tear of living according to these externally imposed definitions can become burdensome.

The self can thus be seen as a culturally constructed constraint—something that our society forces on us, to our discomfort and inconvenience, like neckties or high heels. That view is helpful for understanding the problems and stresses associated with maintaining the self. The more important personal identity is for defining the meaning and purpose of a person's activities, the more disastrous it is when something goes wrong, such as a public scandal or disgrace casting the self in a bad light. A good personal reputation may offer great benefits in dealing with others, but one has to worry constantly about maintaining this good reputation.

Escaping the self is not the same as escaping from oppressive circumstances. The poor, disadvantaged, and downtrodden may periodically desire something to take their minds off their unhappy lives, and their use of drugs or alcohol is readily labeled as escapist. The escapes from the self discussed here, however, appear to be phenomena of material well-being. The social demands of autonomy, responsibility, and self-aggrandizement, of maintaining an inflated image of self, of acting in accordance with exacting standards—these are what increase the burden of selfhood to the point at which a person desires escape.

The type of self that burdens the modern individual is the product of centuries of gradual cultural development that have increased the self's complexity and assigned ever greater importance to it. As religion, tradition, and other long-standing sources of value and meaning have declined in influence, people have turned increasingly to the cultivation of self to give their lives meaning.[15] The self has been made into one of the basic, fundamental values that guide modern Western life and help individuals know what is right and wrong. This emphasis on self is an effective way for society to deal with a shortage of values and to maintain a coherent social order. But it also has costs. Spirituality, for example, to the extent that it relies on submersion of self, becomes increasingly difficult. It is perhaps not surprising that ecstasy seekers turn to drugs or Asian religions: Overcoming the modern Western self requires powerful techniques. Moreover, when events cast the self in a bad light, the modern Western individual has few other sources of value to which he or she can turn.

The modern elevation of the self into a basic source of value is an astonishing turnabout in the relation of self to morality. Concepts of virtue and moral rules historically functioned in opposition to self. Traditional morality opposed and even condemned motives based on benefiting the self. But the twentieth century has developed a new morality that includes obligations to oneself, owing things to oneself, a need and right to do what is best for oneself (even at the expense of other obligations). Spouses and lovers, adolescents, artists, and even athletes and football coaches justify their actions and choices by saying that they have to be themselves. After spending most of human history locked in mortal combat, self and morality have abruptly joined forces.[16]

It would be foolish and excessive to portray the modern self as a blight, an affliction, or a curse. Although this book has focused primarily on the negative aspects of self, there are undoubtedly positive ones as well. My intent has not been to say that the self is all bad, but rather to provide a counterpoint to the deification of individual selfhood that pervades our culture. The self is *not* all good, and the self-seeking tendencies of modern culture have various stressful and dangerous effects.

In short, the modern self is a mixed blessing. It enables society to function, and it offers the individual many sources of pleasure and satisfaction. But it also makes great demands on effort and energy, and the most exalted or overdeveloped selves may require the greatest upkeep. When events cast the self in a bad light, or when the stress of keeping up a good image become excessive, or simply when a person wants access to ecstatic experiences, it may become necessary to set the self aside. In such circumstances, people begin to find ways of forgetting who they are.

Two thousand six hundred years ago, the Greek philosopher Thales coined the maxim "Know thyself." Four hundred years ago, Shakespeare's Polonius advised his son, "This above all: To thine own self be true." These are fine ideals, but they aren't sufficient for people to live by all the time. They are especially difficult admonitions for people who are struggling with personal failures or crises. The weight of self-knowledge can be crushing, especially when one must accept unpleasant facts, and the duty to self can become onerous when the self becomes tyrannical in its demands. People need occasionally to be liberated from the fetters of selfhood, to be allowed to stop being true to their various ideas of self. The self that is known must also, sometimes, be forgotten.

Notes

CHAPTER 1

1. E.g., Shoemaker 1963.
2. E.g., Damon and Hart 1982.
3. Baumeister 1986.
4. Baumeister and Tice 1990; Bowlby 1973.
5. E.g., Darley and Goethals 1980; Taylor and Brown 1988; Baumeister 1982; Zuckerman 1979.
6. See Rothbaum et al. 1982; Langer 1975; Taylor 1983.
7. See Brown 1968 on how emotional responses to losing depend on audience perceptions.
8. Baumeister 1982; Higgins 1987; Markus and Nurius 1986; Rogers, Kniper, and Kirker 1977.
9. Higgins 1987.
10. Zube 1972.
11. Bellah et al. 1985.
12. Triandis 1990.
13. See Altick 1965; Weintraub 1978.
14. See Baumeister 1986; Weintraub 1978.

15. Baumeister 1989.
16. Kiernan 1989.
17. See the research on social comparison, e.g., Festinger 1957; Suls and Miller 1977; Wood 1989. For a more extended discussion of the role of relative superiority in establishing self-esteem, see Baumeister in press.
18. See Crocker and Major 1989.
19. Baumeister 1989.

CHAPTER 2

1. Duval and Wicklund 1972; see also Carver and Scheier 1981.
2. Higgins 1987.
3. This is common knowledge. For example, see Baumeister 1982; Swann 1987; Darley and Goethals 1980; Zuckerman 1979.
4. Baumeister, Tice, and Hutton 1989.
5. Especially McFarlin and Blascovich 1981; see also Swann et al. 1987.
6. Crocker and Major 1989.
7. Duval and Wicklund 1972.
8. Gibbons and Wicklund 1976.
9. Greenberg and Musham 1981.
10. Steenbarger and Aderman 1979.
11. Dixon and Baumeister 1991; Linville 1985, 1987.
12. Baumeister and Tice 1985.
13. E.g., Milkman and Sunderwirth 1986, 15.
14. Lawson 1988; Pines and Aronson 1983.
15. Janoff-Bulman 1989.
16. Taylor 1983.
17. Stephens 1985.
18. Brady 1958.
19. This is common knowledge in stress research. For example, see Monat, Averill, and Lazarus 1972.
20. E.g., Weiss 1971a, 1971b; see also Averill and Rosenn 1972

on the benefits of vigilant coping, which enables a person to know when there are safe periods.

21. Glass, Singer, and Friedman 1969.
22. E.g., Clebsch 1979.
23. E.g., de Rougemont 1956; Morgenthau 1962; Fiedler [1966] 1982.
24. Csikszentmihalyi 1982, 1990.
25. E.g., Herrigel [1953] 1971.
26. Baumeister 1984; Baumeister and Showers 1986.
27. Sarason 1981; Wine 1971.
28. Masters and Johnson 1970; see Baumeister 1989, 124–30 for discussion.

CHAPTER 3

1. Aronson and Carlsmith 1962; Brock et al. 1965; Cottrell 1965; Lowin and Epstein 1965; Ward and Sandvold 1963.
2. Maracek and Mettee 1972.
3. Maracek and Mettee 1972.
4. Baumeister and Tice 1985.
5. Jones 1973; McFarlin and Blascovich 1981.
6. Shrauger 1975; Swann et al. 1987.
7. Horner 1972.
8. Hyland 1989.
9. Zanna and Pack 1975.
10. Baumeister, Cooper, and Skib 1979.
11. Baumgardner and Brownlee 1987.
12. Aronson, Carlsmith, and Darley 1963; Comer and Laird 1975; Foxman and Radtke 1970; Walster, Aronson, and Brown 1966.
13. Curtis, Reitdorf, and Ronell 1980; Curtis, Smith, and Moore 1984.
14. E.g., Eliade 1985.
15. Jones and Berglas 1978.
16. Tice and Baumeister 1990.

17. Baumeister, Hamilton, and Tice 1985.
18. Berglas and Jones 1978; Jones and Berglas 1978.
19. Tucker, Vuchinich, and Sobell 1981.
20. E.g., McCollam et al. 1980.
21. Hull 1981.
22. Wicklund 1975a, 1975b.
23. Dunbar and Stunkard 1979.
24. Sackett and Snow 1979.
25. Meyer, Leventhal, and Gutmann 1975.
26. Becker, Drachman, and Kirscht 1972; Haynes 1976; Zola 1973.
27. Kiernan 1989.
28. Brown 1968, 1970.
29. Brown and Garland 1971; also Baumeister and Cooper 1981.
30. Brown 1968.
31. Trillin 1984, 126–27.
32. Pilkonis 1977a; Pilkonis and Zimbardo 1979; Zimbardo 1977.
33. Arkin 1981; Schlenker and Leary 1982.
34. Schlenker and Leary 1982.
35. Arkin 1981.
36. Carver and Scheier 1986.
37. Cheek and Busch 1981; Jones, Freemon, and Goswick 1981; Maroldo 1982.
38. Maroldo 1982.
39. Leary and Dobbins 1983.
40. Mandell and Shrauger 1980; see also Pilkonis 1977b; Daly 1978.
41. Schlenker and Leary 1982.
42. See Baumeister and Scher 1988.

CHAPTER 4

1. Wegner et al. 1987.
2. E.g., Jones et al. 1981 on biased scanning; see also Markus

1977 on multiplicity of self-schemas; Linville 1985 on self-complexity; Markus and Nurius 1986 on possible selves.

3. E.g., Linville 1985.
4. Cf. Vallacher and Wegner 1985.
5. Wegner and Vallacher 1986.
6. E.g., Lifton 1986.
7. Cf. Vallacher and Wegner 1985, 1987.
8. See Gergen and Gergen 1988 for similar point.
9. Especially Dilthey 1976.
10. E.g., Masters and Johnson 1970.
11. Baumeister, Stillwell, and Wotman 1990.
12. See Vallacher and Wegner 1985.
13. Schachter 1971; Schachter and Singer 1962.
14. Averill 1980.
15. Averill 1980; see also Izard 1977.
16. See Hochschild 1983.
17. Averill 1982.
18. Vallacher and Wegner 1985.
19. Baumeister and Tice 1987, 182; see also Epstein 1973.
20. Carver and Scheier 1990.
21. Carver 1979; Carver and Scheier 1981.
22. Higgins 1987.
23. Keegan 1976.
24. Diener and Wallbom 1976.
25. Masters and Johnson 1970.
26. Vallacher and Wegner 1985, 1987.
27. Vallacher and Wegner 1985, 1987.
28. Wegner 1989.
29. Janoff-Bulman 1985, 1989.
30. Vallacher and Wegner 1985.
31. E.g., Heidegger [1954] 1968.
32. E.g., Janoff-Bulman 1989.
33. Cf. Taylor 1983.

CHAPTER 5

1. Savage 1979, 72.
2. Savage 1979, 72.
3. Savage 1979, 73.
4. Savage 1979, 74.
5. Savage 1979, 76.
6. Cantor 1976; Farmer 1987.
7. Rojcewicz 1970.
8. E.g., Trout 1980.
9. See Kushner 1988 for articulate critique on this point.
10. Bonnar and McGee 1977.
11. Buksbazen 1976.
12. Counts 1987.
13. Shneidman and Farberow 1961, 1970; Hendin 1982.
14. E.g., Hendin 1982, esp. 186.
15. Spengler 1977.
16. Argyle 1987; Lester 1984, 1986, 1987; Farberow 1975; Nayha 1982; Parker and Walter 1982; Shneidman and Farberow 1970.
17. Hendin 1982.
18. Braaten and Darling 1962.
19. Baumeister 1990.
20. *Sports Illustrated*, 16 June 1986, 18–19; *New York Times*, 7 June 1986, 47 and 48.
21. Backett 1987; Bunch 1972; Copas and Robin 1982; McMahon and Pugh 1965.
22. Araki and Murata 1987; Argyle 1987; Holinger 1978; Wasserman 1984 is the best source on general U.S. effects.
23. Breed 1963; Farberow 1975; Maris 1969, 1981.
24. E.g., Argyle 1987; Campbell, Converse, and Rogers 1976.
25. Rothberg and Jones 1987.
26. Bourque, Kraus, and Cosand 1983; Stephens 1985; Maris 1981; Hendin 1982; Loo 1986; Tishler, McKenry, and Morgan 1981; Berlin 1987; Conroy and Smith 1983.
27. Davis 1983; Hendin 1982; Ringel 1976.

28. Douglas 1967.
29. Stephens 1985 found this type of relationship to be the most common one among suicidal women; see also Neuringer's (1972) projective studies and Cantor's (1976) evidence about needs for affiliation, succor, and nurturance.
30. On health, see Bourque, Kraus, and Cosard 1983; Motto 1980; Marshall, Burnett, and Brasurel 1983. On work, see Brodsky 1977; Loo 1986; Motto 1980.
31. Phillips and Liu 1980; Phillips and Wills 1987.
32. Rothberg and Jones 1987.
33. Davis 1983; Hendin 1982.
34. Maris 1981.
35. E.g., Bonner and Rich 1987; Stephens 1987; Tishler, McKenry, and Morgan 1981.
36. Rosen 1976.
37. Rothberg and Jones 1987.
38. Palmer 1971.
39. Gerber et al. 1981; Kaplan and Pokorny 1976.
40. Crocker and Schwartz 1985; Brown 1986.
41. Neuringer 1974.
42. Hendin 1982; on self-consciousness at adolescence, see Simmons, Rosenberg, and Rosenberg 1973; Tice, Buder, and Baumeister 1985.
43. Hendin 1982; Maris 1981; McKenry and Kelley 1983; Roy and Linnoila 1986; on self-awareness and alcohol, see Hull 1981.
44. Greenberg and Pyszczynski 1986.
45. Farberow 1975.
46. Smith and Hackathorn 1982.
47. Henken 1976; Ogilvie, Stone, and Shneidman 1983.
48. This methodology was pioneered by Davis and Brock 1975; see also Carver and Scheier 1978; Hull et al, 1983; Wegner and Giulano 1980.
49. Henken 1976.
50. Henken 1976.
51. Duval and Wicklund 1972; Carver 1979; Carver and Scheier 1981.
52. Hendin 1982.

53. E.g., Bressler 1976; Blachly, Disher, and Roduner 1968.
54. Summarized in Baumeister 1990.
55. See Cole 1988; for a review, see Baumeister 1990, 90.
56. Mehrabian and Weinstein 1985; Bhagat 1976.
57. Weissman et al. 1989.
58. On social bonds and anxiety, see Bowlby 1969, 1973; Baumeister and Tice 1990.
59. Reinhart and Linden 1982; Berlin 1987; Wilkinson and Israel 1984. Of course, this argument is similar to the point made by Durkheim [1897] 1963; see also Trout 1980.
60. E.g., Bancroft, Skrimshire, and Simkins 1976; Birtchnell and Alarcon 1971; Maris 1981.
61. Bancroft, Skrimshire, and Simkins 1976; Birtchnell and Alarcon 1971; Bonnar and McGee 1977; Maris 1981; Hawton et al. 1982.
62. Ringel 1976.
63. Schotte and Clum 1987; see also Asarnow, Carson, and Guthrie 1987.
64. Perrah and Wichman 1987.
65. E.g., Neuringer and Harris 1974; see also Brockopp and Lester 1970. Neuringer and Harris found that suicidals' estimates of the brief durations were more than double the correct answer, and for the longer intervals, one and a half times the correct estimate.
66. Greaves 1971; Yufit and Benzies 1973; Yufit et al. 1970; Iga 1971.
67. Hendin 1982, 140.
68. Henken 1976.
69. Henken 1976.
70. Gottschalk and Gleser 1960.
71. Hendin 1982, 36.
72. Breed 1972.
73. Ringel 1976.
74. Gerber et al. 1981.
75. Neuringer 1964.
76. Linehan et al. 1987.
77. Spirito et al. 1987.

78. Henken 1976.
79. Gerber et al. 1981; Topol and Reznikoff 1982.
80. Mehrabian and Weinstein 1985.
81. Melges and Weisz 1971; see also Connor et al. 1973; Maris 1985; Neuringer 1974; Ringel 1976; Stephens 1985.
82. Bhagat 1976; Cantor 1976.
83. Patsiokas, Clum, and Luscomb 1979.
84. Williams and Broadbent 1986.
85. Williams and Broadbent 1986.
86. Iga 1971; Bonner and Rich 1987; Ellis and Ratliff 1986.
87. Neuringer 1972.
88. Ringel 1976.
89. See Douglas 1967.
90. By Maris 1981.
91. Cf. Taylor 1978.
92. Adams, Giffen, and Garfield 1973; cf. Silberfeld, Streiner, and Ciampi 1985.
93. Allen 1983; Berman 1979; Palmer and Humphrey 1980.
94. See Hendin 1982.
95. Rhine and Mayerson 1973; Hendin 1982.
96. Weiss 1971.
97. See Linehan et al. 1983; see also Baumeister 1990.
98. Hawton et al. 1982.

CHAPTER 6

1. See Baumeister 1988a, 1989 for technical presentation of this material.
2. This example and all others are from the data base used in Baumeister 1988b, 1989 unless otherwise noted.
3. For Sacher-Masoch's life story, see Cleugh 1951.
4. Baumeister 1988b, 1989.
5. Janus, Bess, and Saltus 1977.
6. See Baumeister 1986; Trilling 1971; Weintraub 1978.

7. See Baumeister 1989, 54–56 for review and discussion. See also Gebhard 1971 for similar conclusion.
8. Spengler 1977.
9. Baumeister 1988b.
10. I am grateful to L. Winklebleck, columnist and rational editor of *Spectator*, for supplying this anecdote.
11. Scarry 1985.
12. Hilbert 1984.
13. Califia 1983, 134.
14. Scott 1983.
15. Reik [1941] 1957.
16. Baumeister 1986.
17. Baumeister 1988b, 1989.
18. E.g., Scott 1983.
19. Patterson 1982.
20. Baumeister 1989.
21. Scott 1983.
22. Weinberg and Kamel 1983.
23. Reik [1941] 1957.
24. Scott 1983.
25. See Califia 1982 on disenchantment; Scott 1983; Reage [1954] 1966.
26. Masters and Johnson 1970; LoPiccolo 1978.
27. Baumeister 1989.
28. Also drawn from the data base used for Baumeister 1989.
29. Zoftig 1982, 86–87.

CHAPTER 7

1. I am grateful to the person who furnished this incident. Perhaps understandably, he has expressed a wish to remain anonymous.
2. D. Williamson 1990, 17.
3. Steele and Josephs 1990.
4. Steele and Josephs 1990.
5. Doweiko 1990.

6. Weil 1972.
7. Hull 1981. I shall cover this in more detail in the next part of this chapter.
8. See Baumeister and Placidi 1983.
9. Researchers must obtain permission to administer drugs and then acquire them through legal means, all of which means a great deal of red tape. One researcher, contrasting these legal hurdles with the ready availability of street drugs, concluded that these drugs could easily be obtained and used by anyone *except* a legitimate researcher (Weil 1972)!
10. Hull and Young 1983b.
11. Hull, Young, and Jouriles 1986.
12. See Morrissey and Schuckit 1978; see also Higgins and Marlatt 1973.
13. See especially Hershenson 1965.
14. See Steele and Josephs 1990.
15. See Eliade 1978.
16. See Eliade 1978, 364.
17. Eliade 1978, 365.
18. Eliade 1978, 366.
19. Steele and Josephs 1990.
20. I am grateful to my longtime friend E. P. for recounting this incident.
21. Steele and Josephs 1990.
22. Steele and Josephs 1990.
23. Steele and Josephs 1990.
24. See Doweiko 1990.
25. See Doweiko 1990, 30.
26. Jones and Berglas 1978; Tucker, Vuchinich, and Sobell 1981.
27. E.g. Keegan 1976.
28. Steele and Southwick 1985; see also Steele and Josephs 1990.
29. See Taylor, Gammon, and Capasso 1976; see also Steele and Southwick 1985.
30. Steele and Josephs 1990.
31. Lynn 1988.
32. Steele and Josephs 1990.
33. Steele and Josephs 1990.

CHAPTER 8

1. Tice 1990.
2. Herman and Mack 1975; see Ruderman 1986.
3. I am grateful to D. Hutton for supplying this example.
4. American Psychiatric Association 1987.
5. Hawkins, Turell, and Jackson 1983.
6. Jakobovits et al. 1977.
7. See Heatherton and Baumeister 1991.
8. Heatherton and Baumeister 1991; see American Psychiatric Association 1987; Connors and Johnson 1987; Schlesier-Stropp 1984; Thelen et al. 1987.
9. Fairburn and Beglin 1990.
10. Johnson, Lewis, and Hagman 1984.
11. Herzog et al. 1986.
12. E.g., Polivy and Herman 1985.
13. Nasser 1986.
14. E.g., Herman, Polivy, and Heatherton 1990; Baucom and Aiken 1981; Ruderman 1985b; Heatherton, Herman, and Polivy 1991; Herman et al. 1987.
15. Herman, Polivy, and Heatherton 1990. On fear, see Herman and Polivy 1975; McKenna 1972; Schachter, Goldman, and Gordon 1968. On self-related moods, see Baucom and Aiken 1981; Frost et al. 1982; Herman et al. 1987; Ruderman 1985b; Slochower 1976, 1983; Slochower and Kaplan 1980, 1983; Slochower, Kaplan, and Mann 1981. See also Heatherton and Baumeister 1991 for full discussion.
16. See especially Hudson and Pope 1987; Heatherton and Baumeister 1991; Johnson, Lewis, and Hagman 1984.
17. Brooks-Gunn, Warren, and Hamilton 1987; Garfinkel, Garner, and Goldblum 1987; Garner et al. 1984; Johnson and Connors 1987; Lundholm and Littrell 1986; Smead 1988.
18. Powers et al. 1987; see also Striegel-Moore, Silberstein, and Rodin 1986.
19. Barnett 1986.

20. Herzog et al. 1986.
21. Butterfield and Leclair 1988; Katzman and Wolchik 1984; Mizes 1988; see also Bauer and Anderson 1989; Heatherton and Baumeister 1991.
22. Bauer and Anderson 1989, 417.
23. Blanchard and Frost 1983; see Heatherton and Baumeister 1991.
24. Cash and Brown 1987; Garner, Garfinkel, and Bonato 1987; Powers et al. 1987; D. Williamson 1990; Garfinkel and Garner 1982; Eldredge, Wilson, and Whaley 1990; Mayhew and Edelmann 1989; Garner et al. 1984; Gross and Rosen 1988; Polivy, Herman, and Garner 1988; for review, see Heatherton and Baumeister 1991.
25. Heatherton et al. 1990.
26. Keck and Fiebert 1986.
27. Cattanach and Rodin 1988; Shatford and Evans 1986.
28. D. Williamson 1990.
29. Polivy 1976.
30. Mizes 1988.
31. Heatherton and Baumeister 1991.
32. Abraham and Beumont 1982; Johnson, Lewis, and Hagman 1984; see also Johnson and Pure 1986.
33. Johnson, Lewis, and Hagman 1984.
34. E.g., Knight and Boland 1989; Polivy, Herman, and Kuleshnyk 1984.
35. Lindner 1954.
36. Lindner 1954, 82.
37. Lindner 1954, 82.
38. American Psychiatric Association 1987.
39. Spencer and Fremouw 1979; see also Heatherton et al. 1989; Knight and Boland 1989.
40. Garfinkel and Garner 1982.
41. Smith, Hohlstein, and Atlas 1989; Thompson, Berg, and Shatford 1987.
42. Mizes 1988.
43. Thompson, Berg, and Shatford 1987.
44. Ruderman 1985a.
45. Knight and Boland 1989.

46. Heatherton and Baumeister 1991, for review; evidence on this point is not extensive, however.

47. Johnson, Lewis, and Hagman 1984.

48. Wilson 1988.

49. E.g., Garfinkel and Garner 1982; Hatsukami et al 1984; Hatsukami, Mitchell, and Eckert 1984; Johnson, Connors, and Tobin 1987; Mitchell et al. 1986b; Viessleman and Roig 1985; Yager et al. 1988.

50. Garfinkel & Garner 1982; Yager et al 1988; Mitchell et al. 1986; see also Favazza and Conterio 1989.

51. Garner, Olmstead, and Polivy 1983.

52. See Johnson and Connors 1987.

53. Bauer and Anderson 1989; Johnson and Connors 1987; Baumeister, Kahn, and Tice 1990; Polivy and Herman 1983.

CHAPTER 9

1. Eliade 1982, 198.

2. Rosenthal 1984, 18.

3. Rosenthal 1984.

4. See Graham 1987.

5. See Shafii 1988, 143.

6. Shafii 1988, 55, 144.

7. Merton [1967] 1989, 136.

8. This was a central tenet of the thought of Nagarjuna and other treatments using the concept of "emptiness." On Nagarjuna's thought, see Stcherbatsky 1977, for example.

9. Kapleau 1980, 211.

10. Merton [1967] 1989, 27.

11. See Goleman 1988, 31.

12. Kapleau 1980, 19.

13. See Odajnyk 1988; also Goleman 1988, 30–31; Shafii 1988, 146.

14. Clebsch 1979, 75–76.

15. E.g., Shafii 1988, 60.

16. See Shafii 1988, 185 on Sufism; Eliade 1982, 93–94 on Buddhism.
17. Shafii 1988, 63, 185.
18. Eliade 1982, 84.
19. Kiernan 1989.
20. Many studies use insults to provoke anger, which seems a prerequisite to aggression. Egotism has rarely received full discussion as a causal aspect of aggression (although see Baumeister 1982), but it should not be overlooked. Kernis, Granneman, and Barclay 1989 showed that insecure high self-esteem was associated with the strongest tendencies toward anger and hostility.
21. See Goleman 1988.
22. Shafii 1988, 159.
23. Eliade 1982, 45.
24. Eliade 1982, 46.
25. Tannahill 1980.
26. Shafii 1988, 168.
27. Goleman 1988, 28.
28. Eliade 1982, 99, quoting Buddhist scripture.
29. Kapleau 1980, 239.
30. See Clebsch 1979, 148.
31. Shafii 1988, 154–55.
32. E.g., Goleman 1988; White 1972.
33. Clebsch 1979, 147.
34. Greven 1977; Argyle 1959.
35. E.g., Shafii 1988, 146.
36. E.g., Goleman 1988.
37. Shafii 1988, 146–47.
38. Maupin 1972.
39. E.g., Maupin 1972.
40. Berger and Luckmann 1967.
41. Kapleau 1980.
42. Kapleau 1980.
43. Eliade 1982, 100.
44. Goleman 1988.
45. Shafii 1988, 91.
46. Shafii 1988.
47. E.g., Kapleau 1980, 211.

48. Le Goff 1980.
49. Clebsch 1979.
50. Goleman 1988, 62.
51. Shafii 1988, 235.
52. Shafii 1988, 149.
53. Clebsch 1979, 160.
54. Cf. Goleman 1988.
55. Eliade 1982.
56. For this incident, see Reps 1957. On Hakuin's life, see Hakuin 1971. He is credited with inventing the "one hand clapping" koan.
57. E.g., Goleman 1988; Kapleau 1980, 17–18.
58. Kapleau 1980, 18.
59. E.g., Merton [1967] 1989, 228.
60. Kapleau 1980, 238.
61. De Ropp 1979.

CHAPTER 10

1. See Baumeister 1989, especially chapter 3.
2. Riedel 1990, 13.
3. Bechtel 1990, 35.
4. Yates, Leehey, and Shisslak 1983.
5. Masters 1990.
6. Masters 1990.
7. Masters 1990.
8. Shilts 1987, 414–15.
9. Hull and Baumeister 1976.
10. Fromm 1941.
11. Turner 1969.
12. See Chambers 1903; Cox 1969; Dreves 1894.
13. Turner 1969, 103.
14. Turner 1969, 185.
15. See Baumeister in press.
16. See Baumeister in press, especially chapter 5, for more thorough treatment.

References

Abraham, S. F., and Beumont, P. J. 1982. How patients describe bulimia or binge eating. *Psychological Medicine* 12:625–35.

Adams, R. L.; Giffen, M. B.; and Garfield, F. 1973. Risk-taking among suicide attempters. *Journal of Abnormal Psychology* 82:262–67.

Allen, N. H. 1983. Homicide followed by suicide. Los Angeles, 1970–1979. *Suicide and Life-Threatening Behavior* 13:155–65.

Altick, R. 1965. *Lives and letters: A history of literary biography in England and America.* New York: Knopf.

American Psychiatric Association. 1987. *Diagnostic and statistical manual of mental disorders* 3rd ed., rev. Washington, D.C.: American Psychiatric Association.

Araki, S., and Murata, K. 1987. Suicide in Japan: Socioeconomic effects on its secular and seasonal trends. *Suicide and Life-Threatening Behavior* 17:64–71.

Argyle, M. 1959. *Religious behaviour.* Glencoe, IL: Free Press.

Argyle, M. 1987. *The psychology of happiness.* London: Methuen.

Arkin, R. M. 1981. Self-presentation styles. In *Impression management theory in social psychological research*, ed. J. T. Tedeschi, 311–33. New York: Academic Press.

Aronson, E., and Carlsmith, J. M. 1962. Performance expectancy as a determinant of actual performance. *Journal of Abnormal and Social Psychology* 65:178–82.

Aronson, E.; Carlsmith, J. M.; and Darley, J. M. 1963. The effects of expectancy on volunteering for an unpleasant experience. *Journal of Abnormal Social Psychology* 66:220–24.

Asarnow, J. R.; Carson, G. A.; and Guthrie, D. 1987. Coping strategies, self-perceptions, hopelessness, and perceived family environments in depressed and suicidal children. *Journal of Consulting and Clinical Psychology* 55:361–66.

Averill, J. 1980. A constructivist view of emotion. In *Theories of emotion*, ed. R. Plutchik and H. Kellerman, 305–39. Orlando, FL: Academic Press.

Averill, J. 1982. *Anger and aggression: An essay on emotion*, New York: Springer-Verlag.

Averill, J., and Rosenn, M. 1972. Vigilant and nonvigilant coping strategies and psychophysiological stress reactions during the anticipation of electric shock. *Journal of Personality and Social Psychology* 23:128–41.

Backett, S. A. 1987. Suicide in Scottish prisons. *British Journal of Psychiatry* 151:218–21.

Baechler, J. [1975] 1979. *Suicides*. New York: Basic Books.

Baechler, J. 1980. A strategic theory. *Suicide and Life-Threatening Behavior* 10:70–99.

Bancroft, J.; Skrimshire, A.; and Simkins, S. 1976. The reasons people give for taking overdoses. *British Journal of Psychiatry* 128:538–48.

Barnett, L. R. 1986. Bulimarexia as symptom of sex-role strain in professional women. *Psychotherapy* 23:311–15.

Baucom, D. H., and Aiken, P. A. 1981. Effect of depressed mood on eating among obese and nonobese dieting persons. *Journal of Personality and Social Psychology* 41:577–85.

Bauer, B. G., and Anderson, W. P. 1989. Bulimic beliefs: Food for thought. *Journal of Counseling and Development* 67:416–19.

Baumeister, R. F. 1982. A self-presentational view of social phenomena. *Psychological Bulletin* 91:3–26.

Baumeister, R. F. 1984. Choking under pressure: Self-consciousness and paradoxical effects of incentives on skillful performance. *Journal of Personality and Social Psychology* 46:610–20.

Baumeister, R. F. 1986. *Identity: Cultural change and the struggle for self.* New York: Oxford University Press.

Baumeister, R. F. 1987. How the self became a problem: A psychological review of historical research. *Journal of Personality and Social Psychology* 52:163–76.

Baumeister, R. F. 1988a. Masochism as escape from self. *Journal of Sex Research* 25:28–59.

Baumeister, R. F. 1988b. Gender differences in masochistic scripts. *Journal of Sex Research* 25:478–99.

Baumeister, R. F. 1989. *Masochism and the self.* Hillsdale, NJ: Erlbaum.

Baumeister, R. F. 1990. Suicide as escape from self. *Psychological Review* 97:90–113.

Baumeister, R. F. In press. *Meanings of life.* New York: Guilford Press.

Baumeister, R. F., and Cooper, J. 1981. Can the public expectation of emotion cause that emotion? *Journal of Personality* 49:49–59.

Baumeister, R. F.; Cooper, J.; and Skib, B. A. 1979. Inferior performance as a selective response to expectancy: Taking a dive to make a point. *Journal of Personality and Social Psychology* 37:424–32.

Baumeister, R. F.; Hamilton, J. C.; and Tice, D. M. 1985. Public versus private expectancy of success: Confidence booster or performance pressure? *Journal of Personality and Social Psychology* 48:1447–57.

Baumeister, R. F.; Kahn, J.; and Tice, D. M. 1990. Obesity as a self-handicapping strategy: Personality, selective attribution of problems, and weight loss. *Journal of Social Psychology* 30:121–23.

Baumeister, R. F., and Placidi, K. S. 1983. A social history and analysis of the LSD controversy. *Journal of Humanistic Psychology* 23:25–58.

Baumeister, R. F., and Scher, S. J. 1988. Self-defeating behavior patterns among normal individuals: Review and analysis of common self-destructive tendencies. *Psychological Bulletin* 104:3–22.

Baumeister, R. F., and Showers, C. J. 1986. A review of paradoxical performance effects: Choking under pressure in sports and mental tests. *European Journal of Social Psychology.* 16:361–83.

Baumeister, R. F.; Stillwell, A,; and Wotman, S. R. 1990. Victim and perpetrator accounts of interpersonal conflict. Autobiographical narratives about anger. *Journal of Personality and Social Psychology* 59:994–1005.

Baumeister, R. F., and Tice, D. M. 1985. Self-esteem and responses to success and failure: Subsequent performance and intrinsic motivation. *Journal of Personality* 53:450–67.

Baumeister, R. F., and Tice, D. M. 1987. Emotion and self-presentation, In *Perspectives in Personality: Theory, Measurement, and Interpersonal Dynamics.* Vol. 2, ed. R. Hogan and W. H. Jones, 181–99. Greenwich, CT: JAI Press.

Baumeister, R. F., and Tice, D. M. 1990. Anxiety and social exclusion. *Journal of Social and Clinical Psychology* 9:165–95.

Baumeister, R. F.; Tice, D. M.; and Hutton, D. G. 1989. Self-presentational motivations and personality differences in self-esteem. *Journal of Personality* 57:547–79.

Baumgardner, A. H., and Brownlee, E. A. 1987. Strategic failure in social interaction: Evidence for expectancy disconfirmation processes. *Journal of Personality and Social Psychology* 52:525–35.

Bechtel, J. 1990. Pain is inevitable, suffering is optional. *Ultra Running,* Jan.–Feb., 35.

Becker, M. H.; Drachman, R. H.; and Kirscht, J. P. 1972. Motivations as predictors of health behavior. *Health Services Reports* 87:852–61.

Bellah, R. N.; Madsen, R.; Sullivan, W. M.; Swidler, A.; and Tipton, S. M. 1985. *Habits of the heart: Individualism and commitment in American life.* Berkeley: University of California Press.

Berger, P., and Luckmann, T. 1967. *The social construction of reality: A treatise in the sociology of knowledge.* Garden City, NY: Doubleday.

Berglas, S., and Jones, E. E. 1978. Drug choice as a self-handicapping strategy in response to non-contingent success. *Journal of Personality and Social Psychology* 36:405–17.

Berlin, I. N. 1987. Suicide among American Indian adolescents: An overview. *Suicide and Life-Threatening Behavior* 17:218–32.

Berman, A. L. 1979. Dyadic death: Murder-suicide. *Suicide and Life-Threatening Behavior* 9:15–23.

Bhagat, M. 1976. The spouses of attempted suicides: A personality study. *British Journal of Psychiatry* 128:44–46.

Birtchnell, J., and Alarcon, J. 1971. The motivational and emotional state of 91 cases of attempted suicide. *British Journal of Medical Psychology* 44:42–52.

Blachly, P. H.; Disher, W.; and Roduner, G. 1968. Suicide by physicians. *Bulletin of Suicidology* 2:1–18.

Blanchard, F. A., and Frost, R. O. 1983. Two factors of restraint: Concern for dieting and weight fluctuations. *Behavior Research and Therapy* 21:259–67.

Bonnar, J. W., and McGee, R. K. 1977. Suicidal behavior as a form of communication in married couples. *Suicide and Life-Threatening Behavior* 7:7–16.

Bonner, R. L., and Rich, A. R. 1987. Toward a predictive model of suicidal ideation and behavior: Some preliminary data in college students. *Suicide and Life-Threatening Behavior* 17:50–63.

Bourque, L. B.; Kraus, J. F.; and Cosand, B. J. 1983. Attributes of suicide in females. *Suicide and Life-Threatening Behavior* 13:123–38.

Bowlby, J. 1969. *Attachment and loss: Vol. 1. Attachment.* New York: Basic Books.

Bowlby, J. 1973. *Attachment and loss: Vol. 2. Separation anxiety and anger.* New York: Basic Books.

Braaten, L. J., and Darling, C. D. 1962. Suicidal tendencies among college students. *Psychiatric Quarterly* 36:665–92.

Brady, J. V. 1958. Ulcers in "executive" monkeys. *Scientific American* 199:95–100.

Breed, W. 1963. Occupational mobility and suicide among white males. *American Sociological Review* 28:179–88.

Breed, W. 1972. Five components of a basic suicide syndrome. *Life-Threatening Behavior* 2:3–18.

Bressler, B. 1976. Suicide and drug abuse in the medical community. *Suicide and Life-Threatening Behavior* 6:169–78.

Brock, T. C.; Edelman, S. K.; Edwards, D. C.; and Schuck, J. R.

1965. Seven studies of performance expectancy as a determinant of actual performance. *Journal of Experimental Social Psychology* 1:295–310.

Brockopp, G. W., and Lester, D. 1970. Time perception in suicidal and nonsuicidal individuals. *Crisis Intervention* 2:98–100.

Brodsky, C. M. 1977. Suicide attributed to work. *Suicide and Life-Threatening Behavior* 7:216–29.

Brooks-Gunn, J.; Warren, M. P.; and Hamilton, L. H. 1987. The relation of eating problems and amenorrhea in ballet dancers. *Medicine and Science in Sports and Exercise* 19:41–44.

Brown, B. R. 1968. The effects of need to maintain face on interpersonal bargaining. *Journal of Experimental Social Psychology* 4:107–22.

Brown, B. R. 1970. Face-saving following experimentally induced embarrassment. *Journal of Experimental Social Psychology* 6:255–71.

Brown, B. R., and Garland, H. 1971. The effects of incompetency, audience acquaintanceship, and anticipated evaluative feedback on face-saving behavior. *Journal of Experimental Social Psychology* 7:490–502.

Brown, J. D. 1986. Evaluations of self and others: Self-enhancement biases in social judgments. *Social Cognition* 4:353–76.

Buksbazen, C. 1976. Legacy of a suicide. *Suicide and Life-Threatening Behavior* 6:106–22.

Bunch, J. 1972. Recent bereavement in relation to suicide. *Journal of Psychosomatic Research* 16:361–66.

Butterfield, P. S., and Leclair, S. 1988. Cognitive characteristics of bulimic and drug-abusing women. *Addictive Behaviors* 13:131–38.

Califia, P. 1982. From Jessie. In *Coming to power*, ed. Samois, 154–80. Boston: Alyson.

Califia, P. 1983. A secret side of lesbian sexuality. In *S and M: Studies in sadomasochism*, ed. T. Weinberg and G. Kamel, 129–36. Buffalo, NY: Prometheus.

Campbell, A.; Converse, P. E.; and Rodgers, W. L. 1976. *The quality of American life*. New York: Russell Sage.

Cantor, P. C. 1976. Personality characteristics found among youthful female suicide attempters. *Journal of Abnormal Psychology* 85:324–29.

Carver, C. S. 1979. A cybernetic model of self-attention processes. *Journal of Personality and Social Psychology* 37:1251–81.

Carver, C. S., and Scheier, M. F. 1978. Self-focusing effects of dispositional self-consciousness, mirror presence, and audience presence. *Journal of Personality and Social Psychology* 36:324–32.

Carver, C. S., and Scheier, M. F. 1981. *Attention and self-regulation: A control theory approach to human behavior.* New York: Springer-Verlag.

Carver, C. S., and Scheier, M. F. 1982. Control theory: A useful conceptual framework for personality-social, clinical and health psychology. *Psychological Bulletin* 92:111–35.

Carver, C. S., and Scheier, M. F. 1986. Analyzing shyness: A specific application of broader self-regulatory principles. In *Shyness: Perspectives on research and treatment*, ed. W. H. Jones, J. M. Cheek, and S. R. Briggs, 173–85. New York: Plenum.

Carver, C. S., and Scheier, M. F. 1990. Origins and functions of positive and negative affect: A control-process view. *Psychological Review* 97:19–35.

Cash, T. F., and Brown, T. A. 1987. Body image in anorexia nervosa and bulimia nervosa: A review of the literature. *Behavior Modification* 11:487–521.

Cattanach, L., and Rodin, J. 1988. Psychosocial components of the stress process in bulimia. *International Journal of Eating Disorders* 7:75–88.

Chambers, E. K. 1903. *The medieval stage.* Oxford: Clarendon.

Cheek, J. M., and Busch, C. M. 1981. The influence of shyness on loneliness in a new situation. *Personality and Social Psychology Bulletin* 7:572–77.

Clebsch, W. A. 1979. *Christianity in European history.* New York: Oxford University Press.

Cleugh, J. 1951. *The marquis and the chevalier.* London: Melrose.

Cole, D. 1988. Hopelessness, social desirability, depression, and parasuicide in two college student samples. *Journal of Consulting and Clinical Psychology* 56:131–36.

Comer, R., and Laird, J. D. 1975. Choosing to suffer as a consequence of expecting to suffer: Why do people do it? *Journal of Personality and Social Psychology* 32:92–101.

Connor, H. E.; Daggett, L.; Maris, R. W.; and Weiss, S. 1973. Comparative psychopathology of suicide attempts and assaults. *Life-Threatening Behavior* 3:33–50.

Connors, M. E., and Johnson, C. L. 1987. Epidemiology of bulimia and bulimic behaviors. *Addictive Behaviors* 12: 165–79.

Conroy, R. W., and Smith, K. 1983. Family loss and hospital suicide. *Suicide and Life-Threatening Behavior* 13:179–94.

Copas, J. B., and Robin, A. 1982. Suicide in psychiatric inpatients. *British Journal of Psychiatry* 141:503–11.

Cottrell, N. B. 1965. Performance expectancy as a determinant of actual performance: A replication with a new design. *Journal of Personality and Social Psychology* 2:685–91.

Counts, D. A. 1987. Female suicide and wife abuse: A cross-cultural perspective. *Suicide and Life-Threatening Behavior* 17:194–204.

Cox, H. 1969. *The feast of fools*. Cambridge, MA: Harvard University Press.

Crocker, J., and Major, B. 1989. Social stigma and self-esteem: The self-protective properties of stigma. *Psychological Review* 96:608–30.

Crocker, J., and Schwartz, I. 1985. Prejudice and ingroup favoritism in a minimal intergroup situation: Effects of self-esteem. *Personality and Social Psychology Bulletin* 11:379–86.

Csikszentmihalyi, M. 1982. Toward a psychology of optimal experience. In *Review of personality and social psychology*, Vol. 2, ed. L. Wheeler, 13–36. Beverly Hills, CA: Sage.

Csikszentmihalyi, M. 1990. *Flow: The psychology of optimal experience*. New York: Harper & Row.

Curtis, R.; Rietdorf, P.; and Ronell, D. 1980. "Appeasing the gods?" Suffering to reduce probable future suffering. *Personality and Social Psychology Bulletin* 6:234–41.

Curtis, R.; Smith, P.; and Moore, R. 1984. Suffering to improve outcomes determined by both chance and skill. *Journal of Social and Clinical Psychology* 2:165–73.

Daly, S. 1978. Behavioral correlates of social anxiety. *British Journal of Social and Clinical Psychology* 17:117–20.

Damon, W., and Hart, D. 1982. The development of self-understanding from infancy through adolescence. *Child Development* 53:841–64.

Darley, J. M., and Goethals, G. R. 1980. People's analyses of the causes of ability-linked performances. In *Advances in experimental social psychology*. Vol 13, ed. L. Berkowitz, 1–37. New York: Academic Press.

Davis, D., and Brock, T. C. 1975. Use of first-person pronouns as a function of increased objective self-awareness and prior feedback. *Journal of Experimental Social Psychology* 11: 381–88.

Davis, P. A. 1983. *Suicidal adolescents*. Springfield, IL: Thomas.

De Ropp, R. S. 1979. *Warrior's way: The challenging life games*. New York: Delta/Lawrence.

de Rougemont, D. 1956. *Love in the western world*. 2d ed. New York: Pantheon.

DeSole, D. E.; Aaronson, S.; and Singer, P. 1967. Suicide and role strain among physicians. Paper presented at the meeting of the American Psychiatric Association, Detroit, MI, May.

Diener, E., and Wallbom, M. 1976. Effects of self-awareness on antinormative behavior. *Journal of Research in Personality* 10:107–11.

Dilthey, W. 1976. *Selected writings*. Ed. and trans. H. P. Rickman. Cambridge: Cambridge University Press.

Dixon, T., and Baumeister, R. F. 1991. Escaping the self: The moderating effect of self-complexity. *Personality and Social Psychology Bulletin*. In press.

Douglas, J. D. 1967. *The social meanings of suicide*. Princeton, NJ: Princeton University Press.

Doweiko, H. E. 1990. *Concepts of chemical dependency*. Pacific Grove, CA: Brooks/Cole.

Dreves, G. M. 1894. Zur Geschichte der Fete des Fous (On the history of the feast of fools). *Stimmen aus Maria-Laach* 47:571–

87. Freiburg im Breisgau: Herdersche Verlagshandlung.

Dunbar, J. M., and Stunkard, A. J. 1979. Adherence to diet and drug regimen. In *Nutrition, lipids, and coronary heart disease*, ed. R. Levy, B. Rifkind, B. Dennis, and N. Ernst, 391–423. New York: Raven Press.

Durkheim, E. [1897] 1963. *Suicide*. New York: Free Press.

Duval, S., and Wicklund, R. A. 1972. *A theory of objective self-awareness*. New York: Academic Press.

Eldredge, K.; Wilson, G. T.; and Whaley, A. 1990. Failure, self-evaluation, and feeling fat in women. *International Journal of Eating Disorders* 9:37–50.

Eliade, M. 1978. *A history of religious ideas. Vol. 1: From the Stone Age to the Eleusinian mysteries*. Trans. W. Trask. Chicago: University of Chicago Press.

Eliade, M. 1982. *A history of religious ideas. Vol. 2: From Gautama Buddha to the triumph of Christianity*. Trans. W. Trask. Chicago: University of Chicago Press.

Eliade, M. 1985. *A history of religious ideas. Vol. 3: From Muhammed to the age of reforms*. Trans. A. Hiltebeitel and D. Apostolos-Cappadona. Chicago: University of Chicago Press.

Ellis, T. E., and Ratliff, K. G. 1986. Cognitive characteristics of suicidal and nonsuicidal psychiatric inpatients. *Cognitive Therapy and Research* 10:625–34.

Epstein, S. 1973. The self-concept revisited: Or a theory of a theory. *American Psychologist* 28:404–16.

Fairburn, C. G., and Beglin, S. J. 1990. Studies of the epidemiology of bulimia nervosa. *American Journal of Psychiatry* 127:401–8.

Farberow, N. L. 1975. Cultural history of suicide. In *Suicide in different cultures*, ed. N. L. Farberow, 1–16. Baltimore, MD: University Park Press.

Farmer, R. 1987. Hostility and deliberate self-poisoning: The role of depression. *British Journal of Psychiatry* 150:609–14.

Favazza, A. R., and Conterio, K. 1989. Female habitual self-mutilators. *Acta Psychiatrica Scandinavia* 79:283–89.

Festinger, L. A theory of social comparison processes. *Human Relations* 7:117–40.

Fiedler, L. A. [1966] 1982. *Love and death in the American novel.* New York: Stein & Day.

Foxman, J., and Radtke, R. 1970. Negative expectancy and the choice of an aversive task. *Journal of Personality and Social Psychology* 15:253–57.

Freud, S. 1916. Trauer und Melancholie. *Gesammelte Werke.* Vol. 10, 427–46. London: Imago.

Freud, S. 1920. Ueber die psychogenese eines Falls von weiblicher Homosexualitaet. *Gesammelte Werke.* Vol 12, 269–302. London: Imago.

Fromm, E. 1941. *Escape from freedom.* New York: Holt, Rinehart & Winston.

Frost, R. O.; Goolkasian, G. A.; Ely, R. J.; and Blanchard, F. A. 1982. Depression, restraint and eating behavior. *Behavior Research and Therapy* 20:113–21.

Garfinkel, P. E., and Garner, D. M. 1982. *Anorexia nervosa: A multidimensional perspective.* New York: Brunner/Mazel.

Garfinkel, P. E.; Garner, D. M.; and Goldblum, D. S. 1987. Eating disorders: Implications for the 1990's. *Canadian Journal of Psychiatry* 32:624–30.

Garner, D. M.; Garfinkel, P. E.; and Bonato, D. P. 1987. Body image measurement in eating disorders. *Advances in Psychosomatic Medicine* 17:119–33.

Garner, D. M.; Olmsted, M. P.; and Polivy, J. 1983. Development and validation of a multi-dimensional eating disorder inventory for anorexia nervosa and bulimia. *International Journal of Eating Disorders* 2:15–34.

Garner, D. M.; Olmsted, M. P.; Polivy, J.; and Garfinkel, P. E. 1984. Comparison between weight-preoccupied women and anorexia nervosa. *Psychosomatic Medicine* 46:255–66.

Gebhard, P. H. 1971. Human sexual behavior: A summary statement. In *Human sexual behavior: Variations in the ethnographic spectrum,* ed. D. Marshall and R. Suggs, 206–17. New York: Basic Books.

Gerber, K. E.; Nehenkis, A. M.; Farberow, N. L.; and Williams, J.

1981. Indirect self-destructive behavior in chronic hemodialysis patients. *Suicide and Life-Threatening Behavior* 11:31–42.

Gergen, K. J., and Gergen, M. 1988. Narrative and the self as relationship. In *Advances in experimental social psychology*. Vol. 21, ed. L. Berkowitz, 17–56. San Diego, CA: Academic Press.

Gibbons, F. X., and Wicklund, R. A. 1976. Selective exposure to self. *Journal of Research in Personality* 10:98–106.

Glass, D. C.; Singer, J. E.; and Friedman, L. N. 1969. Psychic cost of adaptation to an environmental stressor. *Journal of Personality and Social Psychology* 12:200–210.

Goleman, D. 1988. *The meditative mind: The varieties of meditative experience*. New York: St. Martin's Press.

Gottschalk, L. A., and Gleser, G. C. 1960. An analysis of the verbal content of suicide notes. *British Journal of Medical Psychology* 33:195–204.

Graham, B. 1987. *Facing death and the life after*. Waco, TX: Word Books.

Greaves, G. 1971. Temporal orientation in suicidals. *Perceptual and Motor Skills* 33:1020.

Greenberg, J., and Musham, C. 1981. Avoiding and seeking self-focused attention. *Journal of Research in Personality* 15:191–200.

Greenberg, J., and Pyszczynski, T. 1986. Persistent high self-focus after failure and low self-focus after success: The depressive self-focusing style. *Journal of Personality and Social Psychology* 50:1039–44.

Greven, P. 1977. *The Protestant temperament*. New York: Knopf.

Gross, J., and Rosen, J. C. 1988. Bulimia in adolescents: Prevalence and psychosocial correlates. *International Journal of Eating Disorders* 7:51–61.

Hakuin. 1971. *The Zen master Hakuin: Selected writings*. Ed. and trans. P. B. Yampolsky. New York: Columbia University Press.

Hatsukami, D.; Eckert, E. D.; Mitchell, J. E.; and Pyle, R. L. 1984. Affective disorder and substance abuse in women with bulimia. *Psychological Medicine* 14:701–4.

Hatsukami, D. K.; Mitchell, J. E.; and Eckert, E. D. 1984. Eating disorders: A variant of mood disorders? *Psychiatric Clinics of North America* 7:349–65.

Hawkins, R. C.; Turell, S.; and Jackson, L. J. 1983. Desirable and undesirable masculine and feminine traits in relation to students' dietary tendencies and body image dissatisfaction. *Sex Roles* 9:705-24.

Hawton, K.; Cole, D.; O'Grady, J.; and Osborn, M. 1982. Motivational aspects of deliberate self-poisoning in adolescents. *British Journal of Psychiatry* 141:286-91.

Haynes, R. B. 1976. A critical review of the "determinants" of patient compliance with therapeutic regimens. In *Compliance with therapeutic regimens*, ed. D. L. Sackett and R. B. Haynes, 26-39. Baltimore, MD: Johns Hopkins University Press.

Heatherton, T. F., and Baumeister, R. F. In press. Binge eating as escape from self-awareness. *Psychological Bulletin.*

Heatherton, T. F.; Baumeister, R. F.; Polivy, J.; and Herman, C. P. 1990. Self-awareness, failure, and dieting. Paper submitted for publication.

Heatherton, T. F.; Herman, C. P.; and Polivy, J. 1991. Effects of physical threat and ego threat on eating behavior. *Journal of Personality and Social Psychology* 60:138-143.

Heatherton, T. F.; Polivy, J.; and Herman, C. P. 1989. Restraint and internal responsiveness: Effects of placebo manipulations of hunger state on eating. *Journal of Abnormal Psychology* 98:89-92.

Heatherton, T. F.; Polivy, J.; and Herman, C. P. In press. Restrained eating: Some current findings and speculations. *Psychology of Addictive Behaviors.*

Heidegger, M. [1954] 1968. *What is called thinking?* Trans J. G. Gray. New York: Harper & Row.

Hendin, H. 1982. *Suicide in America.* New York: Norton.

Henken, V. J. 1976. Banality reinvestigated: A computer-based content analysis of suicidal and forced-death documents. *Suicide and Life-Threatening Behavior* 6:36-43.

Herman, C. P., and Mack, D. 1975. Restrained and unrestrained eating. *Journal of Personality* 43:647-60.

Herman, C. P., and Polivy, J. 1975. Anxiety, restraint and eating behavior. *Journal of Abnormal Psychology* 84:666-72.

Herman, C. P.; Polivy, J.; and Heatherton, T. F. 1990. The effects of distress on eating: A review of the experimental literature. Paper submitted for publication.

Herman, C. P.; Polivy, J.; Lank, C. L.; and Heatherton, T. F. 1987.

Anxiety, hunger and eating. *Journal of Abnormal Psychology* 96:264–69.

Herrigel, E. [1953] 1971. *Zen in the art of archery.* Trans. R. F. C. Hull. New York: Vintage.

Hershenson, D. B. 1965. Stress-induced use of alcohol by problem drinkers as a function of their sense of identity. *Quarterly Journal of Studies on Alcohol* 26:213–22.

Herzog, D. B.; Norman, D. K.; Rigotti, N. A.; and Pepose, M. 1986. Frequency of bulimic behaviors and associated social maladjustment in female graduate students. *Journal of Psychiatric Research* 20:355–61.

Higgins, E. T. 1987. Self-discrepancy: A theory relating self and affect. *Psychological Review* 94:319–40.

Higgins, R. L., and Marlatt, G. A. 1973. Effects of anxiety arousal on the consumption of alcohol by alcoholics and social drinkers. *Journal of Consulting and Clinical Psychology* 41:426–33.

Hilbert, R. A. 1984. The acultural dimensions of chronic pain: Flawed reality construction and the problem of meaning. *Social Problems* 31:365–78.

Hochschild, A. 1983. *The managed heart: Commercialization of human feeling.* Berkeley: University of California Press.

Holinger, P. C. 1978. Adolescent suicide: An epidemiological study of recent trends. *American Journal of Psychiatry* 135:754–56.

Horner, M. 1972. Toward an understanding of achievement-related conflicts in women. *Journal of Social Issues* 28:157–76.

Hudson, J. I., and Pope, H. G. 1987. Depression and eating disorders. In *Presentations of depression,* ed. O. G. Cameron, 33–66. New York: John Wiley & Sons.

Hull, J. G. 1981. A self-awareness model of the causes and effects of alcohol consumption. *Journal of Abnormal Psychology* 90:586–600.

Hull, J. G., and Baumeister, R. F. 1976. Self-awareness and aesthetic pleasure. Manuscript, Duke University, Durham NC.

Hull, J. G.; Levenson, R. W.; Young, R. D.; and Scher, K. J. 1983. Self-awareness-reducing effects of alcohol consumption. *Journal of Personality and Social Psychology* 44:461–73.

Hull, J. G., and Young, R. D. 1983a. The self-awareness-reducing effects of alcohol: Evidence and implications. In *Psychological perspectives on the self*. Vol. 2, ed. J. Suls and A. G. Greenwald, 159–90. Hillsdale, NJ: Erlbaum.

Hull, J. G., and Young, R. D. 1983b. Self-consciousness, self-esteem, and success-failure as determinants of alcohol consumption in male social drinkers. *Journal of Personality and Social Psychology* 44:1097–1109.

Hull, J. G.; Young, R. D.; and Jouriles, E. 1986. Applications of the self-awareness model of alcohol consumption: Predicting patterns of use and abuse. *Journal of Personality and Social Psychology* 51:790–96.

Hyland, M. E. 1989. There is no motive to avoid success: The compromise explanation for success-avoiding behavior. *Journal of Personality* 57:665–93.

Iga, M. 1971. A concept of anomie and suicide of Japanese college students. *Life-Threatening Behavior* 1:232–44.

Izard, C. 1977. *Human emotions*. New York: Plenum.

Jakobovits, C.; Halstead, P.; Kelley, L.; Roe, D.; and Young, C. 1977. Eating habits and nutrient intake of college women over a thirty-year period. *Journal of the American Dietetic Association* 71:405–11.

Janoff-Bulman, R. 1985. The aftermath of victimization: Rebuilding shattered assumptions. In *Trauma and its wake*, ed. C. R. Figley, 15–35. New York: Brunner/Mazel.

Janoff-Bulman, R. 1989. Assumptive worlds and the stress of traumatic events: Applications of the schema construct. *Social Cognition* 7:113–36.

Janus, S,; Bess, B.; and Saltus, C. 1977. *A sexual profile of men in power*. Englewood Cliffs, NJ: Prentice-Hall.

Johnson, C., and Connors, M. E. 1987. *The etiology and treatment of bulimia nervosa*. New York: Basic Books.

Johnson, C.; Connors, M. E.; and Tobin, D. L. 1987. Symptom management of bulimia. *Journal of Consulting and Clinical Psychology* 55:668–76.

Johnson, C.; Lewis, C.; and Hagman, J. 1984. The syndrome of bulimia: Review and synthesis. *Psychiatric Clinics of North America* 7:247–73.

Johnson, C., and Pure, D. L. 1986. Assessment of bulimia: A multidimensional model. In *Handbook of eating disorders,* ed. K. D. Brownell and J. P. Foreyt, 405–49. New York: Basic Books.

Jones, E. E., and Berglas, S. C. 1978. Control of attributions about the self through self-handicapping strategies: The appeal of alcohol and the role of underachievement. *Personality and Social Psychology Bulletin* 4:200–206.

Jones, E. E.; Rhodewalt, F. T.; Berglas, S. C.; and Skelton, J. A. 1981. Effects of strategic self-presentation on subsequent self-esteem. *Journal of Personality and Social Psychology* 41:407–21.

Jones, S. C. 1973. Self- and interpersonal evaluations: Esteem theories versus consistency theories. *Psychological Bulletin* 79:185–99.

Jones, W. H.; Freemon, J. E.; and Goswick, R. A. 1981. The persistence of loneliness: Self and other determinants. *Journal of Personality* 49:27–48.

Kaplan, H. B., and Pokorny, A. D. 1976. Self-attitudes and suicidal behavior. *Suicide and Life-Threatening Behavior* 6:23–35.

Kapleau, P. 1980. *The three pillars of Zen.* Garden City, NY: Doubleday Anchor.

Katzman, M. A., and Wolchik, S. A. 1984. Bulimia and binge eating in college women: A comparison of personality and behavioral characteristics. *Journal of Consulting and Clinical Psychology* 52:423–28.

Keck, J. N., and Fiebert, M. S. 1986. Avoidance of anxiety and eating disorders. *Psychological Reports* 58:432–34.

Keegan, J. 1976. *The face of battle.* New York: Military Heritage Press.

Kernis, M. H.; Granneman, B. D.; and Barclay, L. C. 1989. Stability and level of self-esteem as predictors of anger arousal and hostility. *Journal of Personality and Social Psychology* 56: 1013–22.

Kiernan, V. G. 1989. *The duel in European history.* Oxford: Oxford University Press.

Knight, L., and Boland, F. 1989. Restrained eating: An experimental disentanglement of the disinhibiting variables of calories and food type. *Journal of Abnormal Psychology* 98:412–20.

Kushner, H. 1988. *Self-destruction in the promised land.* New Brunswick, NJ: Rutgers University Press.

Langer, E. 1975. The illusion of control. *Journal of Personality and Social Psychology* 29:253–64.

Lawson, A. 1988. *Adultery: An analysis of love and betrayal.* New York: Basic Books.

Leary, M. R., and Dobbins, S. E. 1983. Social anxiety, sexual behavior, and contraceptive use. *Journal of Personality and Social Psychology* 45:1347–54.

Le Goff, J. 1980. *Time, work, and culture in the Middle Ages.* Trans. A. Goldhammer. Chicago: University of Chicago Press.

Lester, D. 1984. The association between the quality of life and suicide and homicide rates. *Journal of Social Psychology* 124:247–48.

Lester, D. 1986. Suicide and homicide rates: Their relationship to latitude and longitude and to the weather. *Suicide and Life-Threatening Behavior* 16:356–59.

Lester, D. 1987. Suicide, homicide, and the quality of life: An archival study. *Suicide and Life-Threatening Behavior* 16:389–92.

Levenson, M., and Neuringer, C. 1970. Intropunitiveness in suicidal adolescents. *Journal of Projective Techniques and Personality Assessment* 34:409–11.

Lifton, R. J. 1986. *The Nazi doctors: Medical killing and the psychology of genocide.* New York: Basic Books.

Lindner, R. 1954. *The fifty-minute hour.* New York: Bantam Books.

Linehan, M. M.; Camper, P.; Chiles, J. A.; Strosahl, K.; and Shearin, E. 1987. Interpersonal problem solving and parasuicide. *Cognitive Therapy and Research* 11:1–12.

Linehan, M. M.; Goodstein, J. L.; Nielsen, S. L.; and Chiles, J. A. 1983. Reasons for staying alive when you are thinking of killing yourself: The Reasons for Living Inventory. *Journal of Consulting and Clinical Psychology* 51:276–86.

Linville, P. W. 1985. Self-complexity and affective extremity: Don't put all your eggs in one cognitive basket. *Social Cognition* 3:94–120.

Linville, P. W. 1987. Self-complexity as a cognitive buffer against stress-related illness and depression. *Journal of Personality and Social Psychology* 52:663–76.

Loo, R. 1986. Suicide among police in a federal force. *Suicide and Life-Threatening Behavior* 16:379–88.

LoPiccolo, J., and LoPiccolo, L., eds. 1978. *Handbook of sex therapy.* New York: Plenum.

Lowin, A., and Epstein, G. F. 1965. Does expectancy determine performance? *Journal of Experimental Social Psychology* 1:244–55.

Lundholm, J. K., and Littrell, J. M. 1986. Desire for thinness among high school cheerleaders: Relationship to disordered eating and weight control behaviors. *Adolescence* 21:573–79.

Lynn, M. 1988. The effects of alcohol consumption on restaurant tipping. *Personality and Social Psychology Bulletin* 14:87–91.

Mandell, N. M., and Shrauger, J. S. 1980. The effects of self-evaluative statements on heterosocial approach in shy and nonshy males. *Cognitive Therapy and Research* 4: 369–81.

Maracek, J., and Mettee, D. R. 1972. Avoidance of continued success as a function of self-esteem, level of esteem certainty, and responsibility for success. *Journal of Personality and Social Psychology* 22:98–107.

Maris, R. 1969. *Social forces in urban suicide.* Homewood, IL: Dorsey.

Maris, R. 1981. *Pathways to suicide: A survey of self-destructive behaviors.* Baltimore, MD: Johns Hopkins University Press.

Maris, R. 1985. The adolescent suicide problem. *Suicide and Life-Threatening Behavior* 15:91–100.

Markus, H. 1977. Self-schemata and processing information about the self. *Journal of Personality and Social Psychology* 35:63–78.

Markus, H., and Nurius, P. S. 1986. Possible selves. *American Psychologist* 41:954–69.

Maroldo, G. K. 1982. Shyness and love on the college campus. *Perceptual and Motor Skills* 55:819–24.

Marshall, J. R.; Burnett, W.; and Brasurel, J. 1983. On precipitating factors: Cancer as a cause of suicide. *Suicide and Life-Threatening Behavior* 13:15–27.

Masters, K. S. 1990. Hypnotic susceptibility, cognitive dissociation, and runner's high in a sample of marathon runners.

Paper presented at the meeting of the Midwestern Psychological Association, Chicago, IL, May.

Masters, W. H., and Johnson, V. E. 1970. *Human sexual inadequacy.* Boston: Little, Brown.

Maupin, E. W. 1972. Zen Buddhism: A psychological review. In *Highest state of consciousness,* ed J. White, 204–24. Garden City, NY: Doubleday Anchor.

Mayer, W. 1983. Alcohol abuse and alcoholism: The psychologist's role in prevention, research, and treatment. *American Psychologist* 38:1116–21.

Mayhew, R., and Edelmann, R. J. 1989. Self-esteem, irrational beliefs and coping strategies in relation to eating problems in a non-clinical population. *Personality and Individual Differences* 10:581–84.

McCollam, J. B.; Burish, T. G.; Maisto, S. A.; and Sobell, M. B. 1980. Alcohol's effects on physiological arousal and self-reported affect and sensations. *Journal of Abnormal Psychology* 89:224–33.

McFarlin, D. B., and Blascovich, J. 1981. Effects of self-esteem and performance feedback on future affective preferences and cognitive expectations. *Journal of Personality and Social Psychology* 40:521–31.

McKenna, R. J. 1972. Some effects of anxiety level and food cues on the eating behavior of obese and normal subjects: A comparison of the Schachterian and psychosomatic conceptions. *Journal of Personality and Social Psychology* 22:311–19.

McKenry, P. C., and Kelley, C. 1983. The role of drugs in adolescent suicide attempts. *Suicide and Life-Threatening Behavior* 13:166–75.

McMahon, B., and Pugh, T. F. 1965. Suicide in the widowed. *American Journal of Epidemiology* 81:23–31.

Mehrabian, A., and Weinstein, L. 1985. Temperament characteristics and suicide attempters. *Journal of Consulting and Clinical Psychology* 53:544–46.

Melges, F. T., and Weisz, A. E. 1971. The personal future and suicidal ideation. *Journal of Nervous and Mental Disease* 153: 244–50.

Menninger, K. [1938] 1966. *Man against himself.* New York: Harcourt, Brace & World.

Merton, T. [1967] 1989. *Mystics and Zen masters.* New York: Noonday Press.

Meyer, D.; Leventhal, H.; and Gutmann, M. 1985. Common-sense models of illness. The example of hypertension. *Health psychology* 4:115–35.

Milkman, H. B., and Sunderwirth, S. 1986. *Craving for ecstasy: The consciousness and chemistry of escape.* Lexington, MA: Lexington Books.

Mitchell, J. E.; Hatsukami, D. K.; Pyle, R. L.; and Eckert, E. D. 1986. The bulimia syndrome: Course of the illness and associated problems. *Comprehensive Psychiatry* 27:165–70.

Mitchell, J. E.; Hatsukami, D. K.; Pyle, R. L.; and Eckert, E. D. 1988. Bulimia with and without a family history of drug abuse. *Addictive Behaviors* 13:245–61.

Mizes, J. S. 1988. Personality characteristics of bulimic and non-eating-disordered female controls: A cognitive behavioral perspective. *International Journal of Eating Disorders* 7:541–50.

Monat, A.; Averill, J. R.,; and Lazarus, R. S. 1972. Anticipatory stress and coping reactions under various conditions of uncertainty. *Journal of Personality and Social Psychology* 24:237–53.

Morgenthau, H. 1962. Love and power. *Commentary* 33:247–51.

Morrissey, R. E., and Schuckit, M. A. 1978. Stressful life events and alcohol problems among women seen at a detoxification center. *Journal of Studies on Alcohol* 39:1559–76.

Motto, J. A. 1980. Suicide risk factors in alcohol abuse. *Suicide and Life-Threatening Behavior* 10:230–38.

Nasser, M. 1986. Comparative study of the prevalence of abnormal eating attitudes among Arab female students of both London and Cairo Universities. *Psychological Medicine* 16:621–25.

Nayha, S. 1982. Autumn incidence of suicides re-examined: Data from Finland by sex, age, and occupation. *British Journal of Psychiatry* 141:512–17.

Neuringer, C. 1964. Rigid thinking in suicidal individuals. *Journal of Consulting Psychology* 28:54–58.

Neuringer, C. 1972. Suicide attempt and social isolation on the MAPS test. *Life-Threatening Behavior* 2:139–44.

Neuringer, C. 1974. Attitudes toward self in suicidal individuals. *Life-Threatening Behavior* 4:96–106.

Neuringer, C., and Harris, R. M. 1974. The perception of the passage of time among death-involved hospital patients. *Life-Threatening Behavior* 4:240–54.

Odajnyk, V. W. 1988. Gathering the light: A Jungian exploration of the psychology of meditation *Quadrant* 21(1):35–51.

Ogilvie, D. M.; Stone, P. J.; and Shneidman, E. S. 1983. A computer analysis of suicide notes. In *The psychology of suicide*, ed. E. Shneidman, N. Farberow, and R. Litman, 249–56. New York: Aronson.

Palmer, S. 1971. Characteristics of suicide in 54 nonliterate societies. *Life-Threatening Behavior* 1:178–83.

Palmer, S., and Humphrey, J. A. 1980. Offender-victim relationships in criminal homicide followed by offender's suicide, North Carolina, 1972–1977. *Suicide and Life-Threatening Behavior* 10:106–18.

Parker, G., and Walter, S. 1982. Seasonal variation in depressive disorders and suicidal deaths in New South Wales. *British Journal of Psychiatry* 140:626–32.

Patsiokas, A.; Clum, G.; and Luscomb, R. 1979. Cognitive characteristics of suicide attempters. *Journal of Consulting and Clinical Psychology* 47:478–84.

Patterson, O. 1982. *Slavery and social death*. Cambridge, MA: Harvard University Press.

Pennebaker, J. W. 1989. Stream of consciousness and stress: Levels of thinking. In *The direction of thought: Limits of awareness, intention and control*, ed. J. S. Uleman and J. A. Bargh, 327–50. New York: Guilford Press.

Perrah, M., and Wichman, H. 1987. Cognitive rigidity in suicide attempters. *Suicide and Life-Threatening Behavior* 17:251–62.

Phillips, D. P., and Liu, J. 1980. The frequency of suicides around major public holidays: Some surprising findings. *Suicide and Life-Threatening Behavior* 10:41–50.

Phillips, D. P., and Wills, J. S. 1987. A drop in suicides around major national holidays. *Suicide and Life-Threatening Behavior* 17:1–12.

Pilkonis, P. A. 1977a. Shyness, public and private, and its relationship to other measures of social behavior. *Journal of Personality* 45:585–95.

Pilkonis, P. A. 1977b. The behavioral consequences of shyness. *Journal of Personality* 45:596–611.

Pilkonis, P. A., and Zimbardo, P. G. 1979. The personal and social dynamics of shyness. In *Emotions in personality and psychopathology*, ed C. E. Izard, 133–60. New York: Plenum.

Pines, M., and Aronson, E. 1983. Antecedents, correlates, and consequences of sexual jealousy. *Journal of Personality* 51:108–35.

Platt, S. 1986. Parasuicide and unemployment. *British Journal of Psychiatry* 149:401–5.

Polivy, J. 1976. Perception of calories and regulation of intake in restrained and unrestrained subjects. *Addictive Behaviors* 1:237–43.

Polivy, J., and Herman, C. P. 1983. *Breaking the diet habit: The natural weight alternative.* New York: Basic Books.

Polivy, J., and Herman, C. P. 1985. Dieting and bingeing: A casual analysis. *American Psychologist* 40:193–201.

Polivy, J,; Herman, C. P.; and Garner, D. M. 1988. Cognitive assessment. In *Assessment of addictive behaviors*, ed. D. M. Donovan and G. A. Marlatt, 274–95. New York: Guilford Press.

Polivy, J.; Herman, C. P.; and Kuleshnyk, I. 1984. More on the effects of perceived calories on dieters and nondieters: Salad as a "magical" food. Manuscript.

Powers, P. S.; Schulman, R. G.; Gleghorn, A. A.; and Prange, M. E. 1987. Perceptual and cognitive abnormalities in bulimia. *American Journal of Psychiatry* 144:1456–60.

Reage, P. [1954] 1966. *The Story of O.* New York: Grove Press.

Reik, T. [1941] 1957. *Masochism in modern man.* Trans. M. H. Beigel and G. M. Kurth. New York: Grove Press.

Reinhart, G., and Linden, L. L. 1982. Suicide by industry and organization: A structural-change approach. *Suicide and Life-Threatening Behavior* 12:34–45.

Reps, P., ed. 1957. *Zen flesh, Zen bones: A collection of Zen and pre-Zen writings.* Rutland, VT: Tuttle.

Rhine, M. W., and Mayerson, P. 1973. A serious suicidal syndrome masked by homicidal threats. *Life-Threatening Behavior* 3:3–10.

Riedel, R. 1990. Life at a 24-hour run turns out to be far from boring. *Ultra Running* 9(8):13–14 (Jan.–Feb.).

Ringel, E. 1976. The presuicidal syndrome. *Suicide and Life-Threatening Behavior* 6:131–49.

Rogers, T. B.; Kuiper, N. A.; Kirker, W. S. 1977. Self-reference and the encoding of personal information. *Journal of Personality and Social Psychology* 35:677–88.

Rojcewicz, S. J. 1970. War and suicide. *Life-Threatening Behavior* 1:46–54.

Rosen, D. H. 1976. Suicide survivors: Psychotherapeutic implications of egocide. *Suicide and Life-Threatening Behavior* 6:209–15.

Rosenthal, P. 1984. *Words and values: Some leading words and where they lead us.* New York: Oxford University Press.

Rothbaum, F.; Weisz, J. R.; and Snyder, S. S. 1982. Changing the world and changing the self: A two-process model of perceived control. *Journal of Personality and Social Psychology* 42:5–37.

Rothberg, J. M., and Jones, F. D. 1987. Suicide in the U.S. Army: Epidemiological and periodic aspects. *Suicide and Life-Threatening Behavior* 17:119–32.

Roy, A., and Linnoila, M. 1986. Alcoholism and suicide. *Suicide and Life-Threatening Behavior* 16:244–73.

Ruderman, A. J. 1985a. Restraint and irrational cognitions. *Behavior Research and Therapy* 23:557–61.

Ruderman, A. J. 1985b. Dysphoric mood and overeating: A test of restraint theory's disinhibition hypothesis. *Journal of Abnormal Psychology* 94:78–85.

Ruderman, A. J. 1986. Dietary restraint: A theoretical and empirical review. *Psychological Bulletin* 99:247–62.

Sackett, D. L., and Snow, J. C. 1979. The magnitude of compliance and noncompliance. In *Compliance in health care*, ed. R. B. Haynes, D. W. Taylor, and D. L. Sackett, 11–22. Baltimore, MD: Johns Hopkins University Press.

Sarason, I. 1981. Test anxiety, stress, and social support. *Journal of Personality* 49:101–14.

Savage, M. 1979. *Addicted to Suicide*. Cambridge, MA: Schenkman.

Scarry, E. 1985. *The body in pain: The making and unmaking of the world*. New York: Oxford University Press.

Schacter, S. 1971. *Emotion, obesity, and crime*. New York. Academic Press.

Schachter, S.; Goldman, R.; and Gordon, A. 1968. Effects of fear, food, deprivation, and obesity on eating. *Journal of Personality and Social Psychology* 10:91–97.

Schachter, S., and Singer, J. E. 1962. Cognitive, social and physiological determinants of emotional state. *Psychological Review* 69:379–99.

Schlenker, B. R., and Leary, M. R. 1982. Social anxiety and self-presentation: A conceptualization and model. *Psychological Bulletin* 92:641–69.

Schlesier-Stropp, B. 1984. Bulimia: A review of the literature. *Psychological Bulletin* 95:247–57.

Schotte, D. E., and Clum, G. A. 1982. Suicide ideation in a college population: A test of a model. *Journal of Consulting and Clinical Psychology* 50:690–96.

Schotte, D. E., and Clum, G. A. 1987. Problem-solving skills in suicidal psychiatric patients. *Journal of Consulting and Clinical Psychology* 55:49–54.

Scott, G. G. 1983. *Erotic power: An exploration of dominance and submission*. Secaucus, NJ: Citadel Press.

Shafii, M. 1988. *Freedom from the self: Sufism, meditation, and psychotherapy*. New York: Human Sciences Press.

Shatford, L. A., and Evans, D. R. 1986. Bulimia as a manifestation of the stress process: A LISREL causal modelling analysis. *International Journal of Eating Disorders* 5:451–73.

Shilts, R. 1987. *And the band played on: Politics, people, and the AIDS epidemic*. New York: Viking Penguin.

Shneidman, E. S., and Farberow, N. L. 1961. Statistical comparisons between attempted and committed suicides. In *The cry for help*, ed. N. L. Farberow and E. S. Shneidman, 19–47. New York: McGraw-Hill.

Shneidman, E. S., and Farberow, N. L. 1970. Attempted and

committed suicides. In *The psychology of suicide*, ed. E. S. Shneidman, N. L. Farberow, and R. E. Litman, 199–225. New York: Science House.

Shoemaker, S. 1963. *Self-knowledge and self-identity*. Ithaca, NY: Cornell University Press.

Shrauger, J. S. 1975. Responses to evaluation as a function of initial self-perception. *Psychological Bulletin* 82:581–96.

Silberfeld, M.; Streiner, B.; and Ciampi, A. 1985. Suicide attempters, ideators, and risk-taking propensity. *Canadian Journal of Psychiatry* 30:274–77.

Simmons, R.; Rosenberg, F.; and Rosenberg, M. 1973. Disturbance in the self-image at adolescence. *American Sociological Review* 38:553–68.

Slochower, J. 1976. Emotional labelling and overeating in obese and normal weight individuals. *Psychosomatic Medicine* 38: 131–39.

Slochower, J. 1983. Life stress, weight, and cue salience. In *Excessive eating*, ed. J. Slochower, 75–87. New York: Human Sciences Press.

Slochower, J., and Kaplan, S. P. 1980. Anxiety, perceived control and eating in obese and normal-weight persons. *Appetite* 1:75–83.

Slochower, J., and Kaplan, S. P. 1983. Effects of cue salience and weight on responsiveness to uncontrollable anxiety. In *Excessive eating*, ed. J. Slochower, 68–74. New York: Human Sciences Press.

Slochower, J.; Kaplan, S. P.; and Mann, L. 1981. The effects of life stress and weight on mood and eating. *Appetite* 2:115–25.

Smead, V. S. 1988. Trying too hard: A correlate of eating-related difficulties. *Addictive Behaviors* 13:307–10.

Smith, D. H., and Hackathorn, L. 1982. Some social and psychological factors related to suicide in primitive societies: A cross-cultural comparative study. *Suicide and Life-Threatening Behavior* 12:195–211.

Smith, G. T.; Hohlstein, L. A.; and Atlas, J. G. 1989. Race differences in eating-disordered behavior and eating-related expectancies. Paper presented to the American Psychological Association, New Orleans, August 11–15.

256   *Escaping the Self*

Spencer, J. A., and Fremouw, W. J. 1979. Binge eating as a function of restraint and weight classification. *Journal of Abnormal Psychology* 88:262–67.

Spengler, A. 1977. Manifest sadomasochism of males: Results of an empirical study. *Archives of sexual behavior* 6:441–56.

Spirito, A.; Stark, L. J.; Williams, C. A.; and Guevremont, D. C. 1987. Common problems and coping strategies reported by normal adolescents and adolescent suicide attempters. Paper presented to the Association for the Advancement of Behavior Therapy, Boston, November.

Stcherbatsky, T. 1977. *The conception of Buddhist nirvana.* Delhi, India: Motilal Banarsidass.

Steele, C. M., and Josephs, R. A. 1990. Alcohol myopia: Its prized and dangerous effects. *American Psychologist* 45:921–33.

Steele, C. M., and Southwick, L. 1985. Alcohol and social behavior I: The psychology of drunken excess. *Journal of Personality and Social Psychology* 48:18–34.

Steenbarger, B. N., and Aderman, D. 1979. Objective self-awareness as a nonaversive state: Effect of anticipating discrepancy reduction. *Journal of Personality* 47:330–39.

Stephens, B. J. 1985. Suicidal women and their relationships with husbands, boyfriends, and lovers. *Suicide and Life-Threatening Behavior* 15:77–89.

Stephens, B. J. 1987. Cheap thrills and humble pie: The adolescence of female suicide attempters. *Suicide and Life-Threatening Behavior* 17:107–18.

Striegel-Moore, R.; Silberstein, L. R.; and Rodin, J. 1986. Toward an understanding of risk factors for bulimia. *American Psychologist* 41:246–63.

Suls, J. M., and Miller, R. L., eds. 1977. *Social comparison processes: Theoretical and empirical perspectives.* Washington, D.C.: Halstead-Wiley.

Swann, W. B. 1987. Identity negotiation: Where two roads meet. *Journal of Personality and Social Psychology* 53:1038–51.

Swann, W. B.; Griffin, J. J.; Predmore, S. C.; and Gaines, B. 1987. The cognitive-affective crossfire: When self-consistency confronts self-enhancement. *Journal of Personality and Social Psychology* 52:881–89.

Tannahill, R. 1980. *Sex in history*. New York: Stein & Day.

Taylor, S. 1978. The confrontation with death and the renewal of life. *Suicide and Life-Threatening Behavior* 8:89–98.

Taylor, S. E. 1983. Adjustment to threatening events: A theory of cognitive adaptation. *American Psychologist* 38:1161–73.

Taylor, S. E. 1989. *Positive illusions: Creative self-deception and the healthy mind*. New York: Basic Books.

Taylor, S. E., and Brown, J. D. 1988. Illusion and well-being: A social psychological perspective on mental health. *Psychological Bulletin* 103:193–210.

Taylor, S. P.; Gammon, C. B.; and Capasso, D. R. 1976. Aggression as a function of the interaction of alcohol and threat. *Journal of Personality and Social Psychology* 34:938–41.

Thelen, M. H.; Mann, L. M.; Pruitt, J.; and Smith, M. 1987. Bulimia: Prevalence and component factors in college women. *Journal of Psychosomatic Research* 31:73–78.

Thompson, D. A.; Berg, K. M.; and Shatford, L. A. 1987. The heterogeneity of bulimic symptomatology: Cognitive and behavioral dimensions. *International Journal of Eating Disorders* 6:215–34.

Tice, D. M. 1990. Strategies of affect regulation. Presented to the Nags Head Conference on Emotion and Motivation, Nags Head, NC, June.

Tice, D. M., and Baumeister, R. F. 1990. Self-esteem, self-handicapping, and self-presentation: The strategy of inadequate practice. *Journal of Personality* 58:443–64.

Tice, D. M.; Buder, J.; and Baumeister, R. F. 1985. Development of self-consciousness: At what age does audience pressure disrupt performance? *Adolescence* 20:301–5.

Tishler, C. L.; McKenry, P. C.; and Morgan, K. C. 1981. Adolescent suicide attempts: Some significant factors. *Suicide and Life-Threatening Behavior* 11:86–92.

Topol, P., and Reznikoff, M. 1982. Perceived peer and family relationships, hopelessness, and locus of control as factors in adolescent suicide attempts. *Suicide and Life-Threatening Behavior* 12:141–50.

Triandis, H. C. 1989. The self and social behavior in differing cultural contexts. *Psychological Review* 96:506–20.

Trillin, C. 1984. *Killings*. New York: Viking Penguin.

Trilling, L. 1971. *Sincerity and authenticity*. Cambridge, MA: Harvard University Press.

Trout, D. L. 1980. The role of social isolation in suicide. *Suicide and Life-Threatening Behavior* 10:10–23.

Tucker, J. A.; Vuchinich, R. E.; and Sobell, M. B. 1981. Alcohol consumption as a self-handicapping strategy. *Journal of Abnormal Psychology* 90:220–30.

Turner, V. 1969. *The ritual process*. Chicago: Aldine.

Vallacher, R. R., and Wegner, D. M. 1985. *A theory of action identification*. Hillsdale, NJ: Erlbaum.

Vallacher, R. R., and Wegner, D. M. 1987. What do people think they're doing: Action identification and human behavior. *Psychological Review* 94:3–15.

Walster, E.; Aronson, E.; and Brown, Z. 1966. Choosing to suffer as a consequence of expecting to suffer: An unexpected finding. *Journal of Experimental Social Psychology* 2:400–406.

Ward, W. D., and Sandvold, K. D. 1963. Performance expectancy as a determinant of actual performance: A partial replication. *Journal of Abnormal and Social Psychology* 67:293–95.

Wasserman, I. M. 1984. The influence of economic business cycles on United States suicide rates. *Suicide and Life-Threatening Behavior* 14:143–56.

Wegner, D. M. 1989. *White bears and other unwanted thoughts*. New York: Vintage.

Wegner, D. M., and Giulano, T. 1980. Arousal-induced attention to self. *Journal of Personality and Social Psychology* 38:719–26.

Wegner, D. M.; Schneider, D. J.; Carter, S. R.; and White, T. L. 1987. Paradoxical effects of thought suppression. *Journal of Personality and Social Psychology* 53:5–13.

Wegner, D. M., and Vallacher, R. R. 1986. Action identification.

In *Handbook of cognition and motivation*, ed. R. M. Sorrentino and E. T. Higgins, 550–82. New York: Guilford Press.

Weil, A. 1972. *The natural mind.* Boston: Houghton Mifflin.

Weinberg, T., and Kamel, W. L., eds. 1983. *S and M: Studies in sadomasochism.* Buffalo, NY: Prometheus.

Weintraub, K. J. 1978. *The value of the individual: Self and circumstance in autobiography.* Chicago: University of Chicago Press.

Weiss, J. M. 1971a. Effects of coping behavior in different warning signal conditions on stress pathology in rats. *Journal of Comparative and Physiological Psychology* 77:1–13.

Weiss, J. M. 1971b. Effects of coping behavior with and without a feedback signal on stress pathology in rats. *Journal of Comparative and Physiological Psychology* 77:22–30.

Weiss, J. M. 1971c. Effects of punishing the coping response (conflict) on stress pathology in rats. *Journal of Comparative and Physiological Psychology* 77:14–21.

Weissman, M. M.; Klerman, G. L.; Markowitz, J. S.; and Ouellette, R. 1989. Suicidal ideation and suicide attempts in panic disorder and attacks. *New England Journal of Medicine* 321:1209–14.

White, J. 1972. *Highest state of consciousness.* Garden City, NY: Doubleday Anchor.

Wicklund, R. A. 1975a. Objective self-awareness. In *Advances in experimental social psychology.* Vol. 8, ed. L. Berkowitz, 233–75. New York: Academic Press.

Wicklund, R. A. 1975b. Discrepancy reduction or attempted distraction? A reply to Liebling and Shaver. *Journal of Experimental Social Psychology* 11:78–81.

Wilkinson, K. P., and Israel, G. D. 1984. Suicide and rurality in urban society. *Suicide and Life-Threatening Behavior* 14:187–200.

Williams, J. M., and Broadbent, K. 1986. Autobiographical memory in suicide attempters. *Journal of Abnormal Psychology* 95:144–49.

Williamson, D. 1990. Drinking: A sobering look at an enduring Princeton pastime. *Princeton Alumni Weekly* 90(12):14–19 (March 21).

Williamson, D. A. 1990. *Assessment of eating disorders: Obesity, anorexia, and bulimia nervosa.* Elmsford, NY: Pergamon Press.

Wilson, G. T. 1988. Alcohol and anxiety. *Behavior Research and Therapy* 26:369–81.

Wine, J. 1971. Test anxiety and direction of attention. *Psychological Bulletin* 76:92–104.

Wood, J. V. 1989. Theory and research concerning social comparisons of personal attributes. *Psychological Bulletin* 106: 231–48.

Yager, J.; Landsverk, J.; Edelstein, C. K.; and Jarvik, M. 1988. A 20-month follow-up study of 628 women with eating disorders: II. Course of associated symptoms and related clinical features. *International Journal of Eating Disorders* 7:503–13.

Yates, A.; Leehey, K.; and Shisslak, C. M. 1983. Running—an analogue of anorexia? *New England Journal of Medicine* 308:251–55.

Yufit, R. I., and Benzies, B. 1973. Assessing suicidal potential by time perspective. *Life-Threatening Behavior* 3:270–82.

Yufit, R. I.; Benzies, B.; Foute, M. D.; and Fawcett, J. A. 1970. Suicide potential and time perspective. *Archives of General Psychiatry* 23:158–63.

Zanna, M. P., and Pack, S. J. 1975. On the self-fulfilling nature of apparent sex differences in behavior. *Journal of Experimental Social Psychology* 11:583–91.

Zimbardo, P. G. 1977. *Shyness: What it is, what to do about it.* New York: Jove.

Zoftig, S. 1982. Coming out. In *Coming to Power*, ed. Samois, 86–96. Boston: Alyson.

Zola, I. K. 1973. Pathways to the doctor—from person to patient. *Social Science and Medicine* 7:677–89.

Zube, M. J. 1972. Changing concepts of morality: 1948–1969. *Social Forces* 50:385–93.

Zuckerman, M. 1979. Attribution of success and failure revisited, or: The motivational bias is alive and well in attribution theory. *Journal of Personality* 47:245–87.

Index